Professional
Community Server™

Professional
Community Server™

Wyatt Preul

Keyvan Nayyeri

José Lema

Jim Martin

Wiley Publishing, Inc.

Professional Community Server™

Published by
Wiley Publishing, Inc.
10475 Crosspoint Boulevard
Indianapolis, IN 46256
www.wiley.com

Copyright © 2007 by Wiley Publishing, Inc., Indianapolis, Indiana

Published simultaneously in Canada

ISBN: 978-0-470-10828-4

Manufactured in the United States of America

10 9 8 7 6 5 4 3 2 1

Library of Congress Cataloging-in-Publication Data
Professional Community server / Wyatt Preul ... [et al.].
   p. cm.
  Includes index.
  ISBN-13: 978-0-470-10828-4 (pbk.)
  ISBN-10: 0-470-10828-2 (pbk.)
  1. Web servers. 2. Community server. 3. Online social networks — Computer software. I. Preul, Wyatt, 1983-
  TK5105.8885.C555P76 2007
  005.75'8 — dc22
             2006103089

For general information on our other products and services please contact our Customer Care Department within the United States at (800) 762-2974, outside the United States at (317) 572-3993 or fax (317) 572-4002.

Trademarks: Wiley, the Wiley logo, Wrox, the Wrox logo, Programmer to Programmer, and related trade dress are trademarks or registered trademarks of John Wiley & Sons, Inc. and/or its affiliates, in the United States and other countries, and may not be used without written permission. Community Server is a trademark of Telligent Systems, Inc. All other trademarks are the property of their respective owners. Wiley Publishing, Inc., is not associated with any product or vendor mentioned in this book.

Wiley also publishes its books in a variety of electronic formats. Some content that appears in print may not be available in electronic books.

About the Authors

Wyatt Preul works as a software test engineer for Telligent Systems. At age 23 he holds a bachelor's degree in Computer Science and is completing his certification as a Microsoft Certified Technology Specialist. Wyatt has been working with and admiring Community Server since shortly after version 1.1 was released. Since that time he has become a respected member of the community and active participant in the product itself. Wyatt now spends his days happily testing Community Server and trying to locate bugs in the product, about which he reports there aren't many. His thoughts on development, testing, and Community Server can all be found at www.wyattpreul.com. Wyatt currently lives in Philadelphia with his beautiful fiancé Dusti Lyon.

I would like to thank Tony Bierman for first introducing me to Community Server.

Keyvan Nayyeri is a software architect and developer and an active .NET community member with a bachelor of science degree in Applied Mathematics. He began his programming life with over eight years of system programming and much experience with practices. In the development world, Keyvan is a middle-tier developer and an expert in markup languages and their related technologies. Recently he has switched to Service Oriented design and building distributed systems. He is a young community member who has written several articles for .NET communities. Beside this, he's running some open source projects. Keyvan has been a Community Server MVP since April 2006 and primarily focuses on codes and APIs and has written several modules and custom controls for Community Server. He joined the Community Server folks in the early days and actively has helped many Community Server users to find their way in this world. His thoughts on .NET, Community Server, and Technology can be found on www.nayyeri.net.

José Lema, the product unit manager for Community Server, has been developing browser-based applications for the past 10 years. Previous to joining Telligent Systems, he was the lead developer for Microsoft's Hive.net online community. His unique experience with ASP.NET, SQL Server, and Community Server ultimately led him to join Telligent as a senior engineer focused on the forums system. Since that time, his responsibilities have grown to include the entire Community Server product and team. In his free time, José enjoys reading, juggling, playing, and watching/quoting movies with his wife and four boys.

Jim Martin is a software engineer for Telligent. Telligent is a software and solutions company with unique expertise and knowledge of the Microsoft .NET platform. Jim focuses primarily on the services side at Telligent but has also contributed in the development of Community Server, as well as customizing Community Server to fit specific client needs. Jim joined Telligent shortly after the company's birth and has now been there two years. Jim has over eight years of software development experience. He began his career as an information analyst, focusing on custom applications to support company initiatives for Fujitsu Network Communications in Richardson, Texas. After almost five years at Fujitsu he moved to Brink's Inc. where he worked for almost two years as a programmer analyst on a custom solution used to manage the Brink's armored fleet and cash movement.

Jim likes to spend his off time playing in the .NET community. Jim is the treasurer for the North Dallas .NET Users Group in Dallas, Texas. Jim is also a musician and enjoys playing the piano whenever he can find the time. Jim also enjoys the little things in life, such as spending nights reading, drinking coffee, going to the gym, and listening to music.

You can visit Jim's blog at http://JamesDMartin.com or contact him via email at JimMartin@gmail.com.

Credits

Executive Editor
Chris Webb

Development Editor
Rosanne Koneval

Technical Editor
Adonis Bitar

Production Editor
Felicia Robinson

Copy Editor
Foxxe Editorial Services

Editorial Manager
Mary Beth Wakefield

Production Manager
Tim Tate

Vice President and Executive Group Publisher
Richard Swadley

Vice President and Executive Publisher
Joseph B. Wikert

Graphics and Production Specialists
Denny Hager
Joyce Haughey
Barbara Moore
Heather Ryan
Alicia B. South

Quality Control Technicians
John Greenough
Christy Pingleton

Project Coordinator
Erin Smith

Proofreading and Indexing
ConText
Valerie Haynes Perry

Anniversary Logo Design
Richard Pacifico

To Rob, Scott, and Jason – your vision of a platform for online communities is enabling collaboration worldwide.

Acknowledgments

Special thanks are due to Adonis Bitar, who volunteered his time to assist with the editing process of this book. In addition, special thanks are due to Rosanne Koneval for her patience and support during this same editing process. Without you twothis book would not be what it is today.

Rob Howard deserves special thanks for his proofing skills and keen insights, which were vital components in the creation of this book.

Contents

Contents

Contents

Contents

Contents

Contents

Contents

Introduction

Community Server provides a platform that enables communities to be easily created and continuously thrive. It achieves this task by including all of the applications that are useful for the growth of communities. In addition Community Server is extremely flexible and is able to meet the requirements of all types of communities. The combination of simplicity and flexibility makes Community Server an ideal platform.

Who This Book Is For

This book is for both experienced developers and general enthusiasts who are interested in building their site using Community Server. If you are an experienced developer, then it will help if you are experienced with ASP.NET. On the other hand, if you are an enthusiast who is interested in building a site, then it will be helpful if you have some experience working with web applications and administering them.

Aims of This Book

One of the main goals of this book is to provide you with enough insight about Community Server that you will feel comfortable either administering a site or developing a site that is powered by Community Server. In addition, this book aims to provide you with more than adequate knowledge to not only install Community Server but also alter its appearance with little or no development experience. All in all, this book aims to provide you with a single resource to assist in the installation, configuration, and extension of a Community Server–powered site.

What This Book Covers

The book is split into four parts. Part I, "Getting Started," introduces you to Community Server, helps you install a new site, and then walks you through the main components of your site. This part is important for anyone who is new to Community Server as well as anyone who would like to learn more about the various installation methods. It is equally useful for experienced users to review their existing knowledge with these chapters to help build a more solid base.

Part II, "Configuring Community Server," and Part III, "Administering Community Server," target the process of administering a site and walk you through some of the basic configuration changes you can make. In these chapters, you learn about some of the changes you can make to alter the appearance of a site. They also provide advanced topics that take you beyond the installation of your site to actually administering it.

Part IV, "Extending Community Server," targets developers as it demonstrates many ways to extend a Community Server powered sitethrough code. This set of chapters covers everything from creating reports and changing the database to building custom modules and localizing a site. These chapters are intended for developers who have experience with ASP.NET and are at least somewhat familiar with SQL.

Conventions

To help you get the most from the text and keep track of what's happening, we've used a number of conventions throughout the book.

> *Tips, hints, tricks, and asides to the current discussion are offset and placed in italics like this.*

As for styles in the text:

❑ We *highlight* important words when we introduce them.

❑ We show keyboard strokes like this: Ctrl-A.

❑ We show file names, URLs, and code within the text like this: `persistence.properties`.

❑ We present code in two different ways:

```
In code examples we highlight new and important code with a gray background.
```

```
The gray highlighting is not used for code that's less important in the present
context, or has been shown before.
```

Source Code

As you work through the examples in this book, you may choose either to type in all the code manually or to use the source code files that accompany the book. All of the source code used in this book is available for download at `www.wrox.com`. Once at the site, simply locate the book's title (either by using the Search box or by using one of the title lists), and click the Download Code link on the book's detail page to obtain all the source code for the book.

> *Because many books have similar titles, you may find it easiest to search by ISBN; for this book the ISBN is 978-0-470-10828-4.*

Once you download the code, just decompress it with your favorite compression tool. Alternately, you can go to the main Wrox code download page at `www.wrox.com/dynamic/books/download.aspx` to see the code available for this book and all other Wrox books.

Errata

We make every effort to ensure that there are no errors in the text or in the code. However, no one is perfect, and mistakes do occur. If you find an error in one of our books, like a spelling mistake or faulty piece of code, we would be very grateful for your feedback. By sending in errata, you may save another reader hours of frustration, and at the same time you will be helping us provide even higher-quality information.

To find the errata page for this book, go to www.wrox.com and locate the title using the Search box or one of the title lists. Then, on the book details page, click the Book Errata link. On this page, you can view all errata that has been submitted for this book and posted by Wrox editors. A complete book list, including links to each book's errata, is also available at www.wrox.com/misc-pages/booklist.shtml.

If you don't spot "your" error on the Book Errata page, go to www.wrox.com/contact/techsupport.shtml and complete the form there to send us the error you have found. We'll check the information and, if appropriate, post a message to the book's errata page and fix the problem in subsequent editions of the book.

Part I
Getting Started

What Is Community Server?

The following chapter introduces you to Community Server as a platform. You will learn about the various applications that make up this platform and about the different editions of Community Server that are available. Many of these editions are available for purchase, and this chapter covers how you can go about purchasing them. Furthermore, you will also be introduced to some of the add-ins that are available for Community Server. This chapter is intended to provide you with a good basis as well as a basic history of Community Server. The following list is an overview of what is included in this chapter:

- ❑ Definition of Community Server
- ❑ History of Community Server
- ❑ Overview of available editions
- ❑ Feature roadmap

Introduction to Community Server

Community Server is a software platform that can be used to easily activate an online community of any size. The platform consists of several complete applications that include a web log engine (blogs), forums, photo gallery, and file gallery. With this combination, it's easy for online communities to collaborate and share their knowledge with each other and with people outside the community. In addition, the platform is extremely extensible, offering developers the source code used to create Community Server as well as a straightforward API to create additional applications and features.

Community Server is an established and proven software product, which is well recognized by industry experts. Its success is highlighted not only by the awards it has received but also through the appreciation that its users bestow upon it. For example, it was selected by readers of the *asp.netPRO* magazine as the best forums solution for 2005 and 2006. This is a telling indicator of the usefulness of not only the individual applications that compose Community Server but also the platform as a whole.

Community Server is a community product, meaning that its source code is freely available. The core product is also available at no cost in a special personal edition. There are other editions that are available for purchase, which are all geared toward meeting different requirements. That being said, Community Server is definitely a platform that is viewed as meeting the requirements and needs of almost every community imaginable.

Telligent's Role in Community Server

The company that owns Community Server is Telligent Systems. Telligent maintains the source code for Community Server and also provides outstanding support for it. While the source code for Community Server is maintained by Telligent, it is also open to the public. This means that people outside of Telligent are free to contribute source code and feature suggestions. Telligent provides amazing support to those who use Community Server. When you combine this high level of support with an award-winning product like Community Server, the results are phenomenal.

Telligent's main office is in Dallas, Texas, and currently employs more than 50 outstanding people. In addition to those who work in the main office, there are also several other individuals who telecommute to work. These other individuals span all of the time zones in the United States as well as some in other countries, which further improves the level of service that can be offered to customers.

It is also important to understand that Telligent goes beyond Community Server by delivering custom solutions to clients. Telligent also has other products that they have released and are currently in development. One of their more recent and popular products that can be used with a Community Server installation is blogmailr. This tool allows for people to freely post to their blog simply by sending an email.

Previous Versions

From its early releases, Community Server has maintained the goal of enabling online communities to be created quickly and easily. As a result of this goal, people are able to accomplish more with less difficulty with each successive release of Community Server. This goal has been advanced by the addition of new features and the simplification of existing ones. In addition, the feedback provided by community members and customers has helped to shape Community Server through its different versions.

The version numbers of Community Server are tied, in some ways, to the version of .NET that they are able to operate on. Community Server 1.1 runs on .NET 1.1, while Community Server 2.0 and greater are able to run on .NET 2.0. However, it is important to note that Community Server 2.0 and 2.1 can both run on the .NET 1.1 Framework.

Throughout the time that Community Server has existed, it has become more stable as well as more targeted at enabling online communities. For example, with the release of version 2.0, master pages and skin files were introduced. As a result, communities were able to customize the look of their community site with ease. Now, with the release of 3.0, Community Server has simplified the theming process, thus making it even easier to customize the look of a community site. In this way, newer versions of Community Server are constantly improving on existing features and processes. One of the main focuses of each revision of Community Server is simplification. This does not mean that features are removed but that each new version of Community Server is easier to use than the previous one.

Exploring the Applications

The main applications that Community Server offers are a complete blogging engine, forums, photo gallery, and file gallery. All of these applications combine to create a complete community platform that is easily set up to activate online communities quickly. In addition, Community Server also offers a complete way to manage your community members with an enterprise-quality membership system. There are also many features that Community Server includes that are offered across a site, such as searching and syndication. There is a wealth of features that Community Server provides for each application, but for the purposes of this introduction, only the applications themselves are explored here.

❑ **Blogs** — The number of bloggers has been growing over the last few years. A blog itself is nothing more than a web log or online journal that a person or group of people can keep. The entries or posts to a blog are usually organized in a chronological way, where the most recent posts are displayed first. In addition, there is also an archive that is kept of posts for each month that they were created. The blogging engine in Community Server allows every user to a site to have their own blog or even collaborate with others on shared blogs. It is easy to aggregate and search the blog posts using Community Server. You also have the option of allowing visitors to rate and comment on blog posts. This provides an entirely new level of community involvement from people who would not typically be able to contribute their thoughts.

❑ **Forums** — Forums are an important way for community members to be able to collaborate on different ideas. It allows members, and potentially nonmembers, to provide content that relates to specific predefined topics. Community Server allows members to be notified of updates to a forum topic by email or through RSS feeds.

❑ **Photo galleries** — Photo galleries provide a space for community members to share any image files that they have. These images can be well organized and can even be displayed in a slideshow fashion. Individual photos can be rated and commented on just as individual blog posts would be.

❑ **File galleries** — File galleries provide a mechanism for files to be published and shared with the community. The files can be organized into a logical folder structure. Similarly to the previous features, viewers can rate and comment on a file.

Understanding the Role of the First Version

The first version of Community Server was an important milestone because it marked the beginning of a platform offering forums, blogging, and a gallery solution in one package. The main goal for the release of the first version of Community Server was to provide a stable platform with all of the previous features. This first version was available in February 2005. It worked out that the next release, version 1.1, provided bug fixes to this initial version so that it was even more stable. Version 1.1 was available to the public in June 2005.

Community Server 3.0

Community Server 3.0 seeks to drastically improve several core areas of Community Server 2.1. This version contains new features and many bug fixes. The input from community members and clients has an enormous impact on the features that are included and excluded from this and other releases. There is a tremendous amount of energy that goes into Community Server and its useful versions not only from the Telligent employees but also from clients and community members.

New Features

There are several new core features that are contained in the 3.0 release of Community Server. They are described briefly in the following list:

- ❏ *Chameleon* is the name of the new theming engine. This new engine removes complicated skin files and is targeted at making it much easier to customize the presentation of a Community Server site. The themes themselves can be customized from the Community Server Control Panel. This is an improvement over previous releases that required an increased knowledge of web design and skinning. With Chameleon it is easier for nontechnical individuals to alter how their site is presented to visitors.

- ❏ *Zion* is the name of the new file storage system. One of the main attractions of Zion is that it offers a centralized way to store files. This allows for better support for post attachments and for file support.

- ❏ *Morpheus* is the name of the new membership system. This feature allows membership providers to be easily created outside of the standard ASP.NET 2.0 membership store. As a result, existing user stores are able to be utilized and integrated more completely.

- ❏ *Tallyman* is the name of the new Mail Gateway. This new system is important for sites of all sizes as it allows a site to have feature-rich email services. One of the important attractions of Tallyman is that it provides mail list support.

Usage

The new features in Community Server 3.0 will be usable by sites of all sizes. No site is left behind in this release. Existing communities can easily convert their site to Community Server, while new sites can be created quickly and easily with a wealth of advanced functionality.

Choosing the Right Edition for You

To find the most suitable edition of Community Server for your needs, visit the Telligent Store web site at http://store.telligent.com. On this site, there is a listing of all of the available editions as well as commercial add-ins that are available for Community Server. In addition, there is a good description of each edition and a feature matrix to help you identify what features are included.

When deciding on the most appropriate edition of Community Server to purchase, it is important to realize the value of the Gold Support option. This added support is a good option to purchase to help guarantee that your questions will be answered by professionals. While the standard support provided in the open forums is stellar, the Gold Support forums are beyond stellar. Therefore, it is important to consider the importance of purchasing Gold Support with your edition. It is also important to realize that the Enterprise Edition of Community Server includes Gold Support with the license.

Feature Matrix

The following table gives a high-level overview of the features available with each version of Community Server. This feature matrix is available at `http://store.telligent.com/FeatureMatrix.aspx` in a more complete form. If you would like to learn about pricing for each of the editions, please consult the preceding link. Credit is due to Telligent for providing such a useful and well-detailed feature matrix.

	Express Edition	Standard Edition	Professional Edition	Enterprise Edition
Web sites per server	Unlimited	1	10	Unlimited
Users per license	Unlimited	Unlimited	Unlimited	Unlimited
Forums per site	Unlimited	Unlimited	Unlimited	Unlimited
Blogs per site	Unlimited	Unlimited	Unlimited	Unlimited
Photos per site	Unlimited	Unlimited	Unlimited	Unlimited
Files per site (file gallery)	50	500	Unlimited	Unlimited
RSS Reader	250 users	Unlimited	Unlimited	Unlimited
Logo requirement for footer of every page	Yes	No	No	No
Spam blocker	Included	Included	Included	Included
IP Banning add-on	Not available	Yes	Yes	Yes

	Express Edition	Standard Edition	Professional Edition	Enterprise Edition
Member Points System	Not available	Yes	Yes	Yes
Reports	Not available	Yes	Yes	Yes
Web farm support	Not available	Not available	Yes	Yes
Single Sign-on Authentication add-ons	Not available	Add-on available	One included**	All included
Email Gateway	Not available	Add-on available	25 licenses included	100 licenses included

Table continued on following page

	Express Edition	Standard Edition	Professional Edition	Enterprise Edition
Enterprise Search	Not available	Add-on available	Included	Included
NNTP News Gateway	Not available	Add-on available	Add-on available	100 licenses included
FTP Gateway	Not available	Add-on available	Add-on available	100 licenses included
Email Gateway Microsoft Exchange Connector	Not available	Add-on available	Add-on available	Included
Tier II Premium Support included	Not available	Not included	Not included	10 hours

Licensing Community Server

The preceding editions can be purchased from the Telligent Store, and the licenses can be applied to a Community Server implementation easily. In addition, it is also easy to upgrade your license for Community Server. When you decide to purchase Community Server, you can simply navigate to https://store.telligent.com and select the edition that is appropriate for you. The following sections explain more specifics about these editions, and this can help you decide which is most appropriate for your needs. In addition, if you still have questions you can go to the forums at http://communityserver.org and ask for advice. There are many people who are eager to assist you to make the best decision for your situation.

Once you have purchased a license, you can install it through an existing installation of Community Server. To install the license, simply complete the following steps:

1. Log in as an administrator.

2. Click on the Control Panel link.

3. Click on the Administration link.

4. Expand the System Tools menu on the left and select Manage Licenses (see Figure 1-1).

5. Extract the license file provided by Telligent if it is compressed.

6. Click the Browse button on the Manage Licenses page and navigate to the license file you extracted.

7. Click Install, and your new license will be installed and your Community Server site updated.

Figure 1-1: Manage Licenses

Express Edition

You may also find that the Express Edition is referred to as the Personal Edition, as it is targeted more at individual users who need only limited functionality. Furthermore, the Express Edition is the only edition of Community Server that does not cost any money. However, this edition is intended for personal use with small communities. This can be a good starting edition for many people who are starting a small community and do not require the benefits of the other editions.

It is important to understand that if you are going to require any of the commercial add-ons to Community Server, you need to purchase at least the Standard Edition. However, as mentioned previously, it is easy to upgrade your editions using the License Management tool that comes with all versions of Community Server.

Another important aspect of the Express Edition is the fact that you are required to include the Community Server logo at the bottom of every page on your site that is using Community Server. Even though the logo is small and unobtrusive, it is important to realize this requirement.

Gold Support is not available with this edition of Community Server.

Standard Edition

The Standard Edition of Community Server is a step up from the Express Edition, as you receive many new features. One of the most important new features is the addition of reports. These are discussed in more detail in Chapter 9, but they basically allow you to learn more about the current state of your community.

In addition, the Standard Edition provides support for all of the commercial add-ons. If your site requires any of these add-ons, you need to purchase the Standard Edition of Community Server or higher.

The Standard Edition is mainly useful for small to medium-sized community sites; this edition is not for use in a web farm. Additionally, up to 500 files can be stored in the file gallery when the Standard license has been installed.

Gold Support is available with the purchase of the Standard Edition license.

Professional Edition

The Professional Edition of Community Server adds several new features and is designed for all sizes of communities. One of the important distinctions between the Professional Edition and the Standard Edition is that the Professional Edition adds support for web farms.

In addition, it is also important to realize that a Professional Edition allows for up to 10 different web sites running on Community Server to be installed. This is extremely important if you plan on developing multiple communities.

With the purchase of the Professional Edition, you also receive a couple of commercial add-ons at no additional cost. These include the extremely powerful Enterprise Search, Email Gateway, and a Single Sign-on Authentication add-on. If you were planning to purchase any of these add-ons, then definitely consider simply purchasing the Professional Edition, which already includes them.

Also, starting with the Professional Edition you get the ability to have an unlimited number of files per site in the file gallery. This is an important distinction to consider when comparing the Professional Edition to the Standard or Express Edition.

Enterprise Edition

The Enterprise Edition of Community Server is the most feature rich of all of the editions. This edition provides support for Web Farms and will run sites of all sizes. In addition, it includes all of the available commercial add-ons.

An important distinction between the Enterprise Edition and the Standard and Professional Editions is that the Enterprise Edition allows an unlimited number of sites to be installed on the server. If you expect to have multiple communities or a large web farm, then consider the benefits of Enterprise Edition when making your decision.

The Enterprise Edition includes Gold Tier I support at no additional cost. Additionally, it includes 10 hours of Tier II Premium Support. This is extremely important to consider when making a decision between the different editions. The Gold Tier I support allows for any questions about Community Server to be asked in the Gold Forums.

The Future of Community Server

The future of Community Server is so bright that you may have to wear shades. It shows great promise, as each version has attracted many new users and customers. Simplicity of use is one of the main focuses of Community Server; therefore, each new version strives to be even easier to use than the previous one.

Future Support

Community Server has always received excellent support from the Telligent employees as well as community members. The ongoing support of Community Server is some of the best that you will find with any product. If you have purchased Gold Support for Community Server you can expect an even higher-quality answer to any of the questions that you have regarding the product. In addition, there is also a focus to improve the existing level of support that exists. As a result of this outstanding level of support, which is here to stay, you should consider purchasing Gold Support for Community Server.

The Roadmap

Telligent made a roadmap available for Community Server at `http://communityserver.org/i/roadmap.aspx`. This roadmap details the planned features in the next releases of Community Server. If you are interested in a new feature in Community Server, consult this roadmap to learn whether or not it will be included in a future release. If you do not see the desired feature, you can go ahead and post your request in the Community Server forums.

Summary

Community Server is an award-winning platform that offers several enterprise applications. In addition, these applications and the features available vary with each edition of Community Server. Furthermore, the platform itself has been evolving throughout the years so that with each release it becomes easier to use, while providing more useful features.

In the next chapter, you will expand on your understanding of Community Server by learning how to install it. As a result, you will be able to complete an installation of a Community Server site in various ways.

2
Installation

In this chapter you will learn how to install Community Server in an environment that is appropriate for your site. Whether you are upgrading from a previous version or performing a fresh install, this chapter provides adequate instruction on how to perform a new installation. In addition, it also provides the steps necessary for configuring Visual Studio 2005 for use with the Community Server SDK. This chapter is a valuable starting point for getting Community Server running in your environment.

Requirements for Community Server

There are certain system requirements that you should be aware of before you install Community Server. It is important to keep in mind that as newer releases become available, these requirements have the potential to change. After downloading a new version of Community Server, consult the list of system requirements available at `http://docs.communityserver.org` and also the list contained in the Installation Wizard.

System Requirements

Although specific hardware requirements are not defined on the Community Server web site, it is important to understand that they do exist. They exist primarily to provide a means for meeting the software's minimum requirements. For example, one of the software requirements is that you have either Windows Server 2003 or Windows XP Professional installed. Although Windows XP Professional is listed in the requirements, it is recommended that you do not use it to host your site but rather to help you in developing it. In order for either of these products to run correctly, Microsoft recommends (see `http://support.microsoft.com/kb/314865`) that you have the following:

- ❏ At least 300-MHz processor
- ❏ At least 128MB RAM
- ❏ At least 1.5GB of available space on your hard disk

Once you have the appropriate server hardware in place, you need the software to host your web site and a database. Software requirements are detailed in the next section.

While it is possible to run Community Server from a single server running both the Internet Information Server (IIS) web server as well as the database, you may want to consider separating the serving of web content from the performing of database operations. Having two servers can really help boost the performance of your site. To utilize two servers, run SQL Server on one of the servers and IIS on the other. In extreme cases you may decide to run load-balanced web servers and even possibly add redundant warm failover servers for both web and database.

Perhaps dedicated servers aren't the right option for you, and it would be better to utilize a shared server. In most of the shared-hosting plans that are currently available, the SQL Server boxes are separate from the web server boxes, which is a good thing. You should understand that these hosting plans often host multiple sites on the same box, It is important that you plan appropriately for your site visitors' sake. If you have thousands of people hitting your site daily, consider a dedicated hosting package or purchase the Community Server Hosted Edition. The Hosted Edition of Community Server provides you with several options to help target your site's requirements. There is a more detailed explanation of the Hosted Edition of Community Server later in this chapter.

Additional discussion of the various ways in which you could architect your server infrastructure for the deployment of your Community Server site is beyond the scope of this chapter. However, if you can think of an architecture that you would like to deploy, it's likely that Community Server will be perfectly suited for that architecture. Furthermore, you can probably find someone who has already deployed a site with a similar hardware architecture.

Taking into account the requirements of Community Server and the requirements for all of the necessary software programs, the following configuration is recommended:

- ❑ 1-GHz processor
- ❑ 1GB RAM
- ❑ 2.5GB available hard disk space

If you plan on having many sites hosting on the same server, or if your server has a substantial amount of load on it, consider upgrading some of these components, especially the amount of RAM and the processor speed.

Software Requirements

Telligent offers a list of software requirements for hosting Community Server under the Server Requirements and Hosting Suggestions article available at `http://docs.communityserver.org`. Before you install a newer version of Community Server, you should first consult this document. The system requirements recommended by Telligent for hosting Community Server at the time of this writing are the following:

- ❑ Web Server
  - ❑ Microsoft Windows Server 2003 (recommended)
  - ❑ Internet Information Services 6.0 (recommended) or Internet Information Services 5.0
  - ❑ Microsoft .NET Framework version 2.0

❏   Database Server

  ❏   Microsoft SQL Server 2000 or SQL Server 2005

  ❏   Microsoft Desktop Engine (MSDE) 2000 or SQL Server 2005 Express

Your Site's Requirements

There are several editions of both Windows Server 2003 and SQL Server that you should be aware of. Which edition that is right for you depends on the size of your site and the size of your organization. For example, if you are going to install Community Server for a large corporation that has thousands of employees using its web site, then consider purchasing enterprise editions of the various servers. In addition, you want to make sure that the server or servers running the site have adequate resources available to them. If your site has a small number of visitors or users, then consider purchasing a small hosting package. It is not always necessary to have the fastest computers and the most expensive software if only a handful of people are visiting a site. There is no need to go overboard. Ensure that the servers you use meet your minimum requirements, and you should be in good shape. Again, a recommended solution is to simply purchase Community Server Hosted Edition from www.communityserver.com.

Community Server Hosted Edition

Telligent recently released a new edition of Community Server that does not require the purchaser to install it. In addition to installing the site, Telligent hosts the site for you. This is a recommended solution for running your site, because you do not have to worry about the minimum system requirements.

The Hosted Edition comes in three flavors, Standard, Professional, and Platinum. Each of these flavors is targeted at a different-sized community. The Standard version meets the requirements of many small communities, whereas Professional and Platinum both meet the needs of many medium to large communities. If none of these versions adequately meets your community's needs, then contact the sales department at Telligent in order to get a version that is most appropriate for your community.

Shared Hosting of Community Server

There are several hosts that are available that will gladly host your Community Server installation. Before deciding on a host, first consult the http://docs.communityserver.org site because it provides a list of recommended hosts. You should also consult the host where you are considering installing Community Server to determine how many sites are currently hosted on the server your site will reside on. This can be important in determining which host to invest in, because you will know the anticipated bandwidth on the server on which you will be running your site. For example, if one host has 100 sites that it hosts on the server your site will reside on, while another has only 20, then you will be able to make a more informed decision about the host to go with. In addition, it can be helpful in identifying the available bandwidth that each host provides.

Many hosts will even install Community Server for you; this can also be a factor that determines the host to purchase space with. For example, the ASPnix host will install Community Server on your site for an affordable price (only $10 at the time of this writing). Another consideration when deciding on an appropriate host is the limitations the host imposes on your site, such as the number of databases that you can have. If you plan to install other products in addition to Community Server, you may want to consider investing in a host that will allow you to have multiple SQL Server databases without additional cost. There are many things to consider when deciding on a host; therefore, it is important to keep in mind the expected size of your community along with the minimum system requirements outlined previously.

Getting Ready to Install

There are several important steps that you should be aware of before you attempt to install Community Server. First, you need to download the appropriate copy of Community Server. In addition, it is a good idea to have a basic understanding of how the installation files are organized. This section will explore the various areas that will affect you when you begin the installation process.

Where to Download Community Server

The Community Server web site located at `http://www.communityserver.org` contains a Downloads link where you will find a folder called Current Releases. In the Current Releases folder, there is a sub-folder called Community Server that contains the most recent releases of Community Server. In addition to the Downloads link, navigate to the Purchase Now link and purchase an appropriate license for Community Server. Although Community Server is free for personal use, it is not intended to be used commercially without purchasing the appropriate license.

Whenever you view the current releases of Community Server, you will notice several packages that you can download (see Figure 2-1). The Community Server SDK is primarily for developers who are interested in looking at the source code of Community Server and perhaps extending it. The other downloads are divided into a Web Installer and a Microsoft Installer (MSI). The MSI downloads are for installing Community Server locally using a standard Microsoft Install Wizard. The Web Installer is used to install Community Server on a remote machine, requiring only that you have access to upload the installation folders and use your web browser to step through the installation process. If you are installing onto a shared host, then you will most likely need to download the web install package. Make sure that the .NET Framework version on your server matches the version listed on the download file.

File	Date Added	Downloads	
Community Server 2.1 - SDK Community Server 2.1 - Software Development Kit (B... ★★★★★	08-11-2006	2675	⬇ Download File Size 8.1MB
Community Server 2.1 (MSI) - ASP.NET 1.1 Community Server 2.1 - Windows Executable Installe... ★★★★★	08-09-2006	1179	⬇ Download File Size 5.7MB
Community Server 2.1 (MSI) - ASP.NET 2.0 Community Server 2.1 - Windows Executable Installe... ★★★★☆	08-09-2006	4111	⬇ Download File Size 5.7MB
Community Server 2.1 (Web Install) - ASP.NET 1.1 Community Server 2.1 - Web Installer & Upgrade... ★★★★★	08-09-2006	1404	⬇ Download File Size 6.5MB
Community Server 2.1 (Web Install) - ASP.NET 2.0 Community Server 2.1 - Web Installer & Upgrade... ★★★★★	08-09-2006	4351	⬇ Download File Size 6.4MB

Figure 2-1: Community Server Downloads

In order to download any of these files, you need to register on the Community Server site. You may want to go ahead and look at the forums to see if anyone has reported anything about installing Community Server on the host you have selected. For example, GoDaddy may take care of the installation process, but it will not give you access to the installation files. This can cause problems whenever you try to extend Community Server, because you will have no way to access the physical files. It is important that, before installing Community Server, you take the time to look for possible issues with your host. Simply taking five minutes to perform this upfront research can save you time later, if you encounter any issues with the install process.

Understanding the Folder Structure

After you download the SDK or the Web Installer, extract the files inside of the download package. You can do this by using a tool such as WinRar, which is available for free at www.rarlabs.com. Simply extract the package to a folder such as C:\Development\CommunityServer. Executing the MSI will also create a web folder, but this process is discussed later in this chapter.

The SDK comes with many more files and folders than the Web Installer package. Once you have extracted the SDK package, open and browse to the web folder using a file explorer. You should have all of the folders shown in Figure 2-2. Although the content of every folder is not discussed, this book covers the files that you will most likely use often.

Figure 2-2: Community Server Web Folder Structure

❑   **Bin**—Contains the assemblies that are used by the Community Server web project. This is an important folder because it is where you place module assemblies and other assemblies that are used for extending Community Server.

❑   **ControlPanel**—Contains all of the pages used on the Control Panel. This is an important folder because it is where you place extra pages that you use to extend any of the Control Panel's functionality. In addition, this folder is secured and is not accessible on the Web by users who do not have administrative privileges on your site.

❑ **Installer**—Contains the installation page and SQL scripts that are necessary to set up a new installation of Community Server. This folder should be deleted after your new installation is working.

❑ **Languages**—Contains files necessary for localizing and changing the text that is displayed on a Community Server site. In addition, the languages files contain help files, which are accessible by site visitors.

❑ **Themes**—Contains the files that you will use to customize the look of Community Server.

❑ **Utility**—Contains the JavaScript files that provide some of the unique functionality that Community Server offers.

Looking at the Database Schema

The database is set up during the installation process. It can be helpful for the overall understanding of the installation process to look at the database schema used by Community Server. While this is important to understand to gain a better grasp on what occurs during the installation process, if you are not a developer, then it is fine to skip this section and proceed on to "Installing Locally."

During the installation process, you are presented with an option to install ASP.NET Membership tables. However, it is important to understand that in version 3.0 of Community Server, it is optional for these tables to reside in the same database as Community Server. If you already have an existing user store that you would like to use with Community Server, then you don't have to install a new copy ASP.NET Membership schema with Community Server 3.0. However, with previous versions you should make sure that this option is checked unless the database you are installing into already has the ASP.NET Membership schema installed.

After you install Community Server, your database will contain many new tables and stored procedures. There will also be new key constraints between many of the tables. Figure 2-3 shows breakouts of the new tables that are generated as a result of the Community Server installation. Chapter 14 provides a description of each of these tables.

In addition to simply looking at the table structure in the preceding figure, there is a document available on the Community Server web site that diagrams the complete database schema for Community Server 1.1. It is available on the Downloads page under the Community Server Downloads root folder group and then under the Documentation subfolder. The main table that you may need to access during the lifetime of your site is the cs_Exceptions table. The cs_Exceptions table contains an account of the exceptions that occur on your site. These are available in the Exceptions Report, which is discussed in more detail in Chapter 9. You may need to access this table if an exception occurs that prevents you from being able to access the Control Panel of your site, and you want to learn about the actual exception itself—although the chances of this occurring on your site are extremely slim.

Figure 2-3: Database Tables

Installing Locally

The local installation is done through the wizard provided in the MSI download package. This file is available from the Downloads page on www.communityserver.org. In addition, this is perhaps the easiest way to perform an installation of Community Server, because it will create a database for you. Similarly, the MSI will also create a virtual directory for your Community Server installation that points to the appropriate folder.

Configuring the Database Server

Because the Installation Wizard takes care of much of the heavy lifting involved with your database server, there is actually not much that you need to do in order to begin the installation process. You just need to be able to connect to a SQL server that meets the requirements listed in the "Software Requirements" section earlier in this chapter. It is also a good idea to go ahead and create a user account just for Community Server on your SQL Server installation. You should also make sure that you are using a best practice password that is several characters in length and contains at least one nonalphanumeric character. However, if you do not want to require a separate user account for connecting to SQL Server, you can connect to the server using integrated security and a Windows user account by setting `trusted_connection=true` in the connection string. For the purposes of the installation instructions provided as follows, it is assumed that you are using a new user account.

If you are connecting to a database server that is on a remote machine then you should check to make sure that you are able to connect to it from the computer that you are installing Community Server on. You can use the SQL Server Management Studio Express, which is available for free from Microsoft, to test the connection to the remote server. When you have tested your connection and have created an account for Community Server, you can proceed to the next section on running the actual MSI Installer.

Running the Windows MSI Installer

In order to run the MSI Installer, you should first locate it on your computer. It can be found in the folder where you placed the downloaded copy of the MSI version of Community Server. Navigate to this folder and complete the following steps:

1. Double-click the MSI Community Server file to begin the installation process.

2. If you already have Community Server installed, you will be prompted to either Repair or Remove the existing copy. If this is the first time you are installing Community Server, then you should simply press the Next button.

3. The second step of the installer contains an introduction to what you will be installing. Please read through the information and click the Next button to proceed.

4. The third step is the presentation of the license agreement. To complete the installation of Community Server, you first need to agree to the terms and conditions detailed on this page. Take the time to read through these terms, and once you are ready to continue, select the I Agree radio button, indicating that you agree to the terms, and click the Next button.

5. The next screen allows you to control the folder that Community Server will be installed to, as well as what users on the computer will have access to this folder (see Figure 2-4). The default install directory is `C:\Program Files\Telligent\Community Server <version>`, where `<version>` is the version number of the Community Server package being installed. If you do not like the folder destination, then you can change it at this point by clicking the Browse button and navigating to the appropriate directory or by typing the directory. If you are curious whether your computer has enough room for the Community Server installation, you can simply click the Disk Cost button. When you have everything ready to continue, you can click the Next button.

6. The next screen is the Install Confirmation screen, which is the last step before the actual files are copied to the install directory. When you are ready to proceed with the install process, click the Next button.

7. After the files are copied, you are presented with the configuration portion of the Installation Wizard. This is where you set up the database connection and web server, and also optionally install a starter community. Read the welcome screen and when ready, click the Next button.

8. The next screen is the Web Server configuration screen (see Figure 2-5). The default installation will create a new virtual directory called `cs` under the root web site. This means your site will be accessible at `http://localhost/cs`. However, if you decide to install to the root folder then it will be accessible at `http://localhost/`. If you would like to change this path, please do so

now. If you have any questions, you can also click on the Learn more about setup link at the bottom of this screen. When you have made all necessary changes and are ready to proceed, click the Next button.

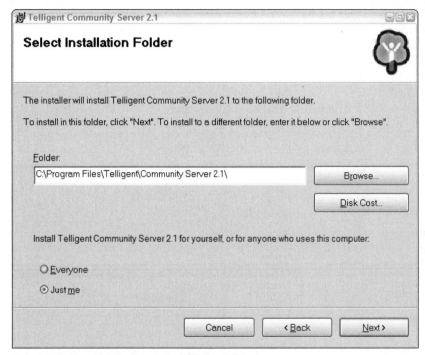

Figure 2-4: Community Server Installation Wizard

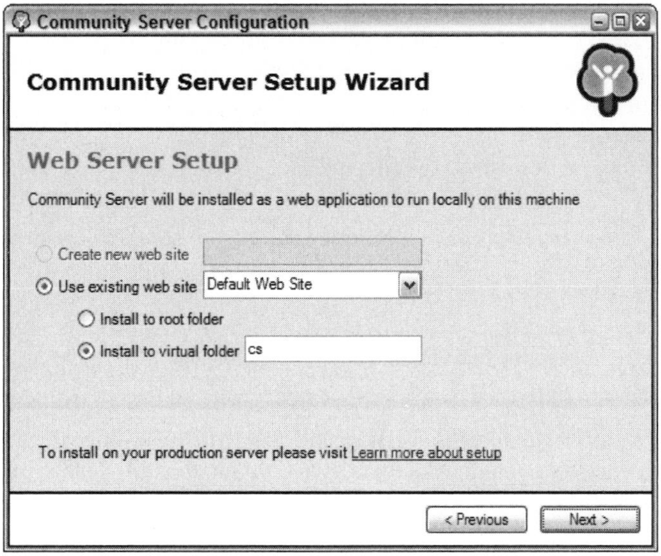

Figure 2-5: Web Server Setup

9. The next screen presents the configuration settings for the database (see Figure 2-6). You should already know the server address for the database server and also the type of authentication you use to connect to the database. The default setup will point to a local database server and try to create a database called CommunityServer. If you want to change any of these settings, you can do so now. After you have everything pointing to the correct server and using the appropriate authentication, click the Next button to test your connection. If you encounter a warning about mixed-mode authentication, then you can try selecting the Windows authentication option.

Figure 2-6: Community Server Database Server Setup

If an error occurs when you try to connect, you are presented with the error message shown in Figure 2-7. If this occurs, it is nothing to worry about; simply click the OK button and change the connection information, and then try again.

Figure 2-7: Database Connection Failed Error Message

10. Whenever the database connection is established, you are prompted to confirm the authentication you use to connect to the database. If everything looks acceptable on this screen, then click the Next button to proceed.

11. The next step is to configure your Community Server site settings (see Figure 2-8). You should provide the login and password fields for the administrative account that you want to install on your community site. In addition, supply an email address that can be used for contacting the site's administrator. When you are ready to continue, click the Next button and your new account will be created in the database.

Figure 2-8: Web Site Configuration

12. The final screen provides you with an overview of the installation process. You are now able to navigate to your site. When you are ready to complete the installation process, simply click the Finish button.

It is important to check the results of your installation whenever it is complete. After you complete these steps, navigate to your new site and try to log in. This is also a good way to start becoming more familiar with Community Server.

Installing on a Remote Server

Like the MSI installation, http://docs.communityserver.org provides a good overview for completing an installation using the Web Installer. Therefore, if at any time during the installation process, you feel the need to consult another source, you should refer to the installation guide on the Community Server site.

Configuring the Server

To run the Web Installer, you need to download the Web Installer package from the Community Server site and extract it to a local temporary directory, such as C:\Temp. By default, for security purposes, the Web Installer is disabled. That way, malicious users are not able to perform an installation on your site. It is also important to disable or remove the installer when you are finished using it. This will be restated in the finals steps below; however, it is important to be are aware of. You also want to configure your web server so that it has a virtual directory location set up at which to install Community Server. You should check the Read and Run Scripts options when configuring this virtual directory.

Aside from configuring the web server, you also want to make sure that the database server is ready for the installation. Create a new database to be used by Community Server and the installation process. Within this database, create a user account with db_owner privileges. You'll provide this username and password during the web installation process. You may choose to add the ASPNET user so it can use Windows authentication. If you use SQL Server authentication, test the new connection by connecting to the database with a tool such as the SQL Management Studio and the newly created account.

Preparing to Run the Web Installer

Once you have the files extracted, you need to follow these steps to prepare them for a Web installation:

1. Open default.aspx under the Installer folder, using notepad as the editor.

2. Change the line toward the top of default.aspx from

   ```
   bool INSTALLER_ENABLED = false;
   ```

   to

   ```
   bool INSTALLER_ENABLED = true;
   ```

3. Save this file and close Notepad.

4. Using a File Transfer Protocol (FTP) tool, such as Smart FTP, upload all of the files and folders in the Web directory to your web server. It is important that everything be copied into a location that is set up as a virtual directory and has ASPNET read permissions. In addition, you may need to grant ASPNET Full Control on the following folders, depending whether you plan to use each function. For example, if you do not plan to use the blogs, then you do not need to worry about changing the permissions on the blogs/files folder.

   ❑ blogs/files

   ❑ photos/cache

   ❑ photos/storage

   ❑ files/storage

   ❑ Utility/RankIcons

   ❑ Utility/RoleIcons

Using the Web Installer

Whenever you are ready to begin using the Web Installer, you simply need to navigate to your site and add the word installer after it. If your site is called wyattpreul.com, then you would navigate to wyattpreul.com/installer. If you encounter an error, such as one stating that directory browsing is not allowed, then you should also add /default.aspx after installer. In addition, you may need to add default.aspx as a valid document in the IIS. When you start the Web Installer, you will notice the screen shown in Figure 2-9, which introduces you to the installation process and reminds you of the requirements. After you have double-checked that you meet these requirements, click the Next button and complete the instructions that follow.

1. Unlike the Windows installer, the Web Installer does not create a new database for you. Therefore, you need to create a database for Community Server on your SQL Server. You can use the freely available SQL Server Management Studio Express to connect to your database server and create a new database. In addition, you should make sure that you know the parameters for connecting to this Community Server database. The parameters that you need are the name of the server that you connect to, and the username and password if you are not using Windows integrated security. When you have all of these details, click the Next button on the Web Installer.

2. The second screen of the installer displays the license agreement for Community Server. Look over this agreement, and if you agree to its terms, check the I Agree checkbox and click the Next button.

3. The screen shown in Figure 2-10 is used to configure the connection to the database server. Input the parameters you gathered in Step 1 into the appropriate fields on this page. When you are ready to test your connection, click the Next button.

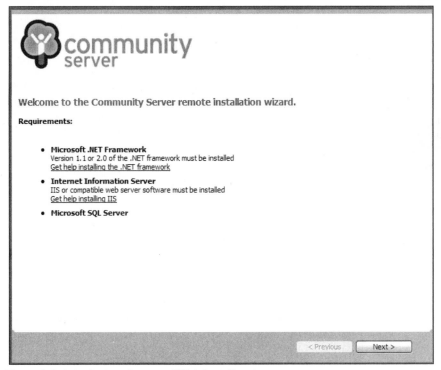

Figure 2-9: Introductory Screen of Web Installer

Figure 2-10: Web Installer Database Configuration

4. The next screen will inform you whether your connection is successful. If the installer is successfully able to connect to the database, you will see a drop-down list with your database as one of the options. If you do not see any databases, you should click the Previous button and double-check your login parameters. If everything looks correct, then simply select the database that you would like to install into, and click the Next button.

5. On the next screen, choose what main components you would like to install. There are three options: Install the ASP.NET Membership, The Community Server database tables, and Create a Community (see Figure 2-11). If you already have a user store or already have ASP.NET Membership installed on the database, then you can unselect the first option. The second option determines if you want to install the Community Server database; you will probably never need to unselect this option. The third option, creating a community, will generally not need to be unselected. If this is your first time installing Community Server, you should leave the checkboxes checked. When you have made your decision, click the Next button.

6. The next step allows you to configure some basic information about the community that you are creating (see Figure 2-12). The Community URL field should be automatically detected by the installer and you do not need to make any changes to it. The other parameters are for setting up the administrator account for your new community. This user account will be granted System Administrator privileges; therefore, it is important that you choose a secure password when creating this account. When you have completed filling in these fields, click the Next button to begin the installation of Community Server with the provided information.

Figure 2-11: Web Installer Installation Options

Figure 2-12: Web Installer Create New Community Screen

7. If everything was successfully installed, you will see a final screen informing you that your
    community was installed (see Figure 2-13). This page also may include several application
    settings that you need to copy into your site's web.config file. If this is the case, a message is
    displayed on the page. It is important that you copy these settings over the appSettings sec-
    tion in the web.config file and test the installation. Also, before you make this change to the
    web.config file, you should make sure to create a backup copy of the file. In addition, this
    page will provide a link to your new community's site. You should click on this link and try to
    log in with the account created in Step 6 to confirm that everything was created appropriately.
    Once you have confirmed your installation, either disable the Installation Wizard or delete the
    installer folder completely. To disable the Installation Wizard, you simply need to change the
    value in the installer/default.aspx page for INSTALLER_ENABLED to false.

Figure 2-13: Web Installer Completion Screen

Manual Installation

Instead of using one of the wizards, you can install Community Server manually. Installing it manually
requires a thorough familiarity with both with IIS and with SQL. The basic process involves creating a
new virtual directory for Community Server and also running several SQL scripts.

Regardless of whether you are manually installing locally or remotely, you need to copy the web folder found in the Web Installer package to the area on the web server where you would like the files to reside. After you have the folder in an appropriate location, you need to create a virtual directory pointing to this location. If you are installing on a remote machine, you will, more than likely, need to use the Control Panel that the host offers so that you can create a new virtual directory pointing to your web folder. To create a new virtual directory in your local IIS, complete the following steps:

1. Run the command `inetmgr` from your Start menu to open the IIS Manager.

2. Inside IIS, you can expand out the Web Sites folder; then right-click on the Default Web Site.

3. In the context menu, choose New ⇨ Virtual Directory.

4. Follow the wizard to create a new virtual directory pointing to the web folder in the location where you would like Community Server to reside.

5. Complete the steps in the preceding "Preparing to Run the Web Installer" section so that the folders have the appropriate permissions.

6. You can test to make sure that you have the virtual directory created appropriately by navigating to the static `error.htm` page in the root of the site. If your virtual directory is called `cs` and it is installed locally, you can go to `http://localhost/cs/error.htm`. If you encounter errors, refer to the "Troubleshooting Installation Issues" section that follows.

7. Create a new database for Community Server. Grant the following roles to the user account that the Community Server installation will be using to connect to this database. You can perform this task using the freely available SQL Server Management Studio Express tool.

   ❑ db_securityadmin

   ❑ db_ddladmin

   ❑ db_datareader

   ❑ db_datawriter

8. Now you need to run the installation SQL scripts located in the `SqlScripts` folder of the root folder of the SDK package. If you look in this same folder, you find a `readme` file that details what these scripts are and how to run them. Run the scripts in the following order to install both Community Server and the ASP.NET Membership schema:

   a. Execute `cs_<YOUR VERSION>_CreateFullDatabase.sql`

   b. Execute `cs_ASPNET2_Membership_Schema_Update.sql`

9. Run the following stored procedure to create a new community in your database. You may notice that the screen shown in Figure 2-12 is used to collect the parameters to call this procedure during the installation process. The capitalized words in the following command should be replaced with your values before running the command.

```
exec dbo.cs_system_CreateCommunity
   @SiteUrl = 'YOUR_URL',
   @ApplicationName = 'dev',
   @AdminEmail = 'YOUR_EMAIL_ADDRESS',
   @AdminUserName = 'admin',
   @AdminPassword = 'YOUR_SECURE_PASSWORD',
   @PasswordFormat = 0,
   @CreateSamples = 1
```

10. Change the SQL connection string in the `web.config` file to represent your connection to your database. For example, if your database was called `cs` and was on a server called SERVERNAME with a trusted connection, then you could use the following connection string to represent this:

```
server=SERVERNAME\SQLEXPRESS;uid=;pwd=;Trusted_Connection=yes;database=cs
```

11. After you have updated the `web.config` file, save it on top of the existing `web.config` file and attempt to connect to your new community. If everything was successful, then using a web browser, you should be able to navigate to your new site. If you do encounter errors with this process, refer to the "Troubleshooting Installation Issues" section that follows.

The documents on the Community Server web site at `http://docs.communityserver.org` are an excellent source for learning how to install Community Server. To learn more about the installation process, visit the site and look at the documentation on the appropriate installation.

Installing a Development Environment

The most detailed document that is available for learning how to install and build a module with the Community Server SDK is available at `www.davestokes.net` and is written by Dave Stokes. This document is much more in depth than the information offered in the following sections. However, the following sections provide a quick guide for configuring Visual Studio 2005 to develop code for Community Server.

Configuring Visual Studio 2005

In order to run the web project from Visual Studio 2005, you first need to install the Web Application Project update. This update allows you to create and run web application projects that are similar to those found in Visual Studio 2003. This update is available at `http://msdn2.microsoft.com/en-us/asp.net/aa336618.aspx` and should be installed prior to launching the Community Server SDK inside Visual Studio 2005.

Configuring IIS or Webdev.Webserver and Database

If you want to debug Community Server on IIS, then you need to complete the installation steps found in the "Manual Installation" section earlier in this chapter. Essentially, you are creating a new installation of Community Server that you will use in order to run and debug code changes.

However, you may also use the built-in web server that comes with Visual Studio 2005, called `webdev.webserver`, to debug your code. This is a web server that can be launched whenever you want to run and debug Community Server. You just need to load it at debug time and do not have to set up a virtual directory. This is important because it allows you to begin debugging without having to manually attach the debugger to the process, and you can also avoid creating a virtual directory. Whenever you are ready to move the installation to quality assurance, you can simply create a new installation that uses IIS and perhaps a different SQL database server.

If you do decide to use the `webdev.webserver` instead of IIS, then you will want to change the properties of the web project in Visual Studio 2005. To use the `webdev.webserver`, complete the following instructions:

1. Right-click on the Community Server web project in Visual Studio 2005, and choose the Properties option from the context menu.

2. Choose the Web tab in the property pages (see Figure 2-14).

3. Under the Servers section select the Use Visual Studio Development Server radio button, and press Ctrl-S to save your changes.

The next time that you want to run the project you simply need to press F5, and a new instance of the web server will start, attaching the debugger to the project. On the other hand, if you decide that you would like to use IIS, you simply need to select it from the web property page in the Servers section, select the option to use IIS, and point it to the URL where Community Server is located. In addition, if you would like to use the `webdeb.webserver` for debugging, while simultaneously running the same web project using IIS, this is also an option.

Figure 2-14: Visual Studio 2005 Servers Configuration

Aside from configuring the web server, you should set up the database that will be used by Community Server during the debugging process. To accomplish this, you should follow the manual installation steps in the "Manual Installation" section earlier in this chapter. You will also need to change the web `.config` connection string to point to your development SQL server.

Opening the Solution

When you are ready to open the Community Server solution, you simply need to open the appropriate solution in the source folder of the SDK package. To do this, you double-click on the solution file and Visual Studio will be launched. Inside this solution, you will find all of the projects that are shipped with the SDK package. A view of some of the projects that are a part of Community Server is displayed in the Solution Explorer screenshot in Figure 2-15. You can browse through these source files and look at how Community Server is built.

Figure 2-15: Solution Explorer Showing Community Server Solution

Debugging

To be able to debug the project, you need to make one final change in the web.config file to enable debugging. This change is made in the compilation section, and the property is to be changed is debug, which you should change to true. In addition, you may also need to set the web project as the startup project by right-clicking on the web project and selecting Set as StartUp Project. If everything was configured correctly, then you will be able to launch the web project with the Visual Studio debugger attached. To launch the project, you simply press the F5 key as you would in other projects. You can also set different breakpoints in the project and use watches and all of the other debugging tools that are common to Visual Studio.

Upgrading from a Previous Version

Community Server is an evolving product, which means that newer versions and service packs are released regularly. One of the many niceties of Community Server is that these new releases do not usually require you to purchase a new license. In addition, new releases typically come with good upgrade instructions. Many people in the community are also good about documenting the upgrade process for new releases and service packs. Therefore, if you would like to read more on how to upgrade from a particular version, you should search the forums on http://communityserver.org.

Backing Up Important Data

Before you complete any upgrade, you should always back up any important data. In the case of Community Server, this should include backing up your database. In addition, you should also back up any theme files that you have used to alter the look of your Community Server site. Last, you will want to also back up the core configuration files so that, if necessary, you can roll back to your previous version. Moreover, you should attempt to perform the upgrade on a copy of your live site locally before actually performing it on the live site itself. You may also need to notify your community members of the pending upgrade before you complete it.

Updating Necessary Files

For many of the service packs, you simply need to overwrite the assembly files located in the `bin` folder. Therefore, you should be able to simply FTP to your `bin` folder on the web server and copy the assemblies in the service pack over any existing assemblies with the same name. Aside from the assemblies, there are also occasional page updates that will need to be upgraded. To perform the file-based upgrades, you will simply need to overwrite the existing files.

Updating the Database Schema

In addition to overwriting updated files, you may also need to update the database schema. To accomplish this task, you need to connect to your database using a tool similar to SQL Server Management Studio Express. Once you are connected, you should only need to run the upgrade script that was packaged with the newer version of Community Server. This script should handle all of the schema upgrade process so that you are not responsible for manually updating tables or stored procedures.

Testing the Results

Once you have updated the appropriate Community Server files and the database schema, the only step left is to test your results. You should fire up a browser and navigate to your site's URL. If everything goes as planned, your site should be updated to the newer version. One of the ways that you can determine the version of Community Server that you are running is to look at the source code of the home page. The `Meta` tag for the `GENERATOR` of the page will tell you the version of Community Server that is installed.

Troubleshooting Installation Issues

Occasionally, people will run into issues with installing a web application such as Community Server. Generally, these issues are a result of environment or configuration changes. It is important that you understand that the environments in which you are installing Community Server are probably different from the next person's. The environment can be different because of the load on servers, potential network outages, and other applications that are installed. If you experience any issues with installing Community Server, you should first look at the most common issues and solutions. If you do not find your issue or solution here, then you should consult the forums on `http://www.communityserver.org` for other people with the same issue. If this fails, then you should post the issue you are experiencing, and someone should get back to you quickly to help get you running with Community Server.

Potential Issues

❑ A *Directory Listing Not Allowed* error can occur if you have not added `default.aspx` as a valid document in the IIS configuration for your site.

❑ A *Prompt for Credentials When Accessing Site* error can occur if you have not allowed anonymous access for your site. This is an IIS setting that you can enable to allow anonymous access to your site.

❑ *General issues* can sometimes be resolved by touching the `web.config` file to cause the application to refresh.

❑ A *SiteUrls Configuration Error* usually means that a section or line is missing in the SiteUrls .config file. This error message can sometimes be resolved by overwriting the SiteUrls .config file with a copy from an installation package. This error can also be caused by the community not being correctly installed; therefore, you can sometimes resolve it by reinstalling the community using the Create Community stored procedure.

❑ *Database connection* issues can occur whenever the connection string is not correct. In addition, you may also encounter issues if the database server does not allow connections from the web server that you are connecting from. Therefore, you should check the connection string in the web.config connectionStrings section and also verify that you can connect to the database server from the web server.

Where to Go for Help

The forums on http://communityserver.org are the premier places to go if you need help. In addition, if you would like to be guaranteed help, you should purchase Gold Support. The Gold Support option for Community Server is a phenomenal solution for resolving any issues with Community Server. You can create an account that will allow you to receive email updates whenever someone responds to your question. Aside from looking in the Community Server forums, you can also search through individuals' blogs because many people in the community are very good about reporting any issues that they run into.

Summary

In this chapter, you learned about the different ways that you can install Community Server. It is possible to install it using the Web Installer, using MSI installer, and manually. In addition to the different ways you are able to install your site, you also learned how to set up Visual Studio to debug a copy of Community Server. This chapter was important in getting you running with Community Server. Now that you have your site installed, you can proceed to Chapter 3 for a guided tour of the applications that compose your new site.

3

Guided Tour

Now that you have completed the installation of Community Server in Chapter 2, let's take a tour of some of its more common capabilities in this chapter. Throughout the tour, you will explore tasks such as adding Google Ads and custom content and organizing your site. In addition, you will explore the common applications that compose this rich platform and their usages; these include the blogs, forums, file gallery, photo gallery, Reader, and Control Panel. Each section will explore an application, as well as provide a step-by-step guide for performing common tasks. By the end of this chapter, you will be familiar with the core Community Server functionality.

Getting Started

To begin with, let's take a look at a typical Community Server page and establish a common vocabulary. You will encounter these terms throughout the remainder of this chapter. Understanding these terms will make it easier to learn some common tasks such as signing in to your newly installed Community Server site.

A Look Around

Go to your site's home page and observe some of the main areas that are displayed (see Figure 3-1).

As shown in Figure 3-1, there are five common areas that exist on a standard Community Server site installation. These sections are highlighted here and labeled with key terms that will be used throughout the chapter to describe these common areas on a Community Server site. Here is a list of the terms and what they represent:

❏   **Header**—Contains the site title and description, as well as the welcome area.

❏   **Welcome Area**—Contains the controls used to link to the login and registration pages and provides an easy way to search the content of a site.

❑ **Navigation Bar**—Contains the main navigation links that bring you to the different applications that are enabled on the site. You will observe later in this chapter that it contains additional links when you are signed in as an administrator.

❑ **Main Content**—Contains the content that is displayed on your site. You will learn later how to easily change this content.

❑ **Sidebar**—Contains the various links and content that are displayed on either the right or left side of your site.

Figure 3-1: Home Page Areas

The parts listed previously will be referred to throughout the remainder of this chapter. For example, the sidebar will be referred to as the sidebar section, and the welcome area will be referred to as the welcome area section. These terms will help you identify areas of your site easily, and this will help you perform the tasks outlined in the following sections.

Signing in as an Administrator

In order to explore your entire Community Server site, which includes many administrative pages, you need to sign in as an administrator. Once you are signed in to your Community Server site with an administrative user account, you can perform administrative tasks from the Control Panel. For the purposes of this demonstration, you will use the special "admin" user account that was created during installation. After you or your site's users create additional accounts, those accounts can also be used to sign in. Community Server supports delegated security permissions, and you can delegate administrative permissions to other accounts besides admin; this is, in fact, recommended. To learn more about setting up additional accounts and delegating permissions, please refer to Chapter 7.

The steps for signing in are the following:

1. Navigate to your site's home page.

2. Click the Sign in link located in the Welcome area section of the home page.

3. On the new page that loads, type in **admin** as the Sign in name and the password you configured for this account during the installation process.

    If you forget your password you can click the I forgot my password link to generate a new one.

4. Click the Sign in button below the password box.

By default, Community Server uses ASP.NET's Forms Authentication. When the sign-on is completed, Community Server relies on ASP.NET to generate a Forms Authentication cookie that stores an encrypted ticket that only that ASP.NET application trusts. Community Server also supports other authentication options using Single Sign-on Modules. Please refer to Appendix A for more information about Single Sign-on Modules.

Congratulations, you are now signed in as an administrator. If you take another look around, you should see some differences. These changes are highlighted in Figure 3-2.

Figure 3-2: Differences When Signed In

In addition to a couple of new menu items in the navigation bar section, such as My Reader and Control Panel, you should also notice some changes to the links in the Welcome area section. The first link, which displays your username, can be used to edit your profile. You can use the second link to sign out. Finally, a link to your private messages (Inbox) also appears whenever you are signed in.

Joining

Now that you are familiar with how to sign in to your site as an existing user, let's take a step back and learn the basics of joining your site from the perspective of a brand-new community member. There are a couple of easy ways to add users to your site:

❏ **Manually Create Accounts** — Have an administrator create the accounts and assign them the appropriate privileges. This task is accomplished through the Membership section of the Control Panel under the Create New Account option. However, this can become cumbersome if you have a rapidly growing community, since you would be forced to create the user account for each user.

❏ **User Created Accounts** — The preferred option for creating accounts is to use the automated registration process built into Community Server.

To understand the registration process from the point of view of new users, follow these steps to join a site:

1. Navigate to the home page of your site and click the Sign out link if you are currently signed in.

2. Click the Join link in the Welcome area section of your site. (Remember: You must be signed-out in order to see this link.)

3. Complete the new user registration form.

   The Sign in Name field should be unique and will be what you use to log in to the site as this user. You can set a friendlier display name in the user profile later on as well. The password in the two password fields must match and should be a strong password. In addition, there are an email and a time zone field that you should use to configure the email address you want associated with the new account and the time zone you live in.

4. Click the Join Now button to complete the new user registration process. Notice that once you click the Join Now button you are signed into your site as the new user that you just created. In addition, you should now see a link with the text of your new username. This link takes you to a page that you can use to change your profile. There is also a new link title inbox that takes you to your private messages, which will be explained later in this chapter in the forums section.

Again, there are several options for new user registration; the one that is presented here is the default configuration. In later chapters, we will examine capturing more user information during the registration process, as well as extending the process itself to include a more complex workflow. However, at this point, it is important to simply understand the basics of how new users can register for your site.

Changing the Content

In 2005, Telligent purchased a Content Management software package and immediately integrated some of its functionality into Community Server. A Content Management tool will be available in 2007 from Telligent, but several key content management capabilities are currently present in Community Server to help site administrators easily edit the site's content. In addition, the controls for enabling content changes are straightforward enough to allow site developers to quickly plug in to just about anywhere inside of a Community Server–powered site.

There are a couple of options for editing content inline on a live site:

❑ **Inline Content** — Inline content controls are typically used for content such as titles and descriptions. These items are typically already styled with Cascading Style Sheets (CSS) and don't require additional editing capabilities beyond changing the text. Inline editing is currently only supported in Internet Explorer.

❑ **Content Parts** — Content parts are used for editing rich content, when you may want to add images, hyperlinks, and any other content beyond simply changing text.

Once you have installed Community Server with the sample data, you can easily experiment with both of these content controls. To begin with, you will walk through how to inline edit site content. Follow these step-by-step instructions for changing your site's title and description using the inline editor:

1. Using Internet Explorer, sign in to your site as a user with administrative privileges.

2. On the home page of your site, click the site's title and notice that the insertion cursor is on the line with the content.

3. Type in a new title for your site; then click outside of the title area to save your changes to the database.

4. Repeat Steps 2 and 3 to change your site's description.

Whenever you explore your Community Server site, you'll find other areas where these inline edits are possible. Furthermore, it is possible to add your own custom editor controls throughout your site, which will be explained in Chapter 5.

Now that you have tried the inline text editor, let's look at the other main content control: content parts. In Chapter 5, you will learn how to use add the `ContentPart` and `InlineTextEdit` controls on your site. To better understand how the `ContentPart` control actually operates, complete the following steps for changing the bulk of your main page's content:

1. Log in to your site as an administrator.

2. Double-click the main content section of the home page (which starts with "Welcome!"). A new window will appear for editing the selected content. Feel free to move, resize, or close this window as you would in any of the popular operating systems.

3. Change the content that appears in the new box, and click the Save Changes button.

As you observed, the content-editing capabilities of Community Server are easy to use and also robust. As a site developer or administrator, you should be pleased to know that your site's content can be easily changed with these simple-to-use tools that come with Community Server. In addition, you should expect to see many great enhancements to the content-management capabilities of Community Server in future releases.

Enabling Google Ads

Ad revenue can be significant when added to sites that generate content, such as blogs or forums. Ad revenue is nothing more than money paid for the placement of advertisements on your web site.

Today, nobody does this better than Google. Google not only has an excellent advertising program but it is also one of the most popular providers and makes it easy for sites of any size to generate revenue.

An explanation of all of the key features of Google's advertising program is beyond the scope of this book. However, if you would like to learn more or register for Google's advertising program, Google AdSense, visit www.google.com/adsense. From this point forward, it is assumed that you have an account with Google AdSense and that you have access to the generated advertisement code for placement on your site.

Placing ads in your Community Server site couldn't be easier; in fact, you can do the majority of the ad management completely through the browser. In previous versions of Community Server, it was required that you edit an .ascx skin file.

To place Google AdSense on your site, please complete the following steps. Please note that these steps assume that you have a copy of the code from Google AdSense that you expect to place on your site.

1. Log in to your site as an administrator.

2. Click the Control Panel link on the navigation bar.

3. Now, click Administration in the resulting navigation bar.

4. Click the System Tools menu option on the left menu to expand out the various tools.

5. Click Manage Ads.

6. Make sure that the checkbox for Enable Ads is checked and click Save.

7. Click the Exit Control Panel and Return to Site link.

8. Now, you will see an Ad Placeholder; double-click it.

9. In the resulting editor box, paste the code from Google AdSense and click Save Changes.

As you have seen, it is rather easy to add a Google AdSense advertisement to your site. This is one way that you can easily profit from a web site powered by Community Server. After you have added the AdSense code, Google will crawl your content and start serving ads targeted toward the type of content your site contains.

If you would like to edit and modify the placement of the ads in your site, this does require that you edit the `Skin-Ads.ascx` file located in your Theme folder's `Skins` subdirectory. In addition to the Google AdSense span tag, you will also find several other placeholder tags for inline ads, the skyscraper, and the footer ads; these are used for more traditional graphical banner ads.

If you want to place the advertisement in a different location, you can do that easily as well. Just place the Community Server Ad control wherever you want advertisements to appear. Once you placed the Ad control in the location that suits your needs, you can again follow the steps outlined previously to change the advertisement that appears in the ad placeholder. The following code snippet will help demonstrate what the ad control looks like:

```
<CS:AdPart runat = "Server" contentname="StandardTop" >
    <CS:Ads Zone="StandardTop" runat="server" id="Ads1" />
</CS:AdPart>
```

In the next version of Community Server, version 3.0, Telligent is doing even more work to make working with ads easier.

Blogs

Key applications that are a part of the Community Server platform are blogs. Furthermore, Community Server comes with an outstanding blogging engine that will help enable your community members to fully share their content. In the following tour of blogs, you will find some key information that will help you get started with understanding not only what blogs are but also how to use them on your new site.

Purpose

Simply put, a blog is a content-publishing tool that orders content chronologically. Blogs can cover a variety of topics from personal to business and have grown in popularity over the last couple of years. What makes blogs so popular is their simplicity. They enable nontechnical people to get a voice on the web.

Community Server offers a powerful blogging engine, allowing for custom themes, advanced and customizable security options, the ability to post using standards-based APIs (the MetaBlog API), and much more. Many large sites rely on Community Server for their enterprise blogging solution. MSNBC, for example, uses Community Server to manage many of their blogs. Community Server is indeed an enterprise-class blogging application.

Create a New Blog

A blog can be created automatically when a user registers with the site or it can be created manually. We will not go into detail on how to automatically create a blog at this point; however, you can learn more about this feature in Chapter 6. In this chapter, we'll look at how you can manually create a blog.

To manually create a blog, simply complete the following steps:

1. Log in as an administrator and navigate to the Administration page in the control panel.
2. Expand the Blogs menu section on the left.
3. Click the Create New Blog option.
4. Provide a name for your new blog in the Name text box and click Save.

Congratulations, you have created a new blog! However, you may be wondering what all of the other options were for when you were on the Create New Blog page. While none of them is actually required to create a blog, they provide you with several options.

Perhaps one of the most useful options, from an organization standpoint, is the Blog Group drop-down list. This allows you to group blogs in a logical manner. For example, if you were running a community site for a team of zoologists that each specialized in a particular type of animal, you could use the blog groups to organize the blogs about each type of animal. You might have a blog group called Mammals, where you placed the blog about tigers and lions. Then, you could have a blog group called Reptiles, where a blog on crocodiles and alligators could be placed. This organizational structure would make it easy to have a section of your site dedicated to each of these types of animals. Later on, we'll look at some other tools for organizing content, such as tags.

Another important option is the radio button to choose whether or not to include the blog in the community aggregate. The community aggregate is nothing more than the list of latest blog posts that can appear on the main page of your site. This option allows you to keep the posts made in a blog from being aggregated with other content outside of the blog itself.

While there are many more options available when creating a new blog, the last option of note at this point is the "enable blog" radio button, which allows you to turn the blog "on" and "off" in a single switch. While the blog is disabled, posts will not be displayed, nor will they be included in search results, and the blog will not show up in any blog lists on your site. To learn more about the remaining options, read the information provided in Chapter 6.

Writing Content for Your Blog

When you are ready to start writing content to your blog, you have a number of options for authoring the content:

❑ Community Server WYSIWYG (what you see is what you get) web editor

❑ Blogging tools such as Live Writer from Microsoft

❑   Sending email to your blog (when the Email Gateway is installed)

❑   Microsoft Word 2007

Community Server provides a great Web-based WYSIWYG editor, the same one you use when editing forum posts or site content. However, if this tool does not meet all your requirements, you may want to use one of the third-party tools described later in this chapter.

In this section, we will go through the basic steps with the WYSIWYG editor. The steps demonstrate how to post new content, and you can use a similar approach to edit and manage existing content. It is also important to note that you can configure a user to have access to multiple blogs, or even have a single post sent to multiple blogs. Community Server is completely flexible in this way, which allows for a wide variety of use cases.

Let's take a look at writing a blog post. It requires that you be logged-in as a user who owns a blog or as an administrator:

1. Click the Control Panel link.

2. Click the My Blogs navigation menu option.

3. At this point, you should ensure that the appropriate blog is selected to be managed. Simply click the Select Blog to Manage button in the top-right area of the main content section and select the blog that you want to make a post to.

4. Under the Common Tasks menu section on the left, select Write a Blog Post.

5. Fill in a title and content in the editable body area.

    If you need more space in which to type, you can click and drag the editable body region so that it is larger by clicking the expandable box icon in the lower-right corner of the body section.

6. Click the Publish button in the lower-right corner of the page.

The Community Server blog post page has been simplified quite nicely in version 2.1. The advanced options are not visible until you check the Advanced Options checkbox. In addition, the actual editing controls have also been simplified to only include the most commonly used options. Among the controls for editing your content is the insert emoticon control, which is useful for helping to convey emotion whenever you are making a post.

It is also important to understand that if you are copying your post from an editor such as Microsoft Word, you should first try copying it into a program such as Notepad and double-check the resulting formatting. This will help protect your post from being formatted incorrectly. Furthermore, with the new spell-check and the option to save a post in the middle of writing it, you can avoid using any external tools completely. This will help ensure consistency as well as a well-formatted post.

Among the new controls for version 2.1 are two new Save buttons. Both buttons allow you to save your post without publishing. Once your post has been published, "Save and Continue Writing" will update the live post on the site, while "Save, But Don't Publish" will effectively save your changes but will not publish the post to the site until you set it to "Published."

The ability to save your writing is quite nice if you are interrupted or unable to finish writing a post in a single sitting. Once you save your post, you can resume your work at a later time from the Manage

Content ⇨ All Posts menu option. In addition to allowing you to write a post during multiple sessions, saving your progress during your writing guarantees that you do not lose any content. This is especially useful when writing long posts.

Aside from all of the other useful features that are a part of the postconstruction editing process, there is one that has been become popular with new Web 2.0 sites, known as tags. Prior to the release of Community Server 2.1, blog posts were organized by using hierarchical categories, where a post could only be associated with a single category. Posts can now be organized with tags. Tags are nothing more than keywords to help people find your post.

For example, if you make a post about a tiger, you could add tags such as mammal, animal, and cat to describe your post. Then, when users want to learn more about different mammals, they only need to click the mammals tag on your site's tag cloud (see Figure 3-3) or do a simple search for mammal. The post about the tiger is returned, even though it may not even contain the word mammal in its content. In addition, the tags do not have to exist prior to your listing them in the tags section of the post page. If they do not exist when you publish your post, they will be created and freely available for you to select in future posts.

Figure 3-3: Popular Blog Tags

Basic Usage

Aside from making posts, bloggers are also able to manage their content after it has been published, control the date and time of publication, and manage user feedback. An important aspect of blogging is readership; if you do not have any readers, then you may consider any thoughtful posts a wasted effort. Fortunately, one of the features of Community Server is a comments tool where readers can leave feedback about your posts. This enables you to have a dialogue with readers, which in turn tends to retain readers. Community Server offers a wonderful way to manage user comments and feedback that will be explored in Chapter 6.

In addition to being able to publish content in the form of text, you can also embed images and video in your posts. Community Server offers a way to reference one video along with several images that you place wherever you want. Even though Community Server provides the ability to reference only a single video, third-party add-ins, such as one for Camtasia Studio, have been developed to include more than one video file in a post.

It is important to understand how the posts from your blog are organized by default in Community Server. By its nature, a blog is supposed to be a type of online journal; therefore, all posts contain a particular date and timestamp. In addition, the posts on your blog are sorted with the posts in descending order according to their publication date.

For example, a post made today will appear above a post made yesterday on your blog. As a result of this organizational structure, you can order your posts however you want simply by changing the timestamp on posts. Community Server does not display a post until the time on the server is past the timestamp of the post. As a result, you can schedule the exact time that a post will be visible to readers. This is quite useful if you are going on vacation but still want to keep your blog active. In this situation, you could write a series of posts and schedule them to post in the future simply by changing the timestamp of each post. This is an extremely nice ability to help to maintain active readership on your site.

Now that you have a firm understanding of the power of changing the date and time of a post, we will go through the basic steps to change an existing post's time value. Before continuing with the following steps, please first log in as an administrator on your site.

1. Select the Control Panel navigational link.

2. Click My Blogs on the navigation bar.

3. Expand the Manage Content menu section on the left by clicking it.

4. Select the All Posts menu option.

5. Click any of the Post Titles that are visible in the main Blog Posts table.

6. Check the Advanced Options checkbox that appears on the far-right side of the Edit Post page.

7. Select the Options tab that appears on the Edit Post page.

8. Now, change the time to a couple of minutes in the future.

    After selecting any of the date fields, you can use the arrow keys on your keyboard to scroll through all of the available options. This is a good way to quickly change the date while guaranteeing its validity.

9. Click the Publish button on the lower right and then return to your blog and wait until the time when your post is supposed to be published. At that time, simply refresh your browser window to see the post appear.

Additional Tools for Authoring Blog Content

There are several other tools you can use to create blog posts inside of Community Server. This section briefly describes a few of them and then provides instructions on using them with Community Server. These tools range from free to supported commercial tools.

If you want to post from a free tool, then I suggest using w.bloggar, which can be downloaded at `wbloggar.com`. This tool allows you to manage your current posts, as well as create new ones, all without having to open a browser window. BlogJet is a commercial blogging tool that works with Community Server and can be found at `blogjet.com`. Besides these two tools, many people are using Microsoft Office 2007 to post to their Community Server blog. Office 2007 offers Community Server as one of its optional blog services for posting to.

In addition to Office 2007, Microsoft provides a tool known as Windows Live Writer, which is designed specifically for making blog posts. A screenshot showing Windows Live Writer being used to make a post to my blog is shown in Figure 3-4. One of the nice things about a tool such as this is that you can easily save your work locally before publishing the post to your blog. You can also edit existing published content easily, as well as insert formatted media objects, such as images, into your posts. Keep in mind that there are several other tools for making blog posts; the only requirement for working with Community Server is that they have MetaBlog support.

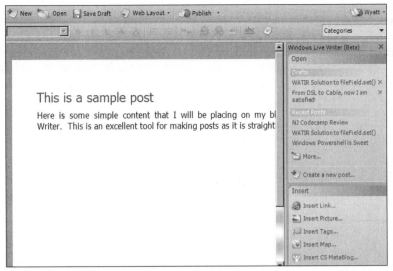

Figure 3-4: Windows Live Writer

To configure your blogging tool to connect to the MetaBlog API on your community site, you need to know the domain of the site and the physical path to the location where Community Server is installed. Once you have this information, simply select the Community Server or MetaBlog provider. For your host, you will need to point to your domain, and for the page, you need to type in the directory where Community Server is installed, along with the Blogs subfolder and path to the `MetaBlog.ashx` file. In a typical Community Server installation, the `MetaBlog.ashx` file is located under the blogs subfolder. Therefore, if your site was installed at `yoursite.com`, you would point to `http://yoursite.com/blogs/metablog.ashx`.

Case Study

In order to better explain the blog capabilities of Community Server, let's look at an example of its use in a real-world web site: `http://communityserver.org`. One of the most heavily trafficked blogs on the `http://communityserver.org` web site is the Community Server Daily News. The Community Server Evangelist at Telligent maintains the content of this news blog, writing fresh content every day of the work week. To assist readers in locating the content on a particular topic, each post uses a standard template. The template is professional looking (see Figure 3-5) and still is completely editable using the blog post editor.

Figure 3-5: Community Server Daily News

The Community Server Daily News goes beyond the way that conventional news is delivered. Instead of simply posting news and then forgetting about it, the author of this news source allows comments to be made. In this way, Community Server enables an active dialogue between the author and the reader. Now, readers have the ability to quickly write a response that is visible to other readers as well as the original author. In this way, the comment feature of the Community Server blog, when used in relation to delivering news, forms a chain of pseudo-letters to the editor.

The Community Server Daily News also allows people to subscribe to its content and be informed when a new edition is published. The ability of readers to effortlessly stay up to date with content is provided either by an RSS feed or through email subscriptions offered to readers. An additional benefit of RSS and email subscriptions is that readers are now able to stay current while they are disconnected by using devices such as a BlackBerry.

Forums

The Community Server forums application, like the blogging application, is enterprise quality. In addition, the forums application helps to provide a community with a common area for group thought and collaboration. Group collaboration is one of the great benefits of implementing a forum. Because of this, several sites will use forums as a way to support products, allowing users to post questions while "experts" provide answers. They also enable group learning, because those interested in a particular forum topic can read the responses and provide their own, hopefully well-formed solutions to a problem. Providing users the ability for discussion in an open atmosphere on a particular subject is the purpose of a forum.

Creating a New Forum

There are actually a couple of ways to create a forum in Community Server. Both of them are quite easy and straightforward. You can create the new forum either by using the Create New Forum button on the Manage Forums page or from the Forums menu in the Administration section of the Control Panel. For the purposes of this demonstration, we will only be looking at only one of these methods. However, after the demonstration is complete, I will show you how to easily switch to a view that allows a forum to be created using a similar method. Before you begin, log in as an administrator. Also, whenever I refer to the context menu that follows, it is the menu that appears when you right-click an item in one of the steps.

1. Click the Control Panel link.
2. Click the Administration link.
3. Click the Forums menu option to expand the suboptions.
4. Click the Forums link that appears.
5. If this is your first time viewing this menu, you will be in the Grid View, in which case you should see a button titled Change to Tree View in the lower-right corner. If you do not see this option, don't worry because that means that you are already in Tree View.

6. Now, you should see a tree view of all of the forums and forum groups currently available. Please right-click the top-level Forum Groups and choose Add Forum Group from the context menu.

7. Under the Group Name, change the name to **Support** and click Save.

8. Right-click the newly created Support Group and choose Add Forum.

9. Type in the name **Technical** for the new forum and click Save.

10. Select the new Forum and make sure that the forum is "Enabled."

As you see, it is quite easy to add both a new forum group and a forum. In addition, you should notice that you are able to edit the name of one of your forum items in the tree view on the left-hand panel. If you would like to try adding a forum using a similar method, click the Change to Grid View button in the lower-right corner of the Forums page. You will notice a new menu option appear on the left, called Create New Forum. All you will need to do to create a new forum is click this option, provide a name for your new forum, and click Save to complete adding it.

Both approaches to creating a new forum are straightforward; it is only a matter of preference as to what view you choose when creating your next forum. You should also notice that you can delete a forum. You can also select to enable or disable one of your forums. This can be a useful option whenever you do not want to lose any of the content from a forum, but you don't want it to be accessible to users.

Posting to a Forum

There are a couple of ways that you can contribute in a forum. Determining which route to take really depends on what information and what posts are already in your forum. What I mean by this is that you should try to avoid creating a new forum thread if there is already a thread with the same topic to which you are planning to contribute. In this situation, you would simply want to add to the conversation already taking place and post a reply to the existing thread.

Community Server disables the ability to have duplicate posts in your forum. This option is available in the Duplicates & Flooding tab under the Global Forum Settings. To assist you in posting information to a forum, you will go through the steps required to first post a new thread to the Technical support forum, which was created in the previous section, and then see how to post a reply to the original thread.

Before beginning this process, log out if you are currently signed in to your site. This will assist you to better understand some of the security implications of allowing anonymous posting, which is discussed further after these posting exercises. Begin by creating a new thread in the Technical forum you just created:

1. Click the Forums option on the main navigation menu.

2. Click the Technical forum link under the Support forum group.

3. You are presented with a message saying "There are no posts to display." Click the Write a New Post button to create a new post.

4. Log in as the administrator.

5. Fill out the form, providing a subject for your post as well as a message. For our purposes, this could simply be a message welcoming new members to your support forum. Also, you should note that you are also able to provide tags to your post to help keep your posts organized and easily accessible.

6. Click the Post button when you are done. This adds your post to the Technical forum and brings you to the page that others will see when viewing it (see Figure 3-6).

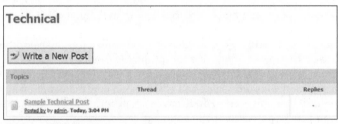

Figure 3-6: Result of Forum Post

Now that you have created a new forum post, you will explore how an individual would go about furthering the discussion and writing a reply to that post. Remember when you are completing these steps that you have the ability to post a reply to a post further along in a thread and are not limited to replying only to the original post. This is a unique feature because it allows one conversation to branch out into several, all within the same forum thread. Again, for this exercise, log out before proceeding, so that you can better understand anonymous posting.

1. Click the Forums option on the main navigation menu.

2. Click the Technical forum link under the Support forum group.

3. Click the Welcome topic that you created in the previous exercise.

4. Click the Reply button, which is visible in the top-right area of the post itself.

5. Log in as the administrator.

6. Simply fill out the body of the message itself. You do not need to change the subject unless you think that it is not descriptive enough for the reply you are posting. You will also notice that the subject begins with a RE: tag, similar to what you would expect when replying to an email message.

7. Add any tags that you think are appropriate to your message, and click the Post button when you are done. Once you click this button, you are brought back to the original thread with your new post visible below the original.

There are a couple of other options that allow you to post a reply to a topic in a forum. The first is the Quote button that appears above each of the messages in the forum. This button will allow you to post a reply while also quoting the original message that you are replying to. This is useful if you want to point out a mistake or applaud a particular point that someone has made. When you click this button, you are able to edit what is actually put into the quote box on your message.

The second option is the Quick Reply link that appears in the lower-right side of messages. When you click this link, a new editor-style window (modal) appears that you can use to quickly post a reply message. When using the Quick Reply option you are not forced to leave the original thread page (see Figure 3-7); instead your new message reply is handled through AJAX, thus making it a quick reply.

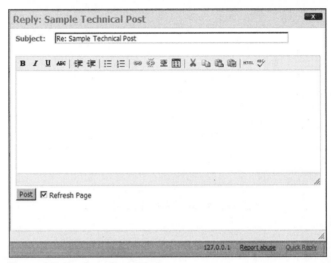

Figure 3-7: Reply to Post Window

Now that you have looked at the many ways to post to forums, let's consider the security option for allowing anonymous posts. Please understand that anonymous posts mean nothing more than being able to make a new post or reply to an existing post without ever having to sign in and identify yourself. Remember in our previous two examples how you were required to log in whenever you were posting a new message; with anonymous posting turned on you would not be required to log in with either situation. Allowing this flexibility can be useful for applications like a technical support forum, where people who are not members of your site can provide possible solutions to your members' problems without having to register. These individuals may not post a reply message that helps someone else if they are forced to register. However, there are security implications for enabling anonymous posting, and you should consider them before allowing anonymous posting. In addition, you can expect that you will need to allow more time to moderate the forum because there is a greater potential for incorrect posting. Fortunately, though, there are censorship filters in Community Server that will help prevent obscene posts from occurring. If you would like to enable anonymous posting, complete the following basic steps:

1. Log in as an administrator.
2. Click the Control Panel.
3. Click Administration.
4. Click Settings in the menu on the left to expand the available options.
5. Click Post Settings.
6. Select the Yes radio button next to the Enable Anonymous Posting text.
7. Click Save.

Now that you have enabled anonymous posting for the entire site, you can enable anonymous posting for forums. In addition, you can also turn on anonymous posting for blogs and the galleries now that you have completed the previous steps. To enable anonymous posting on your forums, complete the following steps:

1. Log in as an administrator.

2. Click Control Panel.

3. Click Administration.

4. Expand the Forums menu on the left.

5. Click the Global Forum Settings menu option.

6. Under the General tab, select the Yes radio button option on the line that says Allow User Posting as Anonymous (see Figure 3-8).

7. Click Save.

Figure 3-8: Enable Anonymous Posting

Basic Usage

There are a couple of personas that participants in a forum may have: the conversation topic's creator and the responder. You may notice that I am not calling the responder the answerer; this is because the responder may not always be answering a question, but may simply be responding. A conversation is started under the appropriate main category, and a new forum post is created under this category. This allows the posts to be organized in a logical way from the standpoint of all participants. For example, if you wanted to create a post about how you are enjoying the forums in Community Server, you could simply make the post under the Forums topical category.

Besides knowing how to create a post, it is also helpful to become familiar with some of the additional features of Community Server forums. One of the main features is the ability to send a private message to other members, which you may think of as a system-only email solution. Another nice feature is being able to add posts and users to a favorites list, which is an excellent way to bookmark people and posts for later reference.

Perhaps one of the most famous features of Community Server, at least from a poster's standpoint, is the point system. The member point system is not unique to forums, but it is widely displayed there. In short, the point system adds points to users for their direct contribution to certain content, such as answering a customer's question or adding important bug details. The point system can be found in the Manage Members Point System menu option under the System Tools menu in the Administration section of the Control Panel. In addition, this is a feature that is enabled whenever you purchase a license for Community Server. Figure 3-9 shows what you will see when you navigate to the members' point system page with the Express or Personal Edition of Community Server.

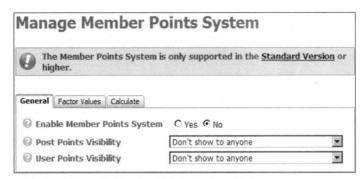

Figure 3-9: Manage Member Points System Page

Case Study

Again, one of the best examples of the usefulness of a Community Server forum setup is the implementation used in `http://communityserver.org`. Telligent is using Community Server forums as a way to provide tiered support for their customers. The `http://communityserver.org` forum is also set up so that anonymous visitors are able to read entries, but only registered users may respond to them. As a result of this structure, Telligent is able to utilize a minimal number of employees for responding to customers while maintaining a steady flow of questions and answers from outside participants. Another important point about this example is that Telligent allows post ratings as well as user ratings. Because of this, the usefulness of a member's answer can be gauged in part to his or her ongoing participation to the overall forum. For example, if two members answer the same question, usually the member with the higher rank will be trusted over the lower-ranked member. As a result, members are encouraged to increase their rank by supporting other members of the community. Furthermore, the `http://communityserver.org` setup provides a solid example of how a relatively small company is able to provide high-quality support to its large customer base.

File Gallery

The file gallery allows a site to offer its users files of any type for easy downloading. Because of the wide range of files that can be organized in the file gallery, its usefulness is vast. A user can upload office document files, software products, or even media files for others to download by employing the file gallery. Therefore, a file gallery is useful for providing a way to deliver a variety of files and file types to community members.

Creating a File Gallery

To better understand how the file gallery functions, you need to create one. For the purposes of this demonstration, you will be creating a file gallery for containing documents that you would normally have organized under your My Documents folder. To create a file gallery, complete the following steps:

1. Log in as an administrator.
2. Click Control Panel.

3.   Click Administration.

4.   Click Files to expand the available options.

5.   Click the Manage All File Groups menu option (if this option isn't available, select Folder Groups and then click the button Change to Tree View).

6.   Right-click Groups on the left panel and choose Add Folder Group from the context menu.

7.   In the Group Name textbox type in **My Documents** and click Save.

8.   Right-click My Documents in the left panel and choose Add Folder from the context menu.

9.   Type in the name **Poems** for the folder (see Figure 3-10).

10. In the right panel, select the Yes radio button next to Enable Folder and click the Save button.

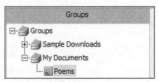

Figure 3-10: File Groups

Something that you should remember is that you can easily delete or disable these folders from the Manage All File Groups page. Explore the various options that are available to you in the gallery by right-clicking the various groups and folders. Now that you have created a new folder group and folder under that group for organizing your documents, you are prepared to publish files to this folder.

Publishing Files

You are ready to begin uploading and publishing files to your gallery. An important thing to remember is that you have the option to keep certain files private and hidden from the public. Therefore, with the file gallery, you have a professional, easy to use file repository for private use. In the following demonstration, you will learn the steps necessary to publish a file.

For the purposes of this demonstration, you will be publishing a text file from your local My Documents folder. Therefore, before proceeding, identify the file that you would like to upload from your computer. You should also understand that this file will be uploaded and will reside on the server that Community Server is using as its file gallery repository.

1.   Log in as an administrator.

2.   Click Control Panel.

3.   Click My Files.

4.   Make sure that the Current File Group that is selected is Poems, if it is not, then click the Select Folder to Manage button on the top right and choose the Poems folder.

5.   Click Upload File.

6.   Click the Pick File button.

7. Click the Browse button, locate the file you want to upload, and choose Save (see Figure 3-11).

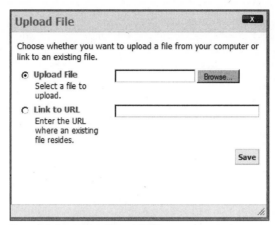

Figure 3-11: Upload File Window

8. Type a title for your file in the Title textbox.

9. Type in a brief description of the file that you are uploading; this is a required field (see Figure 3-12).

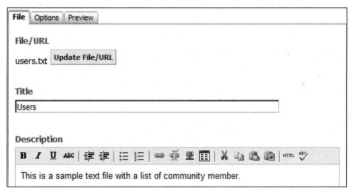

Figure 3-12: Upload File Page

10. Click Save.

When you click the Save button, your file is uploaded and published under the Downloads navigational link. If you want to change whether or not your file is published, you can click it in the list of all files and change this option. Complete the following steps to understand how to change this option:

1. If you do not see a list of all files to manage, then click the Manage Content menu group on the left of the My Files administration navigation bar, and choose the Files menu option.

2. Click the file; then select the options tab.

3. Select either Yes or No next to the Is this file published line.

4. Click Save.

To confirm that everything is in order, log out and return to the main site. Click the Downloads navigational link and you should see your new file. If you want further confirmation that it has been uploaded correctly, download the file and open it to confirm that it is indeed correct. Congratulations, you now have a published document that others can download easily from your site.

One of the nice features of the file gallery is the ability to easily generate a report on the number of downloads and views that a particular file has had. To do this, you can click the Review Files link under the Common Tasks menu of the My Files section of the Control Panel. On this page, you are able to see a listing of all of your files, as well as how many times each file has been downloaded.

You can also use the FTP Gateway add-on to enable FTP tools to communicate with your file gallery (photo gallery, too). This makes it really simple to drag-and-drop files from or to your file gallery. For more information on this tool, you can refer to Appendix A or read the information provided by Telligent on the Community Server web site at www.communityserver.org.

Basic Usage

There are several options for how users and an administrator can use the file gallery. From an administrator's viewpoint, a file gallery can be used to serve and organize file content. The file gallery is organized using a hierarchy starting with the File Group, which can contain many folders, and the folders are capable of containing many files as well as subfolders. To better explain this, let's say that you have a game, Ms. Pacman, and you need to organize it logically for your site users to download. To do so, you would create a Folder Group named **Software**. Then, under this Folder Group you could create a folder named **Games**, and finally you would place Ms. Pacman under the Games folder. In the end, you have a logical progression of Software ⇨ Games ⇨ Ms. Pacman that is easy to traverse (see Figure 3-13).

Figure 3-13: Folder Organization

The user can download files as well as provide feedback regarding these files through the common comment feature that also exists in blogs and photo galleries. The files are often organized in a logical way. Therefore, from the users' perspective it should be easy to know where to locate the file that they are looking for. For example, if they wanted to download a software game using the site in the previous example, they would be able to navigate to your Software Folder Group, and then they would be able to select Games and select the appropriate game. This organizational structure should remind most users of how their personal computers' file structure is organized. When users have feedback to provide, they can add comments to the file's download page. In addition, they can rate files, using a five-star scale.

Limitations

Depending on the Community Server license that you are using, you may notice certain limitations in the number of files you can store. For the Express Edition, you are limited to hosting 50 files in the file gallery. Meanwhile, the Standard Edition allows 500 files to be hosted. If you are going to require more files, then you should use the Professional or Enterprise Editions of Community Server because they each allow an unlimited number of files to be hosted in the file gallery.

Photo Gallery

The photo gallery in Community Server provides an easy way for your community members to share and discuss photos. For example, if your community recently had an event, this would be an easy way for everyone in the community to share and see each other's pictures from that event. Like the other applications that are a part of the Community Server platform, the photo gallery is also an enterprise-grade application.

Standard Features

Community Server goes beyond conventional image galleries in the standard features that it provides. One of the major features that Community Server offers is the photo gallery. Generally, a conventional image gallery is nothing more than a listing of images. Often, these images are organized using the concept of an album or with tags that identify the type of images being grouped. However, beyond this, not much more is required to be considered an image gallery.

Fortunately, Community Server goes beyond these standard requirements and offers additional capabilities. Some of these additional features include the ability to subscribe via RSS to a photo gallery, a way to view detailed EXIF information about image files (such as the camera or application used to create the image), a way to show a slideshow of images, and even the ability to order prints from Shutterfly for selected images.

To better understand some of what the photo gallery offers, you will explore the features further, one at a time. First, let's consider the ability to upload images without size restrictions. What I mean by this is that you can upload a photo that is 1600 pixels by 800 pixels or one by 2024 pixels by 1024 pixels; with the standard setup, you are not restricted to certain dimensions. I bring up this feature mainly because many other services impose restrictions on image size. However, it is important to note that an administrator of Community Server has the option to restrict the physical size of galleries, based upon the number of photos that it can contain or the maximum physical file size of a gallery, through the use of gallery quotas. This topic is discussed further in Chapter 8 in the "Administering Photo Galleries" section.

Another important feature is the expansive way that you are able to organize your photos. Community Server offers a hierarchy of gallery groups, a gallery, and an album to be the parents of an image. In addition, it is important to understand the parent-child relationship between each of these organizational components. Essentially, it breaks down to every parent being capable of having many children. Therefore, a gallery group can contain multiple galleries; just as a gallery can contain multiple albums. In addition, photos can exist in multiple albums. To explain this organizational structure, I was going to look at an example involving cars, but because everyone tends to use cars to explain computer concepts, I will instead use real estate.

Aside from the traditional organization of photos using albums, as of version 2.1 you are able to create tags to organize your photos. Essentially, tags are descriptive labels that you apply to items to group them. For example, you can have tags for Community Server that group sites related to Community Server. This lets you offer users a tag cloud (see Figure 3-3) that contains numerous tags labeling the images contained in a gallery. You may apply the same tag to multiple images, such as European Vacation, which when clicked will reveal all of these images. This is a very flexible approach to organizing images because you can easily add multiple tags to the same image. It is important to note, though, that in version 2.1 you must exclusively use either tags or albums to organize your photos under each gallery; you cannot use both in the same gallery. However, you are able to use tagging in one gallery and albums in another gallery under the same installation.

Another important feature is the ability to view the EXIF data for a particular image file. EXIF stands for Exchangeable Image File Format and contains metadata that can describe information about the camera and settings used to take the picture, copyright, location, and date and time details to name items. It is simply important, at this point, to realize that Community Server offers support for viewing this detail on each image.

Perhaps one of the most popular features of the photo gallery is the slideshow viewer that is shown in Figure 3-14. This allows users of your site to easily play through the images that are contained in a gallery or album. When a user selects this option, a pop-up window appears with a flash control that aggregates the images in the selected album or gallery by displaying those selected images using transitions.

Figure 3-14: Photo Gallery Slideshow Viewer

Speaking of aggregating images, another attractive feature that is becoming more and more widespread is the ability to subscribe to an RSS feed to monitor for new images. This allows people to use a feed aggregator to be instantly notified whenever new images are added to your site, without the need to be actively visiting your site. Users can subscribe to image feeds at differing levels, from the sitewide images to those in a particular album. This is one of the many features that make Community Server stand out among competing image gallery services.

Example Real Estate Scenario Problem

You are an IT professional at a large real estate firm that desires to build a new web site for realtors to use. The firm that you are working for has several offices throughout the world that will benefit greatly from a shared site. This site needs to be done quickly because the realtors were promised that they would have access to it last week, but you were just informed of it today. The purpose of the site is to allow realtors to easily publish their current listings in the form of a photo and short description that can be organized under the type of property being listed.

Example Real Estate Scenario Solution

You decide to use the Community Server photo gallery to meet this challenge. You create a gallery group for each of the offices that your firm owns. Then under each of these groups, you create a gallery for each realtor that is a member of the office labeled in the gallery group. For example, you create a gallery for Tom and Jane, who are members of the same office, and place the galleries under the same gallery group. Now, whenever Tom or Jane logs in they are able to create an album for each property type, such as Farms or Commercial, and upload property images along with a description of each property under the appropriate album. Congratulations, you should feel proud because you were able to create a solution that offers flexibility and stability, and was delivered quickly.

The ability for users to provide feedback regarding a site's content is always important for a site to maintain a relationship with users. For this, and many more reasons, Community Server offers two key ways for users to respond to images that are posted. The first is the ability for users to leave comments regarding a particular image. In addition, users can rate photos using the photo-rating system feature. These features are a way for an image poster to receive feedback, hopefully in the form of praise, for the work he or she has done.

Purpose

At this point, you should have a strong grasp of the main features that are provided by the photo gallery. On the whole, the purpose of collecting these features is to provide a way for the members of your site to create and manage image collections. In addition, they allow a unique way for users to view images and provide feedback about them to other members.

Basic Usage

Many families are using Community Server to bring together their family members by sharing ideas and photos. The photo gallery enables families to share photos of reunions, recent vacations, and the like. Assume that you want to create a site for your family to use to stay in touch with each other easily. As a part of this site you include a photo gallery. Your family members are now able to share images of their lives with other family members, enabling the family on the whole to become better connected. Through the use of a shared photo gallery, distant family members may share pictures of their children, and everyone in the family can experience them growing up even when they can't always be near. You and your parents both subscribe to the RSS feed provided for the album of these children, staying informed of updated images. As a result of the photo gallery, the family is able to feel as though they are close despite the great geographical distances that separate everyone. This is one of the many useful abilities of the photo gallery.

Creating an Album

Now that you have a good understanding of many of the features that are a part of the photo gallery, you can go through the steps for creating a new album. If you installed the sample content with Community Server, then you will already have a sample photo gallery. However, for most purposes, this will not be an appropriate title or setup for publishing photos. Therefore, you will walk through the basic steps for creating a new gallery that will be used to display screenshots. Before proceeding with the following instructions, log in as an administrator.

1. Click Control Panel.
2. Click Administration.
3. Click Photos to expand the available menu options.
4. Click Manage All Photo Galleries.
5. Right-click Gallery in the left panel and choose Add Group from the context menu.
6. Provide a name for your new gallery group and click Save.
7. Right-click the newly created gallery group and choose Add Gallery from the context menu.
8. Type the name **Screenshots** into the name field of the new gallery and select Yes next to the Enable Gallery option to enable it.
9. Click Save.

When you click the Save button, your gallery is created and made visible to others from the photos section whenever you add photos to it. To confirm that the gallery was created successfully, follow the steps in the next section to add a photo to your screenshot gallery.

Publishing Photos

You are ready to add photos to your new Screenshots gallery; therefore you only need to select some images for upload. If you do not have any pictures to publish, simply take a screenshot of your desktop and use that. Before you begin with publishing a photo, log in as an administrator and also locate the image that you would like to publish.

1. Click Control Panel.
2. Click My Photos.
3. Select the Publish New Photo menu option from the menu on the left.
4. Click the Upload Photo button.
5. Click the Browse button, select the photo you want to publish, and click Upload.
6. Click the Save button to publish your photo.

You will notice that the description is not a required field; however, if you want to keep your photos organized and easily find them later, then it is recommended that you provide a description for each photo. In addition, you should also try to add tags to all of your photos to keep them organized and easily accessible. To confirm that your photo was published successfully, log out and click the Photos navigation option. Once you are in your photo gallery you should see the newly published photo from the previous steps. In addition, you may want to experiment with the slideshow and viewing the EXIF data for your photos.

Reader

Many of the users of your site will be new to RSS aggregation and will not necessarily have a tool that allows them to read RSS feeds. A solution for these users is the Community Server Reader, which provides them with an easy-to-use interface for aggregating and reading numerous feeds from both internal and external sources. In addition, the Reader is necessary for the Blog Roller to work properly. This is true because in order to add feeds to your Roller, you will need to first select them from the Reader. For now, though, you only need to understand that the Roller is a simple aggregated presentation of selected RSS feeds that is publicly presented to site viewers. Again, the main purpose of the Reader is to provide members of your site, who have permission for their own Reader, with a simple way to collect RSS feeds and read through them.

Basic Usage

To better understand the basic operations of the Reader, you will go through a couple of basic scenarios: first, adding new feeds to your Reader, and second, viewing the resulting content that is returned. Before you can see the Reader, with the default installation you will need to log in to the site. After you are logged-in, you should be able to see the My Reader link; when you click the link, you will be presented with a blank page (see Figure 3-15) that is similar to Microsoft Outlook's layout. The three window panes are divided in a logical fashion: on the left is a directory tree listing of RSS feeds that you have added, in the middle is a list of the most recent posts from the collection of the feeds, and on the right is where the actual content from a selected post is presented. Additionally, the sections are separated by a collapsible and movable divider.

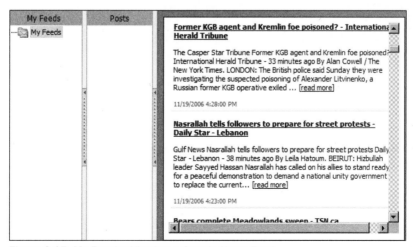

Figure 3-15: My Reader Viewing a Google News Feed

Now that you have gone over the basics, you can add a feed. Simply follow these steps, first for adding a folder to group the feeds and then to add the feed itself. For this example, you will be adding a couple of feeds from popular news sources: CNN and BBC:

1. Navigate to the BBC web site (www.bbc.co.uk) and copy the address to one of their RSS feeds.

2. Select the My Reader navigational link.

3. Right-click the My Feeds main folder (see Figure 3-16).

4. Select New Folder from the resulting context menu.

5. Type **News** as the name for new folder and click Add Folder.

6. Right-click the resulting News folder and select New Feed.

7. Paste the link that you retrieved in Step 1 and click Add Feed.

8. Repeat Steps 6 and 7 for adding a link to the CNN news feed.

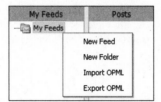

Figure 3-16: Right-Click View of My Feeds

Now that you have added a couple of different news feeds to your Reader, you can more easily stay up to date with what is happening in the news. Before moving on, try adding new folders and feeds of your own choosing. Also, try viewing the content from these feeds by selecting the folder, selecting nothing, and selecting an individual feed. You should notice that the way the resulting content is displayed changes. This is because Community Server allows you to view your content from multiple angles — from seeing all of your feeds collectively to just viewing a single feed's content.

Summary

In this chapter, you learned about the various applications that are a part of the Community Server platform. These include blogs, forums, the file gallery, the photo gallery, and reader applications. All of these applications combine to not only help build your online community but also provide a unique and feature-rich experience to your members. In addition, the applications themselves are feature rich and enterprise ready.

In the next chapter, you will learn how use different configuration options to meet the needs of your new site. This information will be helpful for keeping your site active and responsive as your community grows.

Part II
Configuring Community Server

Configuring a Site to Meet Your Requirements

At this point, you should have a good understanding of how to install Community Server and the features it offers. In this chapter, you will dive a little deeper into the various configuration options available. The option you choose will depend on your specific site requirements. By the end of this chapter, you should be comfortable doing the following:

❑ Defining your specific site requirements

❑ Implementing a small personal site

❑ Implementing a small to medium-sized community

Understanding Your Requirements

Before you can configure Community Server to meet your requirements, you first need to understand what your requirements are. Let's talk about some of the key requirements decisions to consider while defining the requirements. In Chapter 3, you were given a guided tour that provided a general understanding as to what features Community Server provides. You should now have a basic understanding of what is available out of the box. After an installation, you will have the following main sections:

❑ A default home page

❑ Blogs

❑ Photo galleries

❑ Forums

❑ File galleries

There are decisions that need to be made in regard to the five sections mentioned previously. We will not go into the details about what is contained in each of the applications, as that information has already been covered in Chapters 2 and 3, but we will point out the decisions that are useful to be made in regard to each section as it pertains to your site's requirements.

The Default Home Page

Community Server can be configured to bypass the initial home page. For example, you might want your Community Server site to bypass the home page and go directly to your blog's root page or some other application page within your site. You can essentially change your site to focus primarily on one of the applications. Generally, individuals will set up their personal sites so that an individual blog is positioned at the root of the site. Sometimes support sites have a forum located at the root of the site.

Blogs

A site can be configured to host multiple blogs or a single blog. Often a site that has a single blog will place this blog at the root of the site, which is referred to as blogging as root and will be demonstrated later in this chapter. This will allow your Community Server installation to look and function as if it were only a blog, bypassing the default Community Server home page and going directly to your blog when someone navigates to the root of your site. For example, the URL http://yourCSsite.com could take your viewers directly to your blog.

File Gallery

Now is a good time to grab a piece of paper and pencil or open up your text editor of choice. We're going to make a few decisions, and it will be helpful to track these decisions so that you can remember your choices once you get into actual implementation.

The first decision you need to make is which of the sections mentioned previously you want to keep and which you want to hide. For example, you might be interested in setting up a site to host your personal blog, so you don't necessarily need to use the default community server home page, since you don't need forums. You might want to keep the file gallery and photo gallery so that you can host files and photos for your visitors, or you might want to turn off the photo gallery and file gallery altogether and use some other means for hosting your files and folders. Go ahead and write down which sections you would like to keep of those mentioned previously.

Implementing a Personal Site

A personal site is a small site that you can use for your personal blog or for sharing photos with family and friends. In this type of Community Server installation, you are normally dealing with one administrator who is also the provider of all content. While you could turn on features such as forums and a file gallery, these are generally meant for more community-centric collaboration sites; these features will be discussed in the following medium and large Community Server implementation sections.

Having read about installing Community Server in Chapter 2 and taking the guided tour in Chapter 3, you should already have a base Community Server installation and a good overview as to how things work within Community Server. We will now work on customizing the default installation.

Turning Off Unneeded Features

As discussed previously for implementing a personal site, we will only be using blogs and photo galleries. Since we only wish to utilize Community Servers blogging and photo gallery abilities, we need to disable the other Community Server abilities that are enabled by default.

1.   Navigate to Control Panel ➪ Administration ➪ Settings ➪ Applications.

2.   You will see the options that are displayed in Figure 4-1.

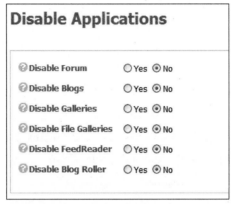

Figure 4-1: Disable Applications Screen

3.   Now, turn all applications to off except for Blogs and Galleries.

4.   Your settings should now resemble the selected options in Figure 4-2.

Figure 4-2: Disable Applications Screen after Applications Are Disabled

Blogging at the Root

Blogging at the root is the term given to a Community Server installation where a user navigates to your site and your blog is immediately displayed, as opposed to the default Community Server home page. For example if my site (www.mysite.com) was configured for blogging at the root, when a user navigates to www.mysite.com it will display as if the user, on a default Community Server installation, has navigated to www.mysite.com/blogs/yourApplicationKey. One important thing to keep in mind is that, for blogs, your application key is usually your username. This is how Community Server determines which blog to display based on the URL a user has issued. For example, www.mysite.com/blogs/jmartin would be jmartin's blog, whereas www.mysite.com/blogs/rsmith would be rsmith's blog. Application keys will come into play here shortly as we make customizations to support blogging at the root.

First, you need to find out what your blog application key is and write it down:

1. Sign in as an admin on your Community Server site.

2. Navigate to <your site>/controlpanel/BlogAdmin/Blogs.aspx.

3. Find the blog name you would like to make the default blog and click the Edit button.

4. The value in the URL textbox is the blog's default ApplicationKey (see Figure 4-3). Write this value down somewhere because it is how you identify the path to your blog.

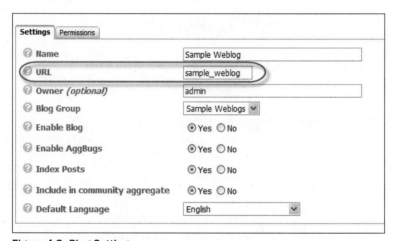

Figure 4-3: Blog Settings

Now that you know your defaultApplicationKey, open your communityserver.config file. This file can be found within your community server installation folder under the web folder.

1. Find the <Weblog>...</Weblog> section.

2. You now need to add the defaultApplicationKey attribute, setting its value to the defaultApplicationKey you wrote down, as shown in Figure 4-4.

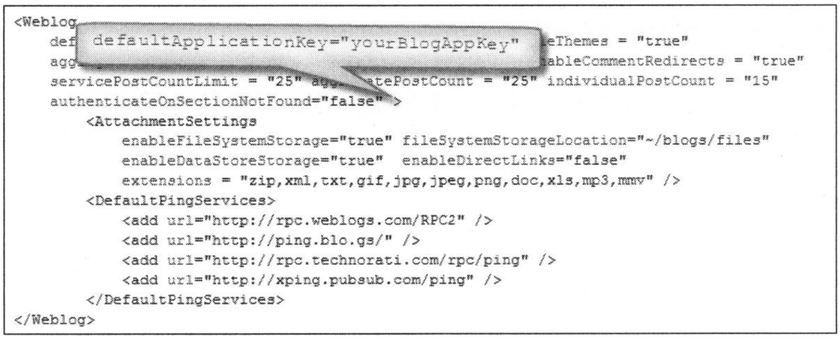

```
<Weblog
    def  defaultApplicationKey="yourBlogAppKey"    eThemes = "true"
    agg                                            ableCommentRedirects = "true"
    servicePostCountLimit = "25" a   tePostCount = "25" individualPostCount = "15"
    authenticateOnSectionNotFound="false" >
        <AttachmentSettings
            enableFileSystemStorage="true" fileSystemStorageLocation="~/blogs/files"
            enableDataStoreStorage="true"  enableDirectLinks="false"
            extensions = "zip,xml,txt,gif,jpg,jpeg,png,doc,xls,mp3,mmv" />
        <DefaultPingServices>
            <add url="http://rpc.weblogs.com/RPC2" />
            <add url="http://ping.blo.gs/" />
            <add url="http://rpc.technorati.com/rpc/ping" />
            <add url="http://xping.pubsub.com/ping" />
        </DefaultPingServices>
</Weblog>
```

Figure 4-4: communityserver.config Weblog Settings

Your `<Weblog>` section should now resemble something like the following:

```
<Weblog
    defaultTheme = "default"
    enableSkinCache = "true"
    enableThemes = "true"
    aggregatePostSize = "250"
    createDirectories = "true"
    enableCommentRedirects = "true"
    servicePostCountLimit = "25"
    aggregatePostCount = "25"
    individualPostCount = "15"
    defaultApplicationKey="Sample_Weblog">
```

The changes just made tell Community Server to use the previously specified `defaultApplicationKey` if one is not provided in the querystring or path.

To get Community Server to use the correct application key, we are going to remove the application key from the `CommunityServer` paths. We do this by editing the "`##blogdirectory##`" transformer in the `SiteUrls.config` file. We will set this value to an empty string. This forces Community Server to use the `defaultApplicationKey`.

```
<add key = "##blogdirectory##" value = "" />
```

Next, we are going to make a change to the "location" tag. This will tell Community Server to still use the files located in the `/blogs` folder even though the physical path will really be at the root. The following is an example of the changes you need to make to the "location" tag. Keep in mind that both the `type` and `physicalPath` are required fields.

```
<location name="weblogs"
    path="/"
    physicalPath="/blogs/"
    type="CommunityServer.Blogs.Components.SingleBlogLocation,
        CommunityServer.Blogs"
/>
```

Finally, we need to make a change to the articles location so that all of your articles will be displayed and published correctly. Open your `SiteUrls.config` file and change the following code from

```
<location name="articles" path="/articles/" />
```

to

```
<location name="articles" path="" />
```

Once you have saved the changes to your `SiteUrls.config` file, you may need to touch the `web.config` file. To touch the `web.config` file, you simply need to change the date that the file was last modified; therefore, you can simply open the `web.config` file in Notepad and save it. This will update the modified time on the file and force your site to refresh its knowledge of the `SiteUrls.config` file, and thus be updated with the changes you have made to it. Now, the next time you browse to your site you should see your blog's content displayed on the homepage.

Implementing a Small to Medium-Sized Community

Many of the communities that are using Community Server will pass through a phase when they are considered either small or medium-sized. Communities are organic and can fluctuate in size; therefore, it is important to understand some of the basic configuration options that can help with running a small to medium-sized community. The size of your site can be determined both from the number of users and through the volume of content. For example, if your site only has 100 users, and each user contributes 20 to 30 posts a day, then you would really have a site that is considered medium-sized.

The boundaries between what is considered a small, medium, and large site are not clearly defined at this point. It is really up to an administrator to determine if a site has grown enough that it should be considered a larger site and tweaks need to occur. Generally, a deciding factor can be that the performance of a site is beginning to suffer. At this point, it may be a good idea to tweak some of your settings and possibly upgrade your hardware.

Optimizations

There are different things you can do to optimize the performance of your site. Many of these recommendations will be basic and logical; others require advanced development knowledge.

One of the basic and more logical things that you can do to help the performance of a site is to improve the hardware that the site uses. Generally, increasing the RAM or processor performance on a site can help with its overall performance. The ability to increase the hardware performance of the server that your site is hosted on requires some level of access to the hardware.

Another basic alteration you can make is to switch to a dedicated host if your site is currently in a shared hosting environment. Usually you will incur additional costs to switch to a dedicated host; therefore, you should weigh the cost benefits.

If you are familiar with Microsoft SQL Server, you can usually increase the performance of your site by tuning the indexes for the most common queries that are made by your site. This will require that you also be familiar with the queries that your site is making frequently. This can be found by running Microsoft SQL Profiler and looking for long-running SQL scripts.

Another thing that you can do to increase the performance of your site is to add more servers and create a web farm. However, there is occasionally a point where too many servers can sometimes be detrimental. This is something that Telligent is best prepared to help you with if you have questions. They have implemented web farms many times and are the premier resource for setting up your own web farm for Community Server.

Configuring a Site to Generate Ad Revenue

Fortunately, Community Server is designed with ad revenue in mind. As a result, there are existing controls that built into Community Server that are used for easily adding advertisements to your site. In addition, these advertisements can be configured from the Control Panel. The configuration screen for advertisements also offers the ability to control what roles the advertisements are displayed to, which is visible in Figure 4-5.

Figure 4-5: Manage Ads Screen

By default, the ads are turned off, which means that you will need to enable ads in the Control Panel if you would like them to appear on the site. In addition, you can also enable the inline ad control that will allow you to easily change the ad that is placed in the ad controls (see Figure 4-6). However, before you do proceed with enabling advertisements it is helpful to first have an ad to be placed on your site. There are many options for companies that will pay you to place ads on your site. One of the popular companies to go through is Google. Once you have registered with their Ad Sense program, you will be provided with a snippet of code that you can then include on your site. Finally, whenever you have this code then you will be ready to enable ads and place the advertisements on the site, which you can do by completing the following instructions:

1. Log in as administrator.

2. Click Control Panel and then the Administration link.

3. Expand the System Tools menu and select Manage Ads.

4. Check Enable Ads and check Enable Inline Ad Control.

5. Click Save to save the updates.

6. Click the Exit Control Panel and Return to Site link.

7. Double-click the Ad via Inline control (see Figure 4-6).

8. Insert the advertisement code into the pop-up window and click Save.

9. Your advertisement should appear after you save and refresh the page.

Once you have saved your advertisement code, you should log out of your site and view it as visitors to your site would. This can be especially helpful for making sure that the advertisements appear correctly for your site visitors.

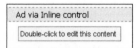

Figure 4-6: Ad Inline Edit

There is already a wealth of information on this topic that exists in the forums at http://community server.org. Therefore, if you would like to discuss this topic with other members of the Community Server community, you can search the forums for the existing threads and participate in them. This serves as a good way for you to learn even more about this important topic and also a way that you can share your ideas with the Community Server development team. Furthermore, this discussion can help provide new avenues for sites to be able to make money using Community Server.

Summary

Community Server is an adaptable platform that is able to meet the requirements of varying-sized communities. There are different configuration changes that you can make to a site to change the way that is operates. One of the common configuration changes is done to make a specific application appear at the root of a site. Additionally, Community Server allows for advertisements to be easily inserted into a site.

In the following chapter, you will learn how to alter the presentation of a site. The information that you gain in this chapter will help you to customize how your site looks.

5

Changing the Look-and-Feel

One of the most important improvements in the 3.0 release of Community Server is the ability for less-technical individuals to be able to modify the presentation of their site. This ability sets Community Server apart from other software that is on the market today that require much more web development expertise.

In this chapter, you will learn many of the basics that are involved with customizing how a Community Server looks. You will learn how to use the new controls that are in the latest release of Community Server to change the presentation of your site. In addition, there will be many basic tips and usage examples for using stylesheets to control some of the presentation. This chapter assumes that you do have some experience with Cascading Style Sheets (CSS) and basic Hypertext Markup Language (HTML) knowledge.

By the end of this chapter, you should feel comfortable with changing the presentation of an entire Community Server blog. In addition, you will also learn about the following items:

- ❑ Using master pages
- ❑ Creating a custom theme
- ❑ Using stylesheets
- ❑ Theme file organization
- ❑ Modifying the presentation of custom controls
- ❑ Using custom themes

Before reading this chapter, it is important to realize that it is targeted at versions of Community Server 2.0 and above, as well as Community Server 3.0. In addition, it is important to realize that Community Server 3.0 has made drastic improvements in the way that it handles the presentation of a site with the creation of the chameleon engine inside of Community Server. To learn more about the differences between Community Server 3.0 and previous versions, read the next section.

Understanding Chameleon

Chameleon is a new engine that was introduced in Community Server 3.0 that makes it easier to change the presentation of a Community Server site. As a result, one of the main differences between Community Server 3.0 and previous versions is that the previous version contained skin files, while the current version does not. While you read through the following examples, it is important to realize that if you see a reference to skin files, it does not concern version 3.0. If you are using a version of Community Server prior to version 3.0, read through the sections in the examples that concern skin files.

In case you are wondering what happened to the information in the skin files, the answer is that they were pulled into the main pages that would have previously used the skin files. As a result, when you are editing a page you do not need to navigate to other files to change the look of the page. That being said, if you do need to change a master layout for a page, there are occasions where you will need to edit a master page.

In addition to the removal of skin files, Chameleon also introduces several new controls to make it easier for developers to modify the presentation of a site. Later in this chapter, some of these controls will be explored so that it is easier to get started using them.

Understanding Themes

Community Server ships with three different themes: default, alternative1, and basic blue. The default theme is what most sites use and is what will be used throughout the following exercises. A theme is a collection of files that can consist of master pages, CSS, images, and skin files that combine in a way that defines the specific presentation of a site.

One of the nice things about a theme is that it can be easily distributed across sites to alter the look of an entire site. In addition, you can easily switch from one theme to the next. A result of this behavior is that a developer can create a theme in a development environment and easily deploy it to a production site, altering the presentation of the production site in one move.

To see a basic example of a theme, you should look at the blog themes. They are complete themes that are much easier to understand than the entire site theme because they do not have the complexity of subthemes.

Again, a theme is really nothing more than a collection of image files, CSS, skin files, and master pages. Of course, a theme does not have to contain all of these types of files; they are merely an example of some of the types of files you can expect to find in a theme.

Understanding Master Pages

With the release of .NET 2.0, several new features were introduced to assist with the development of web applications. One of the main features was the ability to create master pages. Master pages are extremely useful for maintaining consistency across a site. They are also very straightforward, as they look like a normal ASP.NET page, only without a page directive. What makes them so powerful is that you can use them to basically create a template for a site that pages can use. Another nicety of master pages is that they can have parent and child master pages. This allows for a scenario in which you can have a master layout for a site and then different sections of the site that have their own consistent implementation. Aside from consistency, master pages are also useful for reducing the amount of redundant code that would go into the presentation code of a site. A full analysis of master pages is beyond the scope of this book; however, the preceding description is a good introduction or refresher for understanding their concept.

Community Server uses master pages to control the layout and consistency of what visitors observe across a site. However, Community Server does not use the default implementation of master pages that was shipped with .NET 2.0. The reason for this is obvious when you realize that Community Server has supported .NET 1.1 up until the release of Community Server 3.0. In order to have master page support, it was forced to use a solution other than the standard .NET 2.0 master pages. It is also extremely important to realize that the master page syntax in Community Server is close to that of .NET 2.0 master pages. As a result, most developers will be just as comfortable with the master pages in Community Server as they would with those found in any other .NET 2.0 applications. In fact, the master pages in Community Server actually require less code than .NET master pages, which can make them easier to develop.

Default Master Page

To better understand master pages in Community Server, take a look at the following example, which is actually a subset of the root master page. The `Master.ascx` file is the master page that is defaulted to whenever no other master page is defined in the child page. Notice that the extension is the same as a normal ASP.NET control. However, ASP .NET 2.0 master pages would have the extension of master. This is just one of the differences that you should recognize between the two. Without further ado, here is a snippet from root master page with some of the formatting styles removed:

```
<table id="CommonBodyTable">
    <tr>
        <td id="CommonLeftColumn">
            <CS:MPRegion id="lcr" runat="server" />
        </td>

        <td id="CommonBodyColumn">
            <CS:MPRegion id="bcr" runat="server" />
        </td>

        <td id="CommonRightColumn">
            <CS:MPRegion id="rcr" runat="server" />
        </td>
    </tr>
</table>
```

The preceding code snippet was taken from the middle portion of the master page. If you look at the source code that is generated from a Community Server site's `default.aspx` page that is located at the root of the site, you will notice that the `CommonBodyTable` exists with the previous rows. This table defines the standard layout for the main section of a page that uses the `Master.ascx` master page. It defines three main sections to place content on a site:

❑   `lcr`: left column region

❑   `bcr`: body column region

❑   `rcr`: right column region

These different regions are defined by using the MPRegion control, which is similar to the ASP.NET 2.0 ContentPlaceHolder control. Thinking of the MPRegion as a content placeholder is very useful. An MPRegion control is placed in a master page and provides a location for additional controls to be inserted in the page for final rendering. The page that uses the master page as a container uses the MPContent control to declare what MPRegion a section of code will be placed into. For example, the default.aspx page off the root web folder uses the HomeMaster.ascx master page, which then uses the Master.ascx master page. As a result, the default.aspx page can place content in the bcr section defined in Master.ascx by using the MPContent control. Here is what the code looks like for placing content in the bcr region:

```
<CS:MPContent id="bcr" runat="server">
    <div class="CommonContentArea">
        <div class="CommonContent">

            <CS:AdPart runat = "Server" contentname="StandardTop" >
                <CS:Ads Zone="StandardTop" runat="server" id="Ads1" />
            </CS:AdPart>

            <CS:ContentPart runat = "Server" contentname="welcome" id =
                "welcomeContentPart" text=""/>
        </div>

        <div class="CommonContent">

            <CS:AdPart runat = "Server" contentname="StandardBottom" ID="Adpart2">
                <CS:Ads Zone="StandardBottom" runat="server" id="Ads3" />
            </CS:AdPart>

        </div>
    </div>
</CS:MPContent>
```

The previous code generates the main section of the home page of a Community Server site. Using the id attribute, the MPContent control declares that the content contained in it will be used to populate the MPRegion with the id of bcr. As a result, the body column of the home page has an AdPart control located at the top and bottom of this middle cell in the CommonBodyTable. In addition, there is also a ContentPart control that is used to output the welcome text that is easily editable. The ContentPart is an extremely powerful control for making a site easy for nontechnical individuals to edit. All that is required is that they have access to edit the page and can use a WYSIWYG editor.

Another important thing to realize about master pages is where they are located physically in a Community Server site and how to change this location. By default, master pages are located in a subfolder called Masters under the name of the theme that they belong to. Also by default, a theme is located under the themes folder. Therefore, the default theme master pages are located at Themes\default\ masters. The location of these files is defined from the ContentContainer class, which is located in the CommunityServer.Controls namespace.

Creating a Master Page

To create a new master page you simply need to have a layout and know where content can be placed in that layout. For the purposes of this demonstration, assume that you want to create a new master page that will be used for defining the layout of navigation menu. The navigation menu is static and will be on all of the pages of a site; therefore, a master page is appropriate. Here is what the markup of your new master page could look like:

```
<%@ Control Language="C#" %>
<CS:MPContainer runat="server" id="MPContainer" >

    <CS:MPContent id="HeaderRegion" runat="server" >
        <CS:Head runat="Server" >
            <meta http-equiv="Content-Type" content="text/html; charset=UTF-8" />
            <CS:Style id="s2" runat="server" Href="../style/Common.css" />
        </CS:Head>
    </CS:MPContent>

    <CS:MPContent id="rcr" runat="server">

        <ul><strong>Links</strong>
            <li><a href="http://communityserver.org">Community Server</a></li>
            <li><a href="http://google.com">Google</a></li>
            <li><a href="http://yahoo.com">Yahoo</a></li>
            <li><a href="http://amazon.com">Amazon</a></li>
        </ul>

    </CS:MPContent>

</CS:MPContainer>
```

As you can see, the master page is declared to be a control on the first line. There is a new control that is defined called the MPContainer. This stands for *master page container* and is used to wrap the contents of your master page. Inside this container you can see that the MPContent controls are used to occupy the space defined in the MPRegion of the master.ascx master page. This essentially means that these regions are already used; therefore, a page that uses this master page will not need to worry about occupying both the HeaderRegion and rcr regions. Inside the header there is a reference to the common stylesheet, which is located in Common.css. For now, it is important to note that this is included so that the resulting pages will have a presentation that is consistent with other pages in Community Server. The bulk of the usefulness of this master page is located in the rcr content region. In it, there is an unordered list that defines different links that should appear on the sidebar of the pages that use this master page.

In order to use the previous master page, it should be saved in the Masters folder of the default theme and be named SideBarMaster.ascx. Once the file has been saved, you should look at the following .aspx page that uses the SideBarMaster master page:

```
<%@ Page SmartNavigation="False" Language="C#"  enableViewState = "false" %>

<CS:MPContainer runat="server" id="Mpcontainer1"
    ThemeMasterFile = "SideBarMaster.ascx" >

    <CS:MPContent id="bcr" runat="server">
        Here is the body content
    </CS:MPContent>

</CS:MPContainer>
```

In order to view the example, the previous code should be saved in the root of your site and be named `SideBar.aspx`. Notice that the previous page is quite simple, requiring only a few lines of code. However, from just a few lines of code a powerful page is produced because of the use of master pages. Also notice that the previous page defines a content region that will use the `bcr` region that is located on the `Master.ascx` master page. Even though the page declares that it will use the `SideBarMaster.ascx` master page, it will also get access to the `bcr` content region because it is defined on `Master.ascx`, which is the root master page. The resulting page output of the `SideBar` page is quite impressive when you consider the small amount of code that was required. You can observe this output in Figure 5-1.

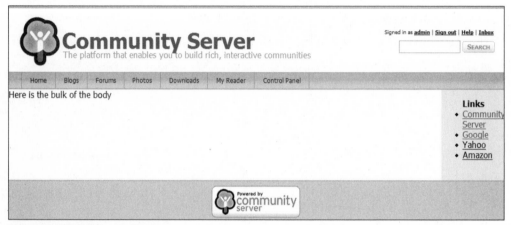

Figure 5-1: SideBar.aspx Output

From the previous example, you can see the power of master pages not only in ASP.NET 2.0 but more importantly in Community Server. In addition, Community Server definitely simplifies the process of creating your own master page with its built-in controls.

Included Master Pages

Community Server ships with several master pages to assist in creating pages for the various areas on a site. It can be helpful to know what master pages exist and what areas of the site they are used for in order to create a consistent look across a site. The following is a list of the standard master pages in Community Server, along with a brief description of each:

- ❏ `BlogControlPanelMaster` defines the layout of the pages in the My Blogs section of the Control Panel.

- ❏ `BlogMaster` defines the layout for pages in the blogs folder. It includes the stylesheets for these blogs' pages.

- ❏ `ControlPanelMaster` defines the layout for the pages in the Control Panel. It also includes some common controls for these pages, such as the Telligent Modal control. In addition, this master page includes the stylesheets that are used in the Control Panel.

- ❏ `ControlPanelModalMaster` defines the layout for the modal dialog box that appears from Control Panel pages.

❑ `FileControlPanelMaster` defines the layout and includes the stylesheets for the pages located under the My Files section of the Control Panel.

❑ `FileGalleryMaster` defines the layout and includes the stylesheets for the pages that present a file gallery to site visitors.

❑ `ForumMaster` defines the layout and includes the stylesheets for the pages under the Forums folder.

❑ `GalleryControlPanelMaster` defines the layout and includes the stylesheets for the My Photos section of the Control Panel. These pages are located under the Photos folder of the ControlPanel folder.

❑ `GalleryMaster` defines the layout and includes the stylesheets for Photo Gallery pages.

❑ `HomeMaster` defines the layout and includes the standard stylesheets for the homepage of Community Server.

❑ `Master` defines the default layout and stylesheets for all of Community Server. If a page uses a master page, and the `ThemeMasterFile` property has not been set, then this master page will be used by default.

❑ `ModalMaster` defines the layout for modal dialog boxes that are used throughout the public area of a site.

❑ `ModerationControlPanelMaster` defines the layout and includes the stylesheets for the pages inside the Moderation section of the Control Panel.

❑ `ReaderMaster` defines the layout and includes the stylesheets for the Reader application pages.

❑ `ReportingControlPanelMaster` defines the layout and includes the stylesheets for the pages located under the Reporting section of the Control Panel.

❑ `RollerBlogsMaster` defines the layout and includes the stylesheets for the roller application pages.

File Organization

In order to be able to change the presentation of a site, you need to alter various files and know where the appropriate files are located. Fortunately, the files that compose Community Server are well organized, making it easier to find them. For the most part, you usually only need to change the files located under the themes folder.

Following are the main subfolders that are found under a themes folder, which is located in the themes directory. Following is a description of the skins directory that is used in Community Server versions before 3.0. Another important change to the folder structure in version 3.0 is that the blogs and galleries folders that are now located under a specific theme folder, such as themes\default. Before version 3.0, blog and gallery themes were listed under the themes root as /themes/blogs/[BlogThemeName] and /themes/galleries/[GalleryThemeName], respectively. Whenever you are editing a blog or gallery theme in Community Server 3.0, you need to look under the specific theme folder, such as "basic blue," which is one of the themes that ships with Community Server.

- ❑ **Blogs** contains the files for changing an individual blog theme. You can add multiple themes in this folder, which will show up as an option for bloggers to change their blog theme. If you are interested in looking at how the blog theme option is presented to users, then you can look at the My Blogs Control Panel section. An example of what this screen looks like is available in Chapter 6.

- ❑ **Common** contains the master pages that are common throughout most of the pages on the site. This includes but is not limited to the default master page and modal page master file.

- ❑ **Files** contain page files that commonly found in the file galleries.

- ❑ **Forums** contain page files that are found in the forums section of a site. If you need to edit the presentation of a sites forum, then you will want to look in this folder first.

- ❑ **Galleries** contain the pages that are used in the galleries section of the site.

- ❑ **Images** contain the image files that are displayed throughout a site. These do not include the images that are uploaded through a photo gallery.

- ❑ **Masters** contain the master pages that are used to control the layout of a site.

- ❑ **Skins** contain the files that are used to control the presentation of specific controls. Under this folder there are also subfolders that contain skin files that control the presentation of controls that relate to that specific folder. For example, there is a forums folder under the skins folder, which contains the skin files for the forums section.

- ❑ **Style** contains the stylesheet files for a specific theme.

Before you proceed with editing different theme files in Community Server, it is usually a good idea to make a backup copy. A simple way to do this is to simply make a backup copy of the entire themes folder. This is useful in case you need to roll back entire folders while editing the presentation of a site.

Editing Stylesheets

Most of the styles that you will need to edit are most likely contained in the `common.css` file. However, there are other stylesheets in the styles folder that you can use to change the presentation of certain areas of a site. For example, if you want to change a style that is specific to the blogs, you can most likely look in the `blog.css` file. Likewise, if you want to change the presentation of a page located in the Control Panel, you can edit the `controlpanel.css` file. The important thing to notice is that the files are organized in a logical manner, so they are easy to find and edit.

If you are unsure about what file you need to edit to change a specific style, you can simply look at the source code of the rendered page. When you look at the source code, you will see a list of the included stylesheets at the top of the page in the HTML head section. This should help narrow down what stylesheet files you need to look at in order to change a style on the page. In addition, you may find it helpful to install and use the web developer toolbars that are available for Firefox, Internet Explorer, and Opera. Each of these toolbars allows you to more easily examine the source and DOM of each of the pages on your site. The web developer toolbar for Firefox can be found at `https://addons.mozilla.org/firefox/60`.

The editor that you choose to use for editing a stylesheet is an important choice. Many developers find that the stylesheet editor inside of Visual Studio is a good option. Other people may prefer an editor such as Notepad that does not have the IntelliSense provided by Visual Studio. The choice of what editor to use is ultimately up to you. It is simply important to realize that you can alter the presentation of a Community Server site by using any standard text editor. As a result, you can edit sites' stylesheets using a non-Windows operating system.

It can sometimes seem difficult to identify what style you need to edit in order to get the desired outcome. Usually, the best approach is to look at the source code of the rendered page that you want to change the presentation of. On this page, you should then navigate to the item that you want to change and find if it has a class or ID attribute defined for it. If neither of these attributes is defined for the element that you want to change, you can always back up to a parent element and locate whether it has an ID or class defined. If it does, then you can always change the presentation of a child element by using the parent's class or ID and the HTML element type of the child. The important thing to realize is that Community Server does a very good job of making sure that all elements are easily identifiable from a stylesheet by either their class or ID.

Changing the Blog Post Header

To better understand how to edit a blog-specific style, consider the situation in which you need to change the way that the title of a blog post is presented. For this example, the header of a post is changed so that it has a different font, is larger, and has a different background color. When you open the `blog.css` file located in the styles directory, the style for the `BlogPostHeader` class should look similar to the following.

```
.BlogPostHeader
{
  color: #666666;
  font-size: 150%;
  font-weight: normal;
  font-family: Tahoma, Arial, Helvetica;
  padding: 4px;
  padding-top: 0px;
  padding-left: 0px;
  margin: 0px;
}
```

The result of the standard `BlogPostHeader` style is pictured in Figure 5-2.

Welcome to Community Server Blogs!

Figure 5-2: BlogPostHeader style

You can change the way that this header is presented to a site visitor by editing the `BlogPostHeader` entry in the `blog.css` file. For the purposes of this demonstration, you will change the font family and font size, and add a background color for this heading, as follows:

```
.BlogPostHeader
{
  color: #666666;
  font-size: 170%;
  font-weight: normal;
  font-family: Arial, Helvetica;
  padding: 4px;
```

```
    padding-top: 0px;
    padding-left: 0px;
    margin: 0px;
  background-color: yellow;
}
```

Welcome to Community Server Blogs!

Figure 5-3: Updated BlogPostHeader style

As a result of the preceding stylesheet change in the blog.css file located in the global styles directory, individual blog themes can override this class. Take a look at the styles section of the rendered HTML on the blog aggregate page of http://communityserver.org (http://communityserver.org/blogs/default.aspx):

```
<link rel="stylesheet" href="/Themes/default/style/Common.css" type="text/css"
media="screen" />
<link rel="stylesheet" href="/Themes/default/style/Blog.css" type="text/css"
media="screen" />
<link rel="stylesheet" href="/Themes/default/style/common_print.css"
type="text/css" media="print" />
<link rel="stylesheet" href="/Themes/default/style/blog_print.css" type="text/css"
media="print" />
```

Note that /themes/default/style/Blog.css comes after Common.css in the previous listing. When a class in blog.css has the same name as a class in common.css, the definition in blog.css will take precedence over common.css. If an attribute in the definition of that class in blog.css is different from the same attribute in common.css, blog.css will override common.css. As a result of the nature of styles, an individual blog theme can override the BlogPostHeader style in its own stylesheet file.

It is also important to realize that the last style will be what it is rendered. If you look inside the controlpanel.css file, you find duplicates of the styles found in the common.css file. The reason for this is that the controlpanel.css styles are included after common.css and therefore are able to override some of the default styles found in common.css. It is also important to realize that controlpanel.css is included only on pages found in the Control Panel of Community Server.

Changing a Site's Header

The default header for Community Server may not be what you have in mind for your site. Perhaps you want to remove the Community Server logo and change the colors so that it looks different from what is shipped by default. The default header for Community Server is pictured in Figure 5-4, and the resulting header that will be produced by the alterations in this section is pictured in Figure 5-5.

Figure 5-4: Default Community Server Header

Figure 5-5: Altered Community Server Header

As you can see from Figure 5-5, the logo image has been removed, the background color has adjusted, the description text color has changed, and the spacing of the text in general has also changed. What you may be surprised to find out is that only one stylesheet was changed, and only a few lines were added to the stylesheet to get the previous outcome.

There are many different ways that you can get the previous outcome; however, for the purposes of this example, you will be adding a few lines at the end of the common.css file that override some of the default styles. This should also demonstrate how the last style will override any preceding style. To get the previous outcome, simply add the following lines to the very bottom of the common.css file. After the code, there will be a discussion that explains the purposes of each line of the code.

```
#CommonHeader
{
   background-color: #BBDE79;
   padding-bottom: 2px;
}

#CommonHeader img
{
   display: none;
}

.CommonTitleBarDescription
{
   margin-bottom: 0px;
   color: #fff;
}
```

If you look for CommonHeader in the common.css file, you find an entry at the top of the file. This is the style that is used for the div that wraps the top header, which includes the navigation bar. The default style for the header only specifies that it takes up 100% of the available width. In the preceding overridden style, notice that there is a background color defined that is the same color as the line at the very top of the page. In addition, bottom padding was used to add a 2-pixel-high line below the navigation bar that will be the same green color as the background.

To remove the default logo image from the presentation of the site, the display property was changed to none so that the image would not be displayed. Note that the image is still included in the rendered HTML, but it is not displayed in the final presentation to the user.

The CommonTitleBarDescription class is defined previously in the stylesheet, but because this new one comes later (below it), it will override the specified styles. The important one is margin-bottom, which was previously defined to be -14px and now is specified as 0px. The reason for having no bottom margin is so that the description text appears below the Community Server title text. The color of the text was changed to white so that it is easier to read on the green background.

In addition to the preceding classes, there are also several other classes that relate to the header on a Community Server site. To help demonstrate what areas of the header each class can alter, the areas in the header have been pictured as follows with a style name that corresponds to the class listed below the picture. The header has also been divided into the top-left (see Figure 5-6) and top-right (see Figure 5-7) areas as well as the navigation bar (see Figure 5-8).

Figure 5-6: Left Header Area Styles

❑ #CommonHeader img — The Community Server logo is accessible through this style.

❑ CommonTitleBarTitle — The title header that is displayed at the top of pages.

❑ CommonTitleBarDescription — The description that is displayed below the title on each page.

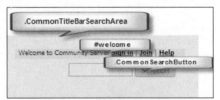

Figure 5-7: Right Header Area Styles

❑ CommonTitleBarSearchArea — This serves as a container for the right side header search area.

❑ #welcome — This is the wrapper for the text and links that show above the search box.

❑ CommonSearchButton — This is the class name used for the search button across the entire site.

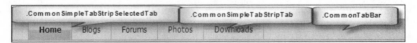

Figure 5-8: Navigation Bar Styles

❑ CommonSimpleTabStripSelectedTab — The style for the selected navigation option

❑ ComonSimpleTabStripTab — The style for all navigation options that are not selected

❑ CommonTabBar — The container class for the entire navigation bar

The important thing to realize when looking at all of the previous styles is that there are actually more in each section. Because of the nature of stylesheets and of the layout of each page, there are parent elements that may have an influence over how a child element is rendered. For example, if the parent of all of the items on the navigation bar specifies that the font is Tahoma, and none of the child elements specifies a different font, then Tahoma will be the font of the rendered children. In addition, it is also important to realize that the previous styles are not an exhaustive list as there are more styles that can impact the appearance of each area.

To learn about all of the styles that are available to edit, you can simply look at the source code of a rendered page. You can also look through the different stylesheet files directly and look for the corresponding style for the element that you want to edit. There are many tools that you can use to look at these files. Many ASP.NET developers will use Visual Studio to look at the source code. However, you can use any basic text editor; you can even use Notepad as an editor to look at these source files.

Changing a Site's Footer

In addition to being able to change a site's header, it is useful to know how to change a Community Server site's footer (see Figure 5-9). Both the header and the footer are visible on all standard pages of a site, so it is important to be able to change the way that the header and footer appear. In this section, the standard styles are examined, and an example is provided, showing how to add rounded corners to the bottom of your site.

Figure 5-9: Footer Styles

❑   `#CommonFooter` — Wraps the entire footer contents on a Community Server site.

To produce rounded corners at the bottom of the footer, an image can simply be placed at the bottom of the footer `div`. This image will be created with Photoshop, although Microsoft Paint will work just as well. Here are the basic steps to create an image with rounded corners using Photoshop:

1. Create a new image that is transparent and has a width of 956 pixels and a height of 7 pixels.

2. Change the foreground color to the hex value 606060.

3. Using the Pencil tool, change the bottom corners of the image so that they are cut off with the new foreground color. As a result, the remaining image should have the bottom corners set to this new color, while the rest of the image is completely transparent. This will allow you to change the background color of the footer while maintaining the look of rounded corners.

4. Select the Save for Web option from the File menu and save it as a `.gif` image with the transparency enabled. Also, save the image with the name `footer-bg.gif` and place it in the `themes\default\images\common` folder of your Community Server installation.

Once you have the image created and saved in the appropriate place, you can begin editing the `common.css` file using your editor of choice. There are a couple of options for adding the new styles: you can either edit the existing `#CommonFooter` that is found in the `common.css` file or you can create a brand-new `#CommonFooter` section at the bottom of the file so that it will override the existing style entry. The important thing to remember when adding a new style at the bottom of the stylesheet instead of altering the existing style by removing the unnecessary entries is that it will make the size of the stylesheet file larger. As a result, the time it takes for new visitors to your site to download the stylesheet will be longer. For the purposes of this example, simply add the following entry to the end of the `common.css` file and save the file:

```
#CommonFooter
{
    background: #D3D3D3 url(../images/common/footer-bg.gif) bottom left no-repeat;
    margin-bottom: 5px;
}
```

This entry for the footer changes the background so that the new image is used and placed at the bottom of the footer `div`, while the parts that are not occupied by the image are replaced with the gray color specified at the beginning of the background line. Notice that the location of the image is relative to the location of the stylesheet. Also notice that it is not a requirement to surround this path with quotation marks. In addition, a bottom margin was added so that it gives more of a rounded corners look that jumps off the page. The result of the previous entry provides the rounded footer look displayed in Figure 5-10.

Figure 5-10: Footer with Rounded Corner

Feel free to experiment with different colored backgrounds for the bottom footer. All you need to do is change the `D3D3D3` entry in the background to whatever color you desire. The nice thing is that the rounded corners will still be visible, as the image used to produce them is transparent throughout the middle region.

Editing Skin Files

To edit the skin files that are a part of Community Server, you should use an editor like Visual Studio. If you do not have access to Visual Studio, use whatever editor you use to edit standard ASP.NET pages. All of the skins that you need to edit are located in the Skins folder in the theme directory.

A common item that makes sense to add to Community Server is a link to sign up for an account that appears on the login screen. Often a visitor to a site will click the sign-in link expecting to find a way to create an account. By default, Community Server does not provide a link to the create account page from the login page. Therefore, for the purposes of this example, the login skin file will be edited and a new link will be added that links to the Create Account page. To begin, simply open the `Skin-Login.ascx` file located in the Skins folder of your site's theme using your editor of choice. For the purposes of this example you are free to use Notepad if you like. Once you have the skin file open, you can add a new anchor tag between the closing `div` tags at the bottom of the skin file, as shown in the following code snippet:

```
      </table>
      </div>
    </div>
    <a href="user/createuser.aspx">Create an account</a>
  </div>
  </div>
```

After you save the `Skin-Login.ascx` page with the updated anchor tag, you get a new link that displays after the login section on the login page. Once again, this addition can be useful for visitors who are new to your site and want to create an account. The preceding code that was added is rendered after the login table, as shown in Figure 5-11.

Figure 5-11: Addition of Login Page Anchor

Creating Stylesheets

Stylesheets are really nothing more than a plaintext file with a `css` extension. You should be able to create new stylesheets using an editor such as Notepad or ultra-edit. Make sure that your stylesheet is named appropriately to help identify what styles are located in it. For example, the Community Server blog stylesheet is named `blog.css`, which makes it very clear that the styles in the file relate to the blog portion of a site.

When creating new stylesheets, you should also make sure that they are properly formed. There are validators that you can use on the Web to make sure that your stylesheet does not break any standards. The World Wide Web Consortium (W3C) offers a free CSS validation service that you can access at `http://jigsaw.w3.org/css-validator`. This allows you to ensure that your stylesheets are following best practices. If you do decide to use the W3C CSS validation service, you may want to tweak some of the advanced settings so that you do not get a large amount of warnings. There are several options for choosing the type of medium that your stylesheet is targeting, such as a `screen` or `tv`.

An example of a stylesheet that you may want to create for Community Server is a stylesheet that targets Internet Explorer 6 and previous versions. This can be helpful for easing the design of your site so that you can target the Internet Explorer 7 browser inside your standard stylesheets. As a result, you're able to fix areas of your site that have issues rendering in Internet Explorer 6 without having to add extra styles and hack your way through your standard stylesheet files. To follow the previous recommendation to name a stylesheet appropriately, you should create a new file called `IE6.css` and place it in your themes style directory. Once you have added the new stylesheet file to your site, you can complete the following steps to add it to the header of all of the pages on your site so that it is included whenever a user accesses your site with an Internet Explorer browser that is less than or equal to version 6:

1. Log in to your site using a System Administrator account.

2. Click the Control Panel.

3. Click the Administration menu.

4. Expand the Settings menu and choose the Site Name & Description menu option.

5. In the Raw Header field, add the following entry:

```
<!--[if lte IE 6]>
<link rel="stylesheet" type="text/css" href="/Themes/default/style/IE6.css" />
<![endif]-->
```

6. Press the Save button.

Now that you have added the previous code to your site's raw header, any time a person visits your site with Internet Explorer 6, the IE6.css file will load. In addition, the stylesheet will load last so that you can override any other styles that are not displayed correctly in Internet Explorer 6. You can use this same strategy for targeting Internet Explorer 7 by replacing 6 with 7 in the example. This way, you can target your development toward Firefox and then fix any inconsistencies with rendering in IE7 as a separate process.

Adding Custom Images

There are some important points that you should consider when adding a custom image to Community Server. First, it is helpful to make sure that your image file is small enough so that it doesn't take visitors a long time to download it. The amount of space that your image file takes up should be balanced with the dimensions of the image while maintaining a reasonable level of quality. Usually, images that are used on web pages are of JPEG, GIF, or PNG type. There are different reasons to go with each of these image choices; here are the most common ones:

❑ **JPEG** is often used for images that you want to be small in file size while still providing a decent level of quality. The level of clarity and file size correlate to the compression level used to produce the image.

❑ **GIF** is often used for the same reasons that a JPEG image would be used. However, the important distinction is that a GIF image allows the image to be transparent, which can be useful for creating things such as rounded corners on a web page.

❑ **PNG** is often used for a similar reason as a GIF image, which is to allow an image to be transparent in places. The important distinction is that a PNG image will allow for alpha transparency. This basically means that an image can have varying levels of transparency. It is important to realize that if you do use a PNG image for alpha transparency that you add special lines in your stylesheet so that Internet Explorer 6 can render the PNG image correctly. All of the other popular browsers today have support for alpha transparency, including Internet Explorer 7.

In addition to choosing the most appropriate image type, it is also important to place your image in the best location in your Community Server site. Images are usually placed in one of the subfolders under the images folder of a specific theme. There are subfolders under the images folder that specify where the each of the images will be located in the site. For example, if you have an image that only relates to pages in the Control Panel, then you should place it under the controlpanel folder. Furthermore, if you have an image that will be used across all areas of the site, such as an image that is in the header of all pages, then you would place it under the images/common subfolder.

Changing the Default Color Scheme

As a result of Community Server relying so much on CSS, it is relatively straightforward to change the default color scheme of a site. To do this, you really only need to edit stylesheet files. For example, if you want to change the colors for the main layout from the green and brown that are set by default to a red and black color scheme, you are able to do so just by editing the `common.css`. This new color scheme replaces all of the background colors with a black background. In addition, it replaces all of the foreground colors and borders with a red color. What the new color scheme looks like can be found in Figure 5-12.

Figure 5-12: Red and Black Color Scheme

There are a few different ways that you can achieve this same color scheme using your default editor with the `common.css` file open. Perhaps the easiest way is to do a find and replace, where you first replace all of the entries for black with red and then replace all of the entries for white with black. This would replace the hex value 000000 with FF002A and then replace FFFFFF with 000. Note that CSS allows for shorthand notation; shorthand 000 is equivalent to the long form of the hex value for black, 000000. After you have replaced the standard colors with these new ones, you can simply search through the `common.css` stylesheet, looking for any remaining colors that need to be updated to either red or black. You can repeat this pattern for any other colors that remain in the stylesheet, such as CCCCCC.

Once you have finished replacing all of the colors with either the black or the red choice, you will only have to update the images with the new colors so that they fit in with the rest of the color scheme. If you do not want to edit some of the images, like the selected tab bar image, then you can simply comment them out or remove them entirely from the stylesheet.

To give you an idea of what some of the updated styles will look like, they are listed as follows. Please note that an entire list of updated styles would be many pages long, which is why not every updated style was included here. When you have finished updating all of the appropriate styles, your new site should look very similar to Figure 5-13.

```
body, html
{
  margin: 0px;
  padding: 0px;
  color: # FF002A;
  font-family: Tahoma, Arial, Helvetica;
  background-color: #000;
}
#CommonLeftColumn
{
  background-color: #000;
```

```
    padding-bottom: 22px;
}

#CommonRightColumn
{
  background-color: #000;
  padding-bottom: 22px;
}

A:LINK
{
  color: #FF002A;

}

A:ACTIVE
{
  color: #FF002A;
}

A:VISITED
{
  color: #FF002A;
}
```

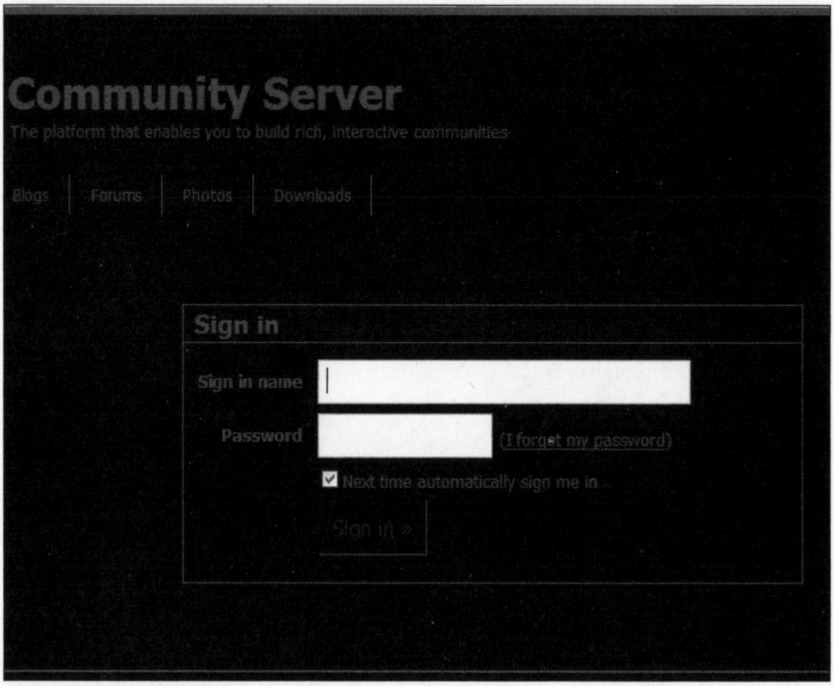

Figure 5-13: Updated Color Scheme

It is important to remember that this is just one of the many color schemes that you can choose to update a site with. Furthermore, the fact that you can change the way a site looks while only touching Cascading Style Sheet files is an important characteristic that demonstrates how flexible Community Server is. Also, realize that to fully change the color scheme of a site, you should make sure to update the images located in the default themes images folder.

Common Community Server Controls

Community Server offers many useful controls that you can use to add functionality to your pages. Some of these controls have already been demonstrated, such as the MPRegion control that was explored toward the beginning of this chapter. However, there are still many more controls that it can be helpful to know about when you are customizing Community Server. The list that follows is not an exhaustive one covering all of the available Community Server controls; instead, it is intended to provide a basic overview of some of the many controls available.

❏   AdPart contains the different ads that can be visible on a site. By default, the AdPart is on the top and bottom of most pages; however, it is only visible whenever ads are enabled from the Control Panel.

❏   AlphaPicker generates a list of links from A through Z to assist users in navigating large groups of information. This control is useful for things such as finding a user quickly, as it allows you to select the letter b to find data that starts with that letter. For example, if you clicked the link represented by the character B, you would get back all data that starts with the letter B.

❏   CollapsableArea is a control that acts similarly to a panel control in that it can wrap a group of children elements. The main difference is that CollapsableArea has the ability to collapse and expand as a user clicks the Collapse and Expand buttons. Also, there is an abstract CollapsableAreaBase class from which the CollapsableArea inherits.

❏   ContentPart creates an editable area on a page that stores the content of the area in the database. When users with the appropriate permissions double-click a ContentPart, they are provided with a WYSIWYG editor for changing the content that is contained in the specific ContentPart.

❏   DatePickerToggle offers a control that allows a user to more easily select a specific date from a calendar. This control serves as a wrapper for a calendar control that you can either hide or show by clicking this control.

❏   DisplayUserWelcome provides the control that shows in the top-right corner of a Community Server site that is using a default theme. It provides the links for users to check their private messages.

❏   Editor is the control that contains the basic elements for the different types of available editors. These editors allow a user to change content in a convenient way as this is a WYSIWYG editor.

❏   Faq is nothing more than a presentation of the frequently asked questions. If you would like to display this content on another page, you can use the Faq control to do so.

❏   Footer provides the control that displays the footer of a page. The default footer will display the Community Server logo. Therefore, if you have purchased a Community Server license and would like to disable this logo, you can do so by editing the footer control.

❑ GenericControl is nothing more than a TemplatedWebControl; it does no more and no less than provide a way to create a templated area of a site.

❑ Head is the control that wraps the content that will be included in the HTML head tag of a page. Inside this control you will often find the Style or Script controls.

❑ InlineContentPart is similar to the ContentPart in that it allows an administrator to edit content on a page without having to leave that page. The inline editor does not display a pop-up window, but instead allows single lines of text to be edited easily. The default installation uses the InlineContentPart for the header and description of a site.

❑ LinkButtonPager is a basic pager control that simply posts back to the same page whenever a new page is selected. This can be useful for cutting down the number of items you return to the user on a single page by effectively splitting those items into multiple pages.

❑ LiteralOrLink is exactly what it says: it will either render a link if a hyperlink value is provided and the TextOnly mode is false, or it will render a literal text control.

❑ Logout wraps the logout functions, which can be useful for having multiple logout methods.

❑ Message is used to render an error message based on an ID that is passed through a querystring. The message itself is nothing more than a title and a body.

❑ ModalLink creates a basic link that when clicked will create a new modal dialog on page.

❑ MPContainer contains various MPContent controls that are used to populate specific areas on a master page.

❑ MPContent is used inside an MPContainer for containing a specific content area of a site that is specified in a master page.

❑ MPForm is a control that serves as a replacement for the HTML form tag inside of master pages.

❑ MPRegion is used on a master page to specify the areas of the page that an MPContent control can populate.

❑ Pager is similar to the LinkButtonPage except that the pager does not post back to the page it is on; instead it relies on the querystring to reload the page by providing a specific page to load.

❑ PostIcons is a control that will render a specific predefined string for a user based on his or her post rank. There are different thresholds for displaying the different text, and the text itself can be configured in the resource files.

❑ RepeaterBar is a control that is used for displaying a navigation bar of different links that can be marked as selected or not.

❑ RepeaterPlusNone is basically like any other repeater control, except that it allows you to specify a template that will be displayed whenever there are no data to be bound. This can be useful for displaying an error message informing the user that no items were found.

❑ ResourceLabel is a control that is used to get the value for a key item in the resource files for the given language.

❑ Script used in the Head control to include JavaScript files. The control will be rendered inside of an HTML head tag.

❑ SearchResults is a control that displays the result items for a given search query.

❑   `SelectedNavigation` is used to select a navigation item on the navigation bar that runs across the site. An example would be that on the blogs page the selected navigation is blogs.

❑   `SiteStats` displays information about the number of forum posts that a site has. It also provides information relating to the most recent posts and the users who have made them.

❑   `StatusMessage` is used mainly in the Control Panel and can provide a success or fail message to the user. It is often used to inform a user that settings have been saved successfully and will be updated.

❑   `Style` is used to include stylesheet files. This will be rendered as a `link` tag inside of the resulting pages `head` tag.

❑   `TagBrowser` is similar to a `TagCloud`, except that instead of displaying the tags in a vertical fashion, they are displayed horizontally.

❑   `TagCloud` is a control used for rendering a tag cloud, which is simply a representation of all of the tags in a particular section of the site.

❑   `ThemedImage` is a control that simply displays an image, with the image source being resolved relative to the location of the theme the control is being used in.

❑   `TitleBar` is the control that appears at the top of the main pages for displaying the title of a site as well as its description.

❑   `UserAttribute` is a control that contains a specific user profile property that you would like to gather from a form, such as a person's birth year or favorite music — basically, anything that you would like to store about that user.

❑   `WhoIsOnline` will display statistics about the current number of users who are online. This is often found on the bottom of the home page or in the forums part of a site.

❑   `YesNoRadioButtonList` is a control that renders two radio buttons for a form field, which provides the options for Yes and No.

Modifying the Look of Custom Controls

Community Server allows you to modify the way that custom controls are presented to a user. These changes are usually done by editing the skin files that correspond to the appropriate control. In Community Server 2.0 and 2.1, there is a skin file that corresponds to the templated controls found in the `CommunityServer.Controls` namespace. As a result, the skin files located in a theme `Skins` directory can be edited and made to contain multiple controls.

To edit the skin files and change the look of the custom Community Server controls, it is helpful if you use a tool such as Visual Studio. The important thing to remember is that these skin files can be edited just as you would edit an HTML page. This means that you can add `div` and `image` tags and other elements that you see necessary. However, before you begin editing these skin files it can be useful to try to edit the look of the control using the CSS that ship with Community Server. This is a handy solution as it allows you to simply apply the same style in future versions of Community Server without having to edit any skin file.

Editing the Sidebar

There are often instances where you want to add or remove content from the sidebar that appears on your site. To do this, you need to edit the `default.aspx` page located in the root of your site. This page adds the sidebar content to the `rcr` content region, which is the right content region or right sidebar. In addition, if you would like the sidebar to appear on the left, then you can change `rcr` to `lcr`. Here is what your code would look like if you changed it to `lcr` so that the sidebar appears on the left side of the screen.

```
<CS:MPContent id="lcr" runat="server" >
   <div class="CommonSidebar">
   ...
   </div>
```

The resulting Community Server home page is pictured in Figure 5-14.

Figure 5-14: Sidebar on Left Side

If you would like to add any content to or remove any content from the sidebar, you simply need to add or remove the appropriate `CommonSideBarArea` div inside of the `default.aspx`. For example, if you want to remove the active section and replace it with a list of links to external sites, you can remove the `ActivePosts ThreadRepeater` control and replace it with the following code:

```
<div class="CommonSidebarArea">
    <h4 class="CommonSidebarHeader">Links</h4>
    <div class="CommonSidebarContent">
        <div class="CommonSidebarContentItem">
            <a href="http:/communityserver.org">Community Server</a>
        </div>
    </div>
</div>
```

When you save the changes to the code and try to run the site, you will notice that there is an error from the page. This is because at the top of the default.aspx page there is a set of server-side scripts that expects there to be a control with an ID of ActivePosts. To make the page run properly, simply remove the following line from the Page_Load code at the top of the default.aspx page:

```
ActivePosts.Visible = ApplicationSet.Applications[ApplicationType.Forum].Enabled;
```

After you make the previous changes, the resulting page will be rendered with the new links section and the active posts removed from the sidebar. In addition, the sidebar will appear on the left side of the page because its ID is still lcr. You can observe the result of these changes in Figure 5-15.

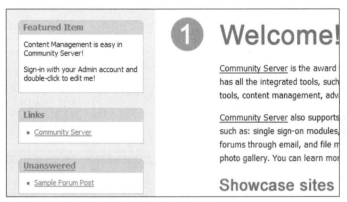

Figure 5-15: Links Section Added to Sidebar

Creating a Blog Theme

As a result of all of the various blog theme examples and Community Server support, the process of creating a new blog has become less challenging. This is a task that will be especially easy if you understand CSS and are able to identify and find the classes of elements on a web page. Before beginning to create your own blog theme, it is usually helpful to have a basic layout in mind for your page. It is also a good idea to have both an editor for the CSS and HTML markup, as well as an image editor in order to help create the theme. In the following example, Visual Studio was used to assist in creating the CSS, and Microsoft Paint was used to create the image.

The directions to create a blog theme are very similar to those for creating a sitewide theme. Therefore, you should be able to apply what you learn here about blog themes to a sitewide theme. A site theme follows the same basic steps, using an existing template and simply modifying it to meet your appearance requirements. Therefore, after you have completed this section, you should also be able to apply your knowledge to the other applications on a site, as well as the entire site itself.

Use Existing Template

It may not be obvious at first glance, but Community Server does provide a template to assist you in creating a blog theme. The template is the default blog theme, which comes packed with all of the various skin files and the basic layout to help get you started. Therefore, the first thing that you will want to do is to make a copy of the default blog theme and rename the copy to the name of your new theme. You can do this using File Explorer in Windows by copying and pasting the default folder in the blogs theme directory back into the directory. This will create a folder called Copy of default, which you can then rename to the name of your new theme. For this example, rename the folder to **Caffeine** as that is the name of the theme that will be created here. After you are done creating the new theme, File Explorer should contain the folders pictured in Figure 5-16.

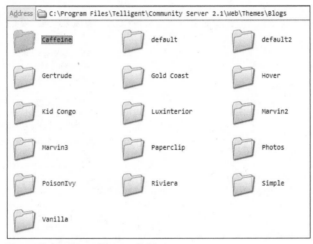

Figure 5-16: Blogs Theme Folder

You have essentially created a new theme as far as Community Server is concerned. To prove this and also to begin editing your new theme, you should navigate to your blog's Control Panel and select the option to change your blog's presentation. When you do this, you will see the option for Caffeine listed; you can now select and then save it to use this new theme. You are now able to edit the theme directly and see the results reflected on your blog.

Edit LayoutTemplate

The LayoutTemplate file in the blog theme folder contains the markup for the layout of each blog. For the purposes of this example, the LayoutTemplate also uses a local BlogMaster master page to helping control the layout. Following is the LayoutTemplate with the changes that should be made to create the new Caffeine theme:

```
<%@ Control Language="C#" %>
<%@ Register TagPrefix="CS" Namespace="CommunityServer.Controls"
Assembly="CommunityServer.Controls" %>
<%@ Register TagPrefix="Blog" Namespace="CommunityServer.Blogs.Controls"
Assembly="CommunityServer.Blogs" %>

<CS:MPContainer runat="server" id="MPContainer"
```

```
        ThemeFolder="~/Themes/Blogs/Caffeine/" ThemeMasterFile="BlogMaster.ascx">
    <CS:MPContent id="bhcr" runat="server">
        <Blog:BlogTitleHeader id="bth" runat="server" />
    </CS:MPContent>
    <CS:MPContent id="bcr" runat="server">
        <div class="CommonContentArea">
            <div class="CommonContent">
                <CS:BodyTemplate id="BodyTemplate" runat="Server" />
            </div>
        </div>
    </CS:MPContent>
</CS:MPContainer>
```

In the previous code there are two different content regions that are used to contain the layout of the Caffeine theme. First is the bhcr, which contains the header portion of the blog theme. In this region, the BlogTitleHeader control is added so that the name of the blog will be visible in the header of a blog. In addition, the bcr content region is also specified, which contains the layout for the main body part of a page. In this region, the only control that is used is the BodyTemplate, which will contain all of the content for the pages on the blog. This is necessary in order for your blog to actually have any of the posts displayed. You should also feel free to add any other content or markup that you would like to this file as it is where the bulk of the blog theme's layout is defined.

The other main file that you can define the layout in is the BlogMaster.ascx file, which is located in the root of the Caffeine theme folder. Here is an example of what the BlogMaster.ascx file should look like in order to create the Caffeine theme:

```
<%@ Control Language="C#" %>
<%@ Import Namespace="CommunityServer.Components" %>
<%@ Register TagPrefix="CS" Namespace="CommunityServer.Controls"
    Assembly="CommunityServer.Controls" %>

<CS:SelectedNavigation Selected="blog" runat="Server" ID="Selectednavigation1"/>
<CS:MPContainer runat="server" id="MPContainer" >
    <CS:MPContent id="HeaderRegion" runat="server" >
        <CS:Head runat="Server" id="h">
            <meta http-equiv="Content-Type" content="text/html;
                charset=UTF-8">
            <CS:Script runat="server" id="s" />
            <CS:Style runat="server"  />
            <CS:Style runat="server" Href="Common.css" id="s1" Enqueue="true" />
            <CS:Style  runat="server" Href="Blog.css" id="s2" Enqueue="true"/>
            <CS:Style  runat="server" Href="common_print.css" media="print"
                ID="Style1" Enqueue="true"/>
            <CS:Style  runat="server" Href="blog_print.css" media="print"
                ID="Style2" Enqueue="true"/>
        </CS:Head>
    </CS:MPContent>

    <CS:MPContent id="rcr" runat="server" >
    </CS:MPContent>
</CS:MPContainer>
```

The previous `BlogMaster` master page serves as a wrapper to the `LayoutTemplate` file defined previously. As you can see in the previous code, the `rcr`, or right content region, is defined but is empty. The reason for this is so that the sidebar does not have any content in it. This prevents the child `LayoutTemplate` page from including any content in this area of the blog. If you would like to add any sidebar controls, you should feel free to do so by adding the controls in the `rcr` content region.

Another important thing to notice is that the selected navigation control specifies that the navigation bar should have the link to the blogs selected. However, the theme itself will not include this navigation bar; therefore, you can omit the line entirely. It was included here as a best practice, so that whenever a navigation menu of some sort is added to the theme, the correct option will be selected.

In addition, the `Head` Community Server control is also included in the previous code. This defines the content that will be placed inside the HTML `head` tag whenever the page is fully rendered in the browser. The default theme includes the `common.css` stylesheet inside the `head` tag. However, because the Caffeine theme does not depend on any of the common site styles, this entry has been removed from the head. As a result, whenever the page is fully rendered, there will be only two stylesheets that are included. The two stylesheets that are included in the head are the `print.css` and `style.css` stylesheets, which can both be found in the theme's style directory. This is a nice feature of Community Server blog themes because by default a theme will link to these two stylesheets.

Editing Style.css

Now that you have the basic layout and master page defined for the new theme, you really only have a couple of tasks left before it is displayed properly. The first of these tasks is to create a new image that will be displayed at the top of the blog theme. To help energize the theme, a picture of a caffeine molecule was selected for inclusion in the page. This will be the only custom image that the new theme requires in order to be rendered properly. You can use any image you would like to display in the header, but to make it match the rest of the theme you should edit its background so that it is black like the other part of theme will be. Furthermore, you should also make sure to create a new directory for your image, called `images`, which is located off the root caffeine directory. The image that is used in the Caffeine theme is called `caffeine-molecule.gif` and was placed in this images folder, the result of which is shown in Figure 5-17.

Figure 5-17: Caffeine Molecule Image

Once you have your new image in place, it is time to begin editing the `style.css` stylesheet. In normal circumstances, you would also proceed by editing the `print.css` stylesheet, which is used for rendering a blog to a print medium. On the other hand, the `style.css` stylesheet is used for rendering a blog to a screen medium. To begin, open the `style.css` file located in the style subfolder of the `caffeine` theme directory, using your Cascading Style Sheet editor of choice. Once you have the `style.css` file open, you should enter the following styles and save the file:

```
body, html
{
  margin: 0;
  padding: 0;
  color: #fff;
  font-family: Tahoma, Arial, Helvetica;
  background-color: #000;
}

a, a:visited, a:link
{
  color: Red;
}

a:hover
{
  color: #fff;
}

#CommonOuter
{
  width: 956px;
  margin-left: auto;
  margin-right: auto;
}

#Common
{
  border: 1px solid red;
  border-bottom: solid 6px red;
  border-top: solid 6px red;
  margin-bottom: 7px;
  padding-bottom: 5px;
}

.CommonTitle
{
  font-size: 200%;
  background: #000 url(../images/caffeine-molecule.gif) no-repeat top right;
  width: 100%;
  height: 200px;
  margin-bottom: -40px;
  text-indent: 30px;
  font-family: Georgia;
}

.CommonTitle a, .CommonTitle a:link, .CommonTitle a:hover, .CommonTitle a:visited
{
  text-decoration: none;
}

#CommonBodyColumn
```

```
{
  padding-left: 10px;
  padding-right: 10px;
}


#CommonCommentForm textarea, #CommonCommentForm input
{
  width: 400px;
}


#CommonFooter
{
  padding-left: 40%;
}
```

As you can see in the previous stylesheet, there are only three colors that are used. The foreground text color is white, the link text and borders are red, and the background is black. One of the important aspects in the previous code is the inclusion of the caffeine molecule as the background image. As you can see, this is done through the stylesheet so that none of the page markup needs to be changed. Another important style to look at is the input and textarea of the `#CommonCommentForm` being declared to have a width of 400 pixels. This is important as the default width of these two elements makes the comment area very small. The result of the previous combination of styles is pictured in Figure 5-18.

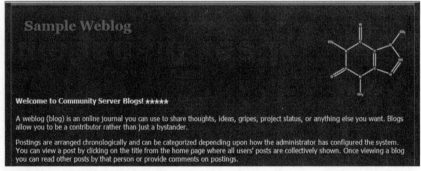

Figure 5-18: Caffeine Blog Theme

Deploying the Theme

To use the new blog theme on a remote web site, you need to deploy it to the site. Fortunately, Community Server makes this process easy to perform even for a novice user because Community Server will automatically detect new blog themes that are added to the blog theme directory. As a result, to deploy your new theme to a remote site you only need to be able to FTP to the blog themes folder and have write access. Here are the basic steps that you can follow in order to deploy the Caffeine theme that was created previously to a fictitious site called Endless Energy:

1. Ensure that the caffeine theme is functioning correctly in a test or development environment.

2. FTP to the Endless Energy site using an FTP client such as SmartFTP.

3. Navigate to the blog's theme directory on the remote site using the FTP client.

4. Upload the entire Caffeine folder to the blog themes directory.

5. Test the site by changing the theme of a blog in Endless Energy to use the new Caffeine theme.

Once you uploaded your new theme, you can disconnect the FTP client from the remote site. In addition, it is also a good idea to make a backup copy of your new theme. If you have a version control system, you can easily do this by checking in the new theme so that it will be versioned.

Using the Theme

To use the theme, your site users will only need to select it from the list of available blog themes. The theme will be automatically detected by Community Server whenever the `caffeine` directory is created in the blog theme folder (see Figure 5-19). Therefore, to use the theme, you simply need to select the Caffeine theme and then click Save.

Figure 5-19: Selecting Caffeine Theme

Packaging the Theme for Distribution

After creating a new blog theme, you most likely want to share it with the rest of the world. In order to do this, there are a few things that you should do to prepare it for global distribution.

First, create a screenshot of the blog theme in action. This means that you should capture an image of your site using the theme. Once you have a screenshot, make sure to save it as a PNG image file and place it in the blog theme folder. You will notice that there is already a PNG file in the root of your blog theme folder that should be named `default@.png`. This is the image that will be displayed in the preview box whenever you select the theme from the drop-down list when changing the look of a blog. Therefore, you should overwrite this image with your screenshot and name it `caffeine@.png` to match the name of your blog theme.

In addition, you should rename the `default@.htm` file to `caffeine@.htm` so that it can be included in the description of the blog whenever it is selected on the blog theme selection page. After you have renamed this file, you should edit it with Notepad or an HTML editor and change the content to reflect your description of the blog. In order to describe the Caffeine theme blog, here is what the `caffeine@.htm` file should look like:

```
<p>
    Here is a Minimalist Caffeine Theme.<BR>
    It features the molecule structure of caffeine and is very simple.
</p>
<p>
    For more skin options see
    <a href=http://communityserver.org/files
        target="_blank">communityserver.org</a>
</p>
```

Once you have made these changes, you are ready to package your theme into a compressed format for easy distribution online. Most often these themes are distributed as either a ZIP or RAR package. You can use a tool such as WinRar to create either one of these packages from your blog theme folder. In the caffeine example, you would compress the entire Caffeine folder using one of these types of compression.

After you have prepared and packaged your new theme, it is time to distribute it. There are a few options for where you can distribute your theme. One is to share it with the community using the forums on the `http://communityserver.org` web site. Another option is to publish the file on your personal site and then inform the community about it and link to its download page. Regardless of the technique you decide to use, you should always make sure to inform the Community Server community about your new creation.

New Theming Enhancements

Before explaining some of the new controls that are available in Community Server 3.0, it is important to give credit and recognition to Ben Tiedt. Ben Tiedt is the person who is responsible for most if not all of Chameleon.

The controls that existed in previous versions of Community Server are now located in the `CommunityServer.Controls.Backport` namespace. One of the reasons for including these controls is to help developers ease into using the new controls. Fortunately, with the straightforwardness and consistency of the new controls, it should be fairly painless for a developer to begin using them.

Another important fact to consider when using the new controls is that they are no longer ID bound. This means that you are not restricted to using the IDs `rcr` or `lcr` to identify the right and left content regions. As a result, it should be more convenient for a developer to modify existing pages in Community Server.

In addition, the new controls now support implicit data binding. This means that a control will be smart enough to know, based on the context of its use, what data should be presented to the user. The example that Ben Tiedt provides is that if a `UserData` control is rendered in a `PostList` parent control, then the `UserData` control will display the data that pertains to the author of each post. This is a tremendous step forward as it eases the task of a developer having to fetch and explicitly include certain data for each control.

Summary

Community Server offers an extremely powerful framework for creating and distributing custom themes. These themes can be tailored for individual applications as well as for an entire site. Furthermore, each theme is able to contain custom CSS, images, skin files, and master pages. The themes inside of Community Server allow developers and individual site members to customize the appearance of the parts of a site that they have access to. To help you understand how to customize a site in this way, you learned about the following main areas:

- ❑ Themes
- ❑ CSS
- ❑ Controls
- ❑ Master pages
- ❑ Skin files
- ❑ Creating a blog theme
- ❑ Recent theme enhancements

In the next chapter, you will learn about the Control Panel. The chapter will teach you how to administer the different applications that make up the Community Server platform.

Part III

Administering Community Server

6

Control Panel

In this chapter, you will learn about the standard organization of the Control Panel. Furthermore, you will learn how to administer the various applications that compose the Community Server platform through the Control Panel. As a result, you will be more prepared to administer a Community Server site. Aside from general instruction on administering applications in Community Server, you will learn about some of the various settings that are available. The following topics are covered in this chapter:

- ❏ Administering blogs
- ❏ Administering photo galleries
- ❏ Administering file galleries
- ❏ Administering the Reader
- ❏ Changing global settings

Accessing the Control Panel

To access much of the administrative functionality of Community Server, you will use the Control Panel. Under the default settings, all administrators and moderators are able to access the Control Panel once they have logged in to their account. In addition, the Control Panel link is displayed to users of roles tagged on the `<link name="controlpanel" />` line in `SiteUrls.config`. It is very rare that you will need to change these roles; however, it is important to know how to do so in case a user has access to a feature on the Control Panel but is not in an administrative role. For example, even though blog owners are able to access the Control Panel, the link for it does not appear under the default settings

Before I explain how you can display the Control Panel link to these individuals, follow these steps to access the Control Panel:

1. Log in to your site using your System Administrator account by clicking the Sign in link in the welcome area section of the home page.

2. Click the Control Panel link that now appears in your navigation bar.

If you have a user who should have access to some of the Control Panel features but can't see the Control Panel, you have two options. First, you can assign the user to a role such as system administrator that will see the link. However, you may not want to assign that person to an administrative account when he or she is simply a blog owner and should not have any extra access rights. Thus, there is option two: create a new role and add it to the list of roles in the `SiteUrls.config` file for which the Control Panel link will be displayed.

Here are the steps for implementing option two:

1. Log in to the Control Panel.

2. Click the Administration link in the Control Panel.

3. Click and expand the Membership options on the left menu bar.

4. Click Manage all Roles.

5. Click the Add New Role button at the top of the grid.

6. Type in the name `AccessControlPanel` and click Save.

7. Open your `SiteUrls.config` file and add `AccessControlPanel` to the Control Panel link roles list.

Now, you have your site configured to display a link any time an account is in the `AccessControlPanel` role. You can now click the membership information for individual accounts and add this new role to their account. The next time that they log in to your site they should see a link to the Control Panel.

Understanding the Layout

In this section, the logical organization of the Control Panel will be explored. You will quickly realize that it is relatively easy to locate a particular administrative page. Aside from exploring the layout, you will learn about the standard features that are a part of the navigation of the Control Panel. This section also demonstrates how easy it is to tie these features together in the dashboard.

Exploring Standard Options

When you first arrive at the Control Panel, you are greeted with a convenient page called the dashboard. The dashboard provides you with links to Control Panel pages that you will use frequently. Notice in Figure 6-1 that these links are grouped according to the section of your site to which they most closely relate. Therefore, you will find a section for managing your blogs with links to common task items such as creating a new post, reviewing blog comments, managing a selected blog, and selecting a particular blog to manage.

For many of the administrative tasks that you will be performing you will more than likely be able to find the link to the appropriate management page on the dashboard. For security purposes, only the links for activities that the particular user has the permission to perform are displayed. Therefore, if a blog administrator logs into the Control Panel, he or she will not see a link for changing how all photo galleries are themed.

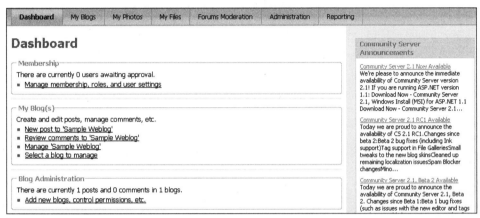

Figure 6-1: Default Dashboard in Control Panel

If you find that you are regularly performing a certain function, such as creating new blog tags, then you can easily add the link to the main dashboard page. This is a simple task for developers to perform because all they need to do is edit the root `default.aspx` page located in the `ControlPanel` directory. When you open this file, you will notice that its code is structured in a similar way to the resulting page's source. Assume that you want to add your new link to the tags management page between the link for Review Comments and Manage Blog. In this case, you would add a link between the following entries in the `/ControlPanel/default.aspx` file:

```
<li runat="server" id="MyBlogsReviewCommentsArea"><asp:HyperLink
    id="MyBlogsReviewComments" runat="server" NavigateUrl=
    "~/ControlPanel/Blogs/comments.aspx?SelectedNavItem=ReviewComments" />
</li>

<li runat="server" id="MyBlogsManageArea"><asp:HyperLink id="MyBlogsManage"
    runat="server" NavigateUrl="~/ControlPanel/Blogs/" />
</li>
```

Looking at the previous two links, you may notice that the text for the link is defined elsewhere (a file called `ControlPanelResources.xml`, to be exact). Therefore, when you add your link, you can either define it in the `HyperLink` explicitly or inside the `ControlPanelResources.xml` file. For the purposes of this example, the text will be defined explicitly. However, keep in mind that if you plan to localize your site you may want to move this text to a resource file. The important part of the entry is the link location, which is defined by `NavigateUrl`. Furthermore, you should also notice that there is an expression `runat="server"` included in the `HyperLink` so that the link can evaluate `"~"` to the site's root folder. The following entry can now be added between the lines shown previously to provide the new shortcut:

```
<li runat="server" id="MyBlogsTagsArea"><asp:HyperLink id="MyBlogsTags"
    runat="server" NavigateUrl="~/ControlPanel/Blogs/postcategories.aspx">Blog
    Tags</asp:HyperLink>
</li>
```

Aside from managing your blogs, the dashboard also provides a system administrator with links to tasks related to managing membership, Photo Galleries, files, forums, the Reader, and general site settings. Therefore, before exploring the other links in the Control Panel, you should first become acquainted with the dashboard because it can allow you to quickly perform common administrative tasks.

Another nicety of the dashboard screen is that it enables you to stay current with what is going on with Community Server. You will notice on the right side of the dashboard a box for displaying Community Server announcements. If you do not want to display these announcements, you can refer to Chapter 10 to learn about disabling this feature in the configuration files. However, if you are interested in staying current with Community Server happenings such as new product releases, then you should make a habit of reading these announcements when you log in to the dashboard.

Understanding Organizational Structure

The Community Server Control Panel is organized so that there is a logical division between system administrative tasks and other application-specific tasks. On the main Control Panel navigation bar, there are links for the management of a specific blog, forum, photo gallery, and file gallery. There is also a link to administration and reporting, which is for linking to the tasks that a system administrator would perform.

Because of the separation of administrative tasks, it should be simple to find the action you need to perform. If you want to write a new blog post, for example, you can either click the New Post link from the dashboard or go to the blogs management section under My Blogs and select Write a Blog Post.

Note that when you need to change a sitewide setting or a setting that affects multiple blogs or galleries, you should start in the Administration link. For example, if you want to set how all blogs should look by default, select the Administration section of the Control Panel and then expand the Blogs menu option. Here, you will find and can set the Default Presentation.

In addition to providing access to change sitewide settings for a specific application, such as forums, you are also presented with the means to control membership, adjust general sitewide settings, view basic reports, and use system tools. All of these capabilities are geared toward enabling system administrators to perform their job more easily. Aside from the reports found in the Administration link, you will also notice several more in the reporting tab. To learn more about these reports, refer to Chapter 9.

When you are trying to locate a setting in the Control Panel, you should first ask yourself if the setting is sitewide. If the setting is sitewide, then you should navigate to the Administration link. Otherwise, you should try to locate the setting under the main link that it relates the most to (My Photos, My Blogs). If you have navigated to the main administration page, you should now ask yourself if the setting relates to a specific feature, such as a blog or forum. If it does, then you should expand the menu for that particular link (Blogs, Photos, Files, Forums, Reader). Otherwise, navigate to one of the remaining menus that relates most to the topic of your setting (Membership, Settings, Reports, System Tools). The organizational structure of the Control Panel makes it is convenient to locate a particular setting just by simply asking these questions.

Administering Blogs

The administration of blogs can be as complex or as simple as you want to make it. Blogs can be administered at many levels by many user roles, or you might only have one blog on a site administered by a single individual. Part of the beauty of Community Server blogs is how flexible they are. If an organization wants to have many bloggers without any limitations on how their blog looks or behaves, you can configure Community Server to do this. On the other hand, if an organization wants to place limitations on what blogs look like or who can place comments on them, Community Server can be configured to meet these demands as well. In addition to exploring how to accomplish both of the previous examples, this section will address everything from the basics, such as posting to a blog, to more advanced topics such as changing how a blog looks.

In Chapter 3, the details for creating a blog and blog post were discussed. Therefore, the following will be used to simply provide a review and an expansion of the blogging section of Chapter 3.

Creating a New Blog

To create a new blog, you need to first be signed in as a blog administrator or system administrator. After you have logged in, navigate to the Control Panel and complete the following basic steps:

1. Click Administration.

2. Expand the Blogs menu and select Create New Blog; the page that loads looks like Figure 6-2.

3. Under the Settings tab, provide a name for your blog, which does not have to be unique. However, if you do provide the same name as another blog, you will need to specify a unique URL; otherwise, you will not need to even provide the URL.

4. Click Save and your new blog will be created.

As you have witnessed, it is quite easy to create a new blog in Community Server. There are really only a couple of fields that need to be filled in order to get a blog running. Beyond the basic fields several more do exist for customizing a new blog. Fortunately, there is a question mark icon next to each of the fields that provides additional information to help you understand what each field represents. Therefore, the following information about the fields on the create blog screen will be more advanced. If you are interested in learning only the basic information about each field, consult the administration screen for creating a blog and hover over the question mark next to a field to learn more about it.

The Enable Blog radio button option controls whether or not you want a blog to be enabled and visible to others. It is important to notice that if you disable a blog it can still be managed under the My Blogs main Control Panel tab.

New Blog

Set the properties for this blog

Settings | Permissions

- Name
- URL /cs21/blogs/
- Owner (optional)
- Blog Group Sample Weblogs ▾
- Enable Blog ⦿ Yes ○ No
- Enable AggBugs ⦿ Yes ○ No
- Index Posts ⦿ Yes ○ No
- Include in community aggregate ⦿ Yes ○ No
- Default Language English ▾

Figure 6-2: New Blog Screen

Creating a New Post

There are a couple of different ways that you can create a new post for your blog in Community Server. One way is to use the Control Panel and the built-in text editor. The second option is to use a third-party tool that is designed specifically for posting to blogs. If you do decide to use an external tool to create your blog, make sure that it supports the MetaBlog API. The following list contains a few popular tools that are available that work with Community Server, along with the web site where you can purchase or freely download the tool:

❑ **Qumana:** www.qumana.com

❑ **Blogjet:** www.blogjet.com

❑ **Microsoft Word 2007:** www.microsoft.com/office

❑ **Windows Live Writer:** windowslivewriter.spaces.live.com

The previous list is obviously not comprehensive, but it is a good starting point for trying out various tools, both free and commercial, that will work well with Community Server.

Now that you have a basic idea of what tools are available for writing posts for a Community Server blog, let's now proceed to exploring how to create a post using the default post creation method. To create a blog post, you will need to be either an administrator or the owner of a blog.

1. Log in to your site and navigate to the Control Panel.

2. Click the My Blogs link in the navigation bar.

3. Select the blog that you want to post to; refer to Figure 6-3 for an example of what the Select Blog to Manage link looks like.

4. Click the Write a Blog Post link under the Common Tasks menu on the left.

5. Fill out the Title and Body fields of the post, and click one of the following options:

Save and Continue Writing

Save, but don't Publish

Publish

The three options are a new feature for Community Server and now allow you to save your work as it progresses. Therefore, if for any reason your browser window closes or your computer crashes before you are done with the post, you can easily return to where you left off. One of the differences between Save and Continue Writing and the Save, but don't Publish buttons is that the second will switch a published post to being not published. Therefore, if you have a post that is currently published and you want to make it unpublished, you can click the Save, but don't Publish button.

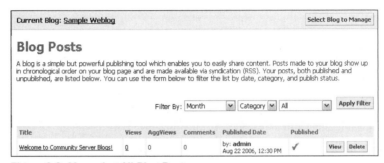

Figure 6-3: Managing All Blog Posts

Modifying an Existing Entry

The Community Server Control Panel does a good job of separating the management of existing entries from the creation of new ones. To modify existing content, you simply need to navigate to the menu section entitled Manage Content. This section of the blog Control Panel allows you to manage posts, comments, pages, tags, lists, snippets, and the information about a particular blog. In the following example, however, you will be concentrating on changing the content of a particular blog post.

1. Inside the Control Panel, click the My Blogs navigational link.

2. Click Manage Content to expand the menu options.

3. Click the All Posts menu option.

4. Click the title of the post you want to modify (see Figure 6-3).

5. Change any of the content of the selected post, and click one of the save options at the bottom. Note that if you do not want to modify whether the post is published or not, you can safely click the Save and Continue Writing button. The other buttons allow you to specify if you want this post to be published or not.

Understanding Blog Groups

The ability to assign a set of blogs to a particular group is a powerful feature. Often, you will want to group blogs that share a common characteristic so that you can keep them in manageable blocks. For example, if you have a large number of blogs that often talk about technology then you could easily place the blogs into a blog group called Technology. The simple act of grouping blogs into an organized structure can make the management of blogs less confusing.

One of the benefits of grouping blogs is that you are able to present the blogs to site visitors in an organized way. Instead of simply presenting a long listing of different blog posts, you can present the blogs in related groups. A good example of a site utilizing blog groups to present an organized listing of blogs to the user is www.3cords.org. This is a site that I helped develop that groups blogs into one of three groups. As a result of this organized structure, the main page of the site presents each of these groups in a unique way.

Currently, Community Server does now allow a blog to belong to multiple groups. Therefore, you are required to choose a single blog group to assign each blog to. However, you are able to change what blog group a blog is assigned to after you initially create the blog. To do this, you simply need to click the Administration link of the Control Panel and complete the following steps:

1. Expand the Blogs menu and select the Blogs menu option.
2. Select the blog that you want to change the blog group for.
3. Change the Blog Group drop-down option to the blog group that you want to assign the blog to.
4. Click Save.

Modifying Default Settings

The default blog settings are located in the Default Settings menu option on the blogs menu, which is located in the Administration tab of the Control Panel. These settings control specific properties for all blogs. It is important to realize that a couple of these settings can be overridden at the blog level. For example, a blogger on your site can override what services are pinged whenever they create a new blog post. Here is a listing of the available settings on this page and a brief description of each:

❑ **Create Directories** will create a directory for each of the blogs on your site. If you have `default .aspx` enabled as a default document, then your site visitors can navigate to a blog simply by using the blog's name, without having to provide the `default.aspx` page. In addition, you should make sure that the account your application is running as has write access to the blog's directory. Otherwise, you will encounter a warning message when you create a new blog.

❑ **Auto Create**, when enabled, will create a blog for new users. This is disabled by default, and you may want to keep it this way unless you are certain you want all new users to get a blog. Also, before you enable this setting, realize who has access to register on your site. If anyone is able to register and create an account, then you should realize that there is a potential for a rapid increase in the number of blogs on your site.

❏ **Enable Cross-Posting**, when enabled, allows for a post to be published to different blogs. This option is disabled by default and can be controlled at both the individual blog level and further at the post level. The blog level can be found in the Default Post Settings menu option of the blog itself. Meanwhile, the post level option is found in the Advanced Options under the Advanced Options tab. You can set up blogs to cross-post to under the Spam, Ping and Cross-Posting Settings menu option of the individual blog under the Global Settings menu section.

❏ **Enable Blog Owners to add content to HTML Head** is disabled by default, meaning that bloggers are unable to add content to the <head> section of their blog. If you enable this setting, then you can make it easy for bloggers to add tracking information to their blog, as well as any custom JavaScript or HTML tags that they deem useful. When this option is enabled, a new textbox is provided in the Control Panel for each blog under the Title, Description, and News menu option called Raw Header.

❏ **Default Group** specifies what blog group you want to assign to new blogs if no other group is specified. This option can be changed when creating the actual blog; it merely selects the default group when creating a new blog. This is especially useful in conjunction with the Autocreate option because this is the group that will be used when blogs are created automatically.

❏ **Default Ping Services** is a list of the ping services that you want to ping whenever a new post is created. Essentially, it is a list of services that are notified when new content is added to your blogs. This option can be overridden at the blog level; however, it can be useful to ping more than the default services if you want to help increase awareness about your site.

❏ **Default Aggregate Tags** lists the tags that you want to use to filter content by for a site's aggregate blog control. Therefore, if you only wanted to include those posts that relate to politics in Canada on your main page, then you would add Politics; Canada to the list of aggregate tags. By default, the list is blank, meaning that all posts that are marked for aggregation will be included on your site's aggregation controls.

❏ **Service Post Count Limit** is the maximum number of posts returned to requests made from the various Community Server services. If you want to change the number of posts returned to third-party tools using the MetaBlog API, for example, you can change this number from the default of 25.

Managing Comments

There is an inherent responsibility for bloggers to allow site visitors to post comments to their blog. Often, these comments are directed at the author or authors of the blog and almost always demand some level of response. As a result, bloggers must not only create new posts for their blog, but they should also manage and respond to comments made on their blog.

It is important to realize that comments should be managed. By this, I mean that inappropriate comments should be deleted and inquisitive ones should be responded to. Fortunately, Community Server does an excellent job in assisting bloggers with managing their comments. One of the ways that it does this is through the use of spam filters that prevent spam from being displayed. Furthermore, additional custom spam filters can be developed to aid in the removal of spam from your site.

From the Review Comments screen (see Figure 6-4), you are able to easily manage all of the comments on a particular blog. The Review Comments screen allows you to edit, unpublish or publish, and delete comments. To edit a comment, simply click the comment link found under the title column, change the comments text, and then save it. In addition, you are able to perform bulk commands, such as deleting or unpublishing several comments. The important thing is that you check this screen on a regular basis to manage your blog's comments.

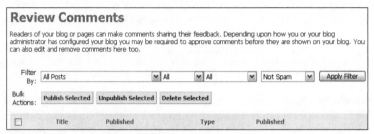

Figure 6-4: Review Comments Screen

Tweaking the Presentation

There are a few different levels from which you can tweak the presentation of a blog. First, you can set a default presentation as a system administrator at the site level. This can be done either by editing the `CommunityServer.config` file or by changing the default presentation settings under the administration blog's menu. If you want to force all blogs to have the default theme, then you simply need to uncheck the Enable Themes box in the Default Presentation administration screen for blogs and have the default theme selected. Similarly, you can configure your site to start all new blogs with a particular theme by selecting a default theme from the default presentation. However, users are able to change their particular default theme at the blog level whenever themes are enabled.

In addition to selecting different themes, users are also able to override the stylesheet of a theme at the blog level. This allows for blogs to share the same theme but still look very different. You can modify these styles by selecting the CSS Overrides tab on the Change how my Blog Looks menu option of a particular blog when themes are enabled. For example, let's assume that you have the default theme selected and want to change the background of the page to black. In addition, you want to remove the site header at the top of your blog as well as make all of the links blue until hovered over, when their background color will change. To do all of this, you only need to add the following to your CSS Overrides tab and click Save:

```
body {
   background-color: #000;
}

a:link, a:visited, a:active {
   color: #0000FF;
   text-decoration: none;
}

a:hover {
   background-color: #EEE;
```

```
    }

    .CommonTitleBar {
        display: none;
    }
```

As you can see, it really does not require that many lines of code to drastically alter the way your blog looks. If you would like to change your blog's presentation further using the CSS overrides, then you should first become familiar with Cascading Style Sheets (CSS). There are many books available and many free tutorials online that can help you become more familiar with using stylesheets. A couple of sites that I have found to be useful in learning more about CSS are www.cssbeauty.com and www.csszengarden.com.

If you want to learn about what class styles are available on your blog, the best method may be to view the actual source code of your blog. You can do this easily in your web browser by navigating to your blog site and selecting the View Source option that is usually located on the browser's View menu. Then, when you are sifting through the source, simply look for an ID or class on the tag that you want to manipulate. In addition, you can also override the stylesheet for an HTML element itself. A good example of this is the anchor and body elements that were changed in the previous example.

Under the covers, all that happens when you add custom CSS overrides is that an extra stylesheet is included after the default stylesheets. This is true for the CSS overrides for both blogs and galleries. You can even control the name of the custom CSS file by editing the SiteUrls.config file's blog_customcss entry. The actual style that each user enters for their blog is added to the cs_Sections table as an extended attribute value for the respective blog.

Global Settings

There are additional settings that are available to configure all of the blogs on a site. These additional settings are found in the blog's menu section of the administration page in the Control Panel. To access these settings, you will need to be logged in with an administrator account.

One of the more interesting and unique settings is the Post Relevance Sorting. This feature can be used to control how your aggregate posts are sorted on the aggregate blog page (the page that a user sees when he or she clicks the blog's link in the top navigation bar). By default, posts are sorted by date only. After you enable Post Relevance Sorting, you have a great deal of control over how posts are displayed on the aggregate page.

There are standard values that are populated in the Post Relevance Sorting function to get you started. If you wanted to display the posts with the highest rating above all other posts, then you would simply set the Rating Factor as the highest to sort by. You can always tweak these settings until you arrive at the appropriate sorting method for your site. Note that the first option after enabling the sorting system is Number of Posts, which represents the size of the set of posts that will be scored to determine sort order. By default, the top 250 posts are scored and sorted, and older posts are ignored.

Another setting that you can configure for all blogs is the Global Permissions setting. To edit this setting, simply navigate to the Global Permissions menu option of the Blogs menu on the administration screen. On the leftmost column of the permissions display are the names of all of the roles on your site. Once you locate the role that you want to change the permissions for, you simply need to place a check in the box in each of the columns for granting this role access to the respective blog ability. To help you locate the appropriate role, you can also click the columns on this page to sort the entries differently.

Additional Options

Community Server provides the functionality to easily manage list content. Lists may be used to link to your favorite blogs, resources, news sites, and so on. Lists are managed through the My Blogs link of the Control Panel, under the All Lists menu option on the Manage Content menu. You may create a single list or group list elements into many sections. For example, you could create a list called Search Engines, which would contain links to all of your favorite search engines. In addition, as mentioned previously, you could have a second list of your favorite bloggers.

Along with the link title, each list element can have an associated short description, which will be displayed below the link. Furthermore, you can even specify how the link is related to you. If, for example, the link was to a friend's blog, then you could state that the list item is a friend.

Another nice option in the blog Control Panel is the ability to create snippets for use on your blog. A snippet is a keyword that the system will convert when you save your post. These are typically used to make linking to common resources easier. For example, through the use of a snippet, you can add the link to www.google.com as a snippet and then reference it by putting brackets around your text. In your post, you simply need to say [google], and a link will be created for you in place of [google].

If you find that you are creating links to the same pages often, then you may want to create an abbreviated way to reference them. For example, if you are referencing the Community Server Daily News often, you could abbreviate your snippet to CSDN and reference it as [CSDN]. Then, you only need to type Community Server Daily News in the text field of the snippet, which will replace [CSDN] with the link and text. You should also note that the name of the snippet is not case sensitive, so you can reference the Community Server Daily News as [csdn], [CsdN], [CSDn], and so on.

Aside from replacing your text with links, you can also use snippets to replace part of your blog posts with other text. The link URL is not a required field when you create a snippet, which allows you to specify the text that will replace the snippet in your post. As a result, you are able to create your own language set for quickly creating posts. Perhaps the most useful type of text to replace will be acronyms. However, you can use snippets to create your own shorthand language for quickly inserting common phrases or words. In short, you can use snippets to replace anything you don't want to type out in full any more.

Administering Photo Galleries

Photo galleries can be administered quite similarly to the management of blogs. They support a lot of the same types of options, such as changing the presentation or grouping of a gallery. They additionally support comments in much of the same way that comments are supported in blogs. Therefore, the following may sound familiar after reading about administering blogs. One of the benefits of this consistency is that the administration of blogs and galleries is easier to remember because they are both so similar.

Creating a New Gallery

The ability to create new photo galleries in Community Server is quite simple. After you have created a new photo gallery, you can immediately begin adding new photos to it and share those photos easily with others. Here are the basic steps required to create a new photo gallery. Remember that you should first be signed in as an administrator to your site:

1. Click the Administration link on the Control Panel navigation bar.

2. Click the Photos menu to expand it.

3. Click the Create New Gallery menu option (see Figure 6-5).

4. Enter a name for your new gallery.

5. Change any default settings that you see fit to, and click Save.

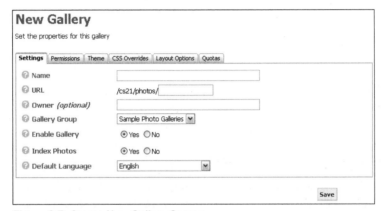

Figure 6-5: Create New Gallery Screen

Publishing New Photos

By default, only gallery owners, gallery administrators, and site administrators can publish new photos. When you log in as one of these accounts, you will be able to see a link to the Publish New Photo under the My Photos Administration link.

To publish new photos, complete the following instructions:

1. Click the My Photos link on the Control Panel navigation bar.

2. If a gallery has not already been selected or if the gallery you want to publish the photo to is not selected, click the Select Photo Gallery to Manage button and select the appropriate gallery.

3. The Common Tasks menu section should be expanded; if it is not, then click it to expand it.

4. Click the Publish New Photo menu option.

5. Click the Upload Photo button to select the photo that you want to publish.

6. The name of the photo will appear in the subject line; if you want to provide anything more descriptive, provide it now.

7. Click Save to publish your photo. You can optionally change any of the default settings first so that you do not have to worry about modifying them later.

When you click the Save button your photo will be published to your photo gallery at the time specified in the Options tab. If you would like to have your photo published at a particular time, you can change the time of your post under the Options tab. Also, if you do not want your photo to be published at all, save it in your gallery and, under the advanced Options tab, set it to Not Published.

In addition, if your photo has metainformation for the other fields, such as a description, then it will be populated once you click Save. However, if you want to provide a more detailed description of your photo, it is helpful to add the additional details when you are publishing it.

Reviewing Comments

A detailed explanation of why you should manage comments was provided in the "Managing Comments" section earlier in this chapter. Therefore, I will not go into much detail here about why it is important to keep track of your photo comments. Instead, I will provide you will the information you will need in order to locate these comments and review them. The options for managing photo gallery comments are very similar to those of blogs. You are able to approve, unapprove, and delete comments, allowing you to control whether a comment is visible or not in a gallery. Remember, though, that comments must be enabled on your gallery before any will exist. If you would like to enable comments on your gallery first, make sure that they are enabled globally on the site; then complete the following steps to enable them at the gallery level.

1. Click My Photos on the Control Panel navigation bar.
2. Click Settings to expand the menu options.
3. Click the Default Post Settings menu option.
4. Select the Yes radio button next to the Enable Comments text and click Save.

To access the comments of a particular photo gallery, log in to your site as an administrator or gallery owner and navigate to the Control Panel. Once you are in the Control Panel, you simply need to complete the following instructions to access your photo gallery comments:

1. Click My Photos on the Control Panel navigation bar.
2. Click Manage Content to expand the menu options.
3. Click the All Comments menu option.

Managing Content

The Managing Content screen is a useful way to quickly add new photos and manage existing ones. In addition, it provides a nice thumbnail preview for each of the photos to allow you to quickly locate a desired photo. It is important that you manage your photos so that you do not have a large number of photos that are no longer useful floating around your site. To access the Manage Content section of your photo gallery, simply navigate to your My Photos navigation link in the Control Panel and click the Manage Content menu section to expand the various options.

One of the most useful features of the Manage Content screen is the Quick Add option for adding photos. This can prove to be extremely useful when a photo gallery owner needs to upload a large number of photos at once. If you are interested in uploading large quantities of photos easily, there are a couple of solutions. You can use an open source tool called Chiwis that is available at `https://sourceforge.net/projects/csgallerytool`. The other option is to use the bulk import feature that is found in photo galleries' Advanced Photo Settings Administration screen. To bulk import a selection of photos, simply upload the photo files, using an FTP tool, to your galleries folder and then use the advanced photo settings Import tab to import them. Thus, if your gallery were named Vacation, you would upload your photo files to Photos/vacation.

All that is required to add a new photo to the selected gallery is to click the Browse button and select the image. The image will automatically be uploaded and added to the list of photos on the screen. If you want to provide more of a description of each photo, you can click the thumbnail and then type a description and tags on the resulting screen. In addition, you can also use the advanced options of a photo to make it unpublished.

Managing Quotas

Community Server provides an easy-to-use, yet very powerful quota management system for photo galleries. As an administrator, you are able to define a set quota for all users for both the amount of storage they can utilize and the number of photos that they can upload. In addition, you can optionally override these default settings on a per-role basis. To access the Quota Management screen, please follow these instructions:

1. Log in to your site as an administrator.
2. Click the Control Panel and then the Administration link.
3. Click the Photos menu option to expand it.
4. Select the Global Storage Quotas menu option.
5. Either edit the settings per role by clicking Edit or select the Global Quotas tab to change the settings for the entire site.

These quotas are extremely useful when you have a limited amount of storage on your site, or you may want to provide varying levels of accounts on your site. For example, if you were charging people a hosting fee to have a photo gallery, you might want to offer them a different amount of storage than what you would offer people for free. Therefore, you could offer people who have a professional account, and thus in the professional role, 50MB of storage, while free accounts may only receive 5MB. How you decide to use this powerful feature is up to you; just remember that it exists at the global level and at the role level for both the maximum amount of space a gallery can utilize and the maximum number of photos that a gallery can contain.

Tweaking Gallery Presentation

Changing the way that a gallery is presented to a site visitor is similar to changing the presentation of a blog. You are able to select a gallery theme as well as override the gallery's CSS. If you would like an example of changing a site's CSS, refer to the presentation section on blogs earlier in this chapter. It can be important for your general understanding, though, to realize that the resulting stylesheet when you override a gallery theme is called `customcss.ashx`. Therefore, when you look at the source code of a gallery page that you have overridden the CSS on, you will notice that this file is the last stylesheet listed.

To change the theme of your gallery, you need to log in and access the My Photos section of the site, where you can expand the Settings and select Change how my gallery looks (see Figure 6-6). On the next screen, you can choose the theme you want to use from the Theme tab. In addition, you can specify custom CSS overrides for your gallery. The last tab is Layout Options, which you can use to specify how to arrange your photos when they are presented in tabular fashion. Furthermore, this tab also allows you to change how your photos are sorted when they are presented. The default layout is to have a table of four rows and four columns with the photos sorted by the date that they were created.

Figure 6-6: Change how my gallery looks

Administering File Galleries

The Community Server offers many tools for administering file galleries. In this section, you learn how to create new folders as well as how to upload files to the file gallery. Another important area that you learn is how to manage and edit files that are currently uploaded to your site.

Creating a New Folder

You can think of a file folder in Community Server as being similar to a gallery or blog. The folder holds a specific grouping of files that can be managed separately from other folders. In addition, a folder can be organized into folder groups just as similar galleries or blogs can be organized into groups. To create a new folder, you must be an administrator and have access to the administration section of the Control Panel. Complete the following steps to create a new folder on your site:

1. Click the Administration navigation link in the Control Panel.

2. Click Files to expand the menu options.

3. Select the New Folder menu option.

4. Provide a descriptive name for your new folder, and select the appropriate folder group to place it in.

5. If you would like to restrict or allow certain file extensions for your new folder, click the Options tab and type those extensions, separated by commas.

6. Click the Save button to create your new folder.

Adding Files

Once you have a folder created, you can start adding files to it that do not have restricted extensions. To begin adding files to your folders, you must be an administrator or folder owner, or have been granted access to add files to the folders. When you are ready to proceed with one of these accounts and after you have selected a file that you would like to add to one of your folders, complete the following steps:

1. Click the My Files navigation link on the Control Panel navigation bar.

2. Select Upload File on the Common Tasks menu.

3. Under the File tab, click the Pick File button, choose the file that you want to upload or link to, and click Save (see Figure 6-7).

4. Provide a title and description for your new files; at this point you are able to click Save.

5. Provide any tags that you would like to use to help organize this file.

6. If you do not want your file to be published, select the options tab and select the No option, which determines that this file is not to be published.

7. Click Save to upload the file and add it to the selected folder.

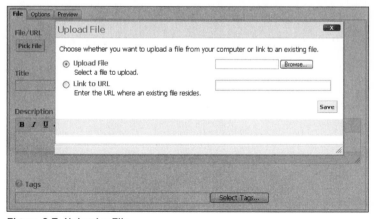

Figure 6-7: Upload a File

Editing Files

Occasionally, a file in the gallery will need to be updated; perhaps it is a package and new items have recently been added. Another common example is when a .pdf or Word document is published to your file gallery and the content needs to be updated. Whatever the reason may be, it is important to understand that the file gallery allows a file to be updated.

If you have a file that is currently in the file gallery and it needs to be updated, you can simply complete the following steps to accomplish this task:

1. Log in to the Control Panel and navigate to My Files.

2. Click the Manage Content menu option to expand the menu.

3. Click Files to see a list of the current files on the server in the selected folder.

4. Select the appropriate folder where your file resides by clicking Select Folder to Manage.

5. Click the title of the file that you want to update.

6. The file's title and description are presented, along with a link for updating the file. Click the Update File/URL link and upload the updated version of the file.

7. Change the title or description if appropriate, and click the Save button to complete the update.

Additional Settings

The file gallery contains several additional settings for administering the gallery. These settings will allow you to manage tags, comments, and other more-advanced settings. Because the comment moderating and tagging concepts have already been explored, they will not be explained here. Instead, the advanced options, which mainly relate to Figure 6-8, will be explored.

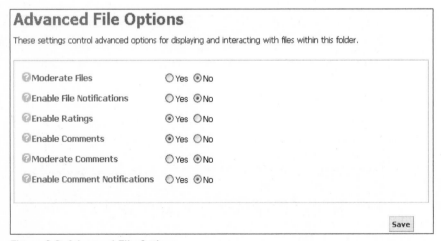

Figure 6-8: Advanced File Options

The first option on the Advanced Options screen, which is located under the Settings menu of the My Files page, allows an administrator to require that new files by nonadministrator and gallery owners be moderated. In other words, if a general site user who is not a member of an appropriate administrator role uploads a file, that file will not be published until an administrator or owner of the file gallery approves it.

The other options are explained quite well by the Community Server help buttons next to each option. Therefore, the only other options that need to be discussed here are the Advanced Syndication Settings available in the menu directly below Advanced File Settings. The two options on this page allow an administrator or gallery owner to toggle whether or not site visitors will be able to subscribe to the gallery. Keeping these options enabled can be important to allow visitors to easily stay up to date when you add new files. An example of when this becomes extremely useful is when you are publishing software in the gallery that is supported with patches. Allowing your software users to stay up to date with new patches in this way will help enable them to always have current versions of your software installed.

Administering Forums

Moderating and administering forums is quite easy with Community Server. There are several options that allow an administrator or forum moderator to easily manage the content on a forum as well as manage more advanced settings. It is important to note that to accomplish many of the following tasks you should be logged in as a system administrator, forum administrator, or moderator. While these are not the only roles that are available for changing some of these settings, they will work for what is going to be discussed below. Also, it is important to note that these three roles all share the same permissions regarding forums. You should know that there is also an editor role that can be used to edit the content of forums.

Creating a New Forum

Aside from forum groups, there are also forums that can be parents of other forums. This is a vital feature because it allows discussions to branch out into subtopic areas. For example, a forum relating to software could have subforums for support and bug reporting. A forum is not required to have a parent, but it is still a good idea to identify if it is appropriate for the forum that is being created before proceeding with creating it.

1. Click the Administration tab.
2. Click the Forums menu and expand the options.
3. Click the Create New Forum menu option. If you do not see this option, then you should select Manage All Forums and click the Change to Grid View button in the lower-right corner of the resulting page. After you have enabled the Grid View, you should see an option for Create New Forum.
4. Type in the name of the forum and select any of the other options that are appropriate, such as selecting the forum group.
5. Click the Save button, and a forum is created.

Creating Posts

The interesting thing about the creation of forum posts is that they occur outside of the Control Panel. It is still important to know how they are created and how an administrator or moderator can manage who has access to create them. The management of posts in a forum can be thought of as being similar to the management of comments for a particular blog, in that both allow for posting to be disabled for anonymous users at a global and application level. By default, anonymous users are not allowed to make posts to any of the forums until an administrator enables this at the global level under the Global Forum Settings menu option.

In addition, new posts can be set for moderation, meaning that they require approval before being published. Under the covers, whenever a forum has Moderate Posts enabled and the user is not moderated, new posts are simply marked as not approved in the database. However, these new posts are only marked as not approved when they are not coming from an administrator or moderator. In most situations, these would be posts from registered users or anonymous users. Whenever a moderator or administrator reviews the post and decides to approve it, the post is marked as approved in the database.

Whenever going through the following steps for creating a new post, it's important to notice that all new posts come from the `AddPost.aspx` page of the `/forums` directory. This page handles the creation of new posts, responses to existing posts, reporting post abuse, and creation of other types of new posts. It determines what type of post is being created from the querystring; therefore, if you try to navigate directly to the page with nothing on the querystring, you will encounter an error.

1. Click the Forums tab on the main navigation menu of your site.
2. Click a forum title to select it.
3. Click the Write a New Post button.
4. Type your new post for this particular forum and click Post.

Managing Ranks

The ability to rank users based on the number of posts that they contribute to forums is something that can greatly encourage more participation among users. With the Community Server ranking system, users can now automatically be recognized for their hard work and participation in all of the forums.

To understand ranking a little better, consider the following example. You are administering a role-playing community, and you want to encourage forum participation among your role players. You decide that you will use the ranking system and provide your members with fun titles depending on how many posts they contribute. You set up the ranking so that users who have posted fewer than 100 posts are titled Peon, while users with 100–500 posts are lvl 5 Barbarians, participants with 500–1000 posts are lvl 10 Warriors, and those with greater than 1000 posts are called lvl 20 Dungeon Masters. In this way, users are now recognized and feel a level of competition that leads them to participate more in the community.

To manage ranks, you should log in as an administrator with access to the forum Control Panel. Log in and click the Administration link on the Control Panel, and complete the following instructions to establish a new rank:

1. Click the Forums menu to expand the menu options.

2. Click Manage Ranks.

3. Click Add a New Rank.

4. A new modal box will appear where you can enter the name of the new rank, the minimum number of posts to be considered part of this rank, the maximum number of posts, and an optional rank icon that will be displayed with the rank.

5. Click the Save button, and the new rank is added to the list of ranks.

Global Settings

Changing the global settings for forums allows an administrator to help manage what posts are considered popular, prevent duplicate posts and flooding, change the settings for file attachments to posts, change how posts can be edited after being published, and handle other general settings. To see what this page looks like in your site, you can refer to Figure 6-9. There is a lot of power located in this administrative page; therefore, it is important that you understand it fully.

Figure 6-9: Global Forum Settings

The Popular Posts tab allows an administrator to configure the requirements for a post to be considered popular. Whenever a post becomes popular, the icon next to it will gain a star so that it stands out more than other posts. The amount of site traffic and post feedback should determine the requirements for a post to become popular. For example, if most posts only have a couple of replies, then perhaps it would be appropriate to lower the Popular Post Replies number to five or something more suitable for your site. If your posts generally only have around 20 views, then the Popular Post Views number should also be lowered. On the other hand, you do not want to create a situation in which all posts are marked as popular; therefore, you may need to increase these numbers if your site draws large amounts of traffic or post replies. Again, this is a way to distinguish those posts that draw the most attention from others. In some ways, it can help encourage contributors to make their posts meaningful so that they will eventually become popular.

The Duplicates & Flooding tab allows an administrator to control how often a user is allowed to post and if they are allowed to duplicate their posts. By default, both of these options are disabled, meaning that users can post as often as they want and duplicate their posts. In many situations, this is fine to leave as is. However, if you start to notice that users are flooding your forums, then you should consider enabling this option and setting the time to a value that you feel is appropriate.

The Attachments tab is important because it controls whether or not forums posts are allowed to have file attachments, and almost more importantly what types of files are allowed to be attached. In addition, there is a maximum file size that you can specify to control the size of files that can be attached. The type of forums that are being run should determine these various settings. The default configuration is to enable file attachments that are less than 64KB and to disable images from being displayed inline. However, it may be appropriate to enable image attachments to be displayed inline so that they can be embedded in posts. Another important setting is controlling the types of file extensions that are allowed to be attached. If your community shares a lot of `.pdf` or `.doc` files, then they need to be added to the valid extensions. To accomplish this, simply append the following to the list of extensions: `;pdf;doc`.

The Editing tab allows you to control whether or not posts can be edited after they are published and what is associated with this editing process. By default, a person can edit a forum post that they made at any time and do not have to explain why they are editing it. However, you can use the Age Limit value to specify the maximum length of time after a post has been published that it can be edited. In addition, edit notes can be required so that whenever users are changing the content of a post they have to explain why it was changed. This can be thought of as being similar to a check-in message that is entered whenever someone is changing a file on a source control system. Being able to edit a post after it has been published can be a lifesaver for many users, especially given how easy it is to make a mistake the first time around.

On the General tab, there are several remaining settings that should also be considered when administering forums. The first option enables a link to be added for RSS syndication for subscribing to the content on public forums. Another option that is important for organizational purposes is the ability to tag individual posts. By default this is enabled, which means that posts can all be organized into the subject that they relate to. In addition to the other settings, the ability to change how many posts are on a single page can be very valuable.

Administering the Reader

The Reader is a slightly different feature to administer because aspects of it are located outside the Control Panel. Whenever you are logging in to your site as an administrator, you should notice that a new link is added to the menu called My Reader. This is where the feeds can be added to the reader; meanwhile, there is also a piece that sits in the Administration menu for controlling which of these feeds are visible in the reader. The reader is really more of a personal feature for staying current with whatever it is that you are interested in.

Managing Feeds

To manage feeds, you should navigate to your personal Reader by logging in to the site and selecting My Reader from the top navigation bar. Once you are in the Reader, add several feeds. Community Server does a good job of making this an easy task to complete because there is a simple-to-use context menu on the My Reader page. Therefore, simply right-click the My Feeds entry on the left window pane and choose New Feed. In addition to the New Feed button, there are also New Folder, Import OPML, and export OPML buttons. The New Folder option allows you to create a new folder for grouping similar feeds. For example, a folder could be created for Community Server that would contain feeds from `http://communityserver.org`, Rob Howard's blog (`weblogs.asp.net/rhoward`), and Scott Watermasysk's blog (`www.scottwater.com`). These various subscriptions will help enable you to stay current with what is happening in the Community Server world.

The option to import or export feeds using the Outline Processor Markup Language (OPML) standard is important because it means that your feeds are easily transferable between different readers. Perhaps you are already using a feed reader and want to now switch to the Community Server Reader. With these options you can easily import your existing feeds using the OPML format. In addition, if you want to switch away from Community Server, or simply want to share your feeds with a friend or coworker, you can export them, again using OPML. This is an important feature and should not go ignored when using the Reader.

To control these feeds further, an administrator can go to the Reader menu under the Administration tab and click the Manage Feeds menu option. On this page, a listing of the subscribed feeds is provided, along with a convenient button to edit the feed. Whenever you do edit the feed, you can update the URL that the feed comes from. This is important for a situation where a blog has moved and the URL needs to be updated.

Additional Settings

Aside from the standard management of feeds link, there are also a few other links that are a part of the Administration menu for the Reader. An important one is the Manage Access setting, which allows a system administrator to specify what roles are able to control the Reader. In addition, the Settings menu option also has a few important options. The Last Modified Interval setting is especially important because it allows you to determine how often the content from feeds is updated.

Managing Settings

The last section that will be explored in this chapter is the management of sitewide settings located under the Settings menu of the Administration link in the Control Panel. Under this menu are links to several pages that allow you more advanced control over the content and behavior of an entire site. These settings can override application-level settings, such as who is allowed to create posts and even the sizes of syndicated content. Therefore, it is important to understand that whenever you are editing these settings, they are sitewide and should be changed with caution. Fortunately, these settings are often only changed when originally configuring and setting up a site; therefore, they should not need to be changed often. It is also important to realize that changes to some of these settings may not be reflected immediately because they are often cached for performance reasons. Therefore, if you make a change and do not see it reflected immediately, you may want to wait a few minutes.

General Site Settings

Review Figure 6-10 to see a listing of the settings that are available on this page. They mainly change how information will be displayed on your site. The first option, for enabling Ink, is useful if your site contributors are using computers with a screenwriter enabled, such as a tablet. The second option, for enabling the site description to be displayed, is useful if the site header has not been changed drastically. If this is enabled, the description that is provided in the Site Description field of a separate administration page to be displayed on the home page. The other settings are well described in the help icons, so it is easy to learn more about each option.

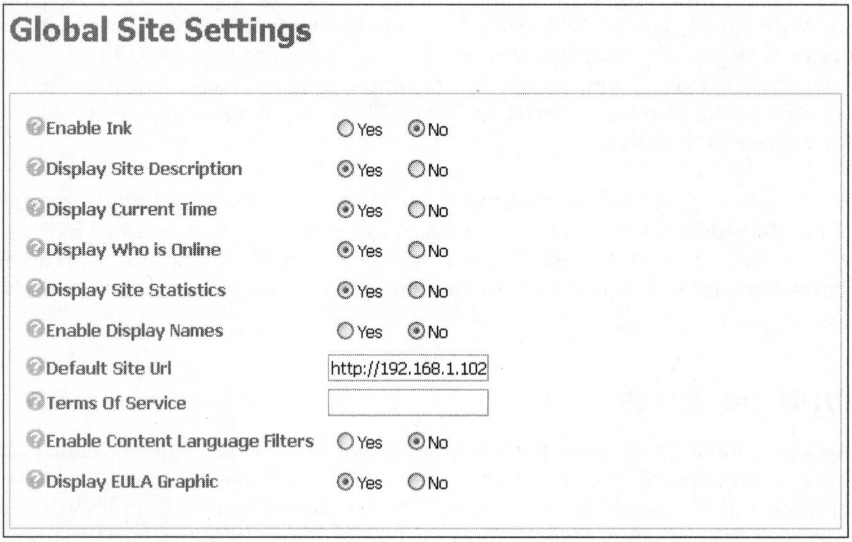

Global Site Settings

Enable Ink	○ Yes ⊙ No
Display Site Description	⊙ Yes ○ No
Display Current Time	⊙ Yes ○ No
Display Who is Online	⊙ Yes ○ No
Display Site Statistics	⊙ Yes ○ No
Enable Display Names	○ Yes ⊙ No
Default Site Url	http://192.168.1.102
Terms Of Service	
Enable Content Language Filters	○ Yes ⊙ No
Display EULA Graphic	⊙ Yes ○ No

Figure 6-10: Global Site Settings

Site Name & Description

The Site Name & Description page allows for the identification of a site and also control over the head tag of each page on your site. If, for example, you want your site to be identified specifically by certain keywords by search engines, then you can include a list of those keywords in the Search Meta Keywords list. Likewise, the Search Meta Description can also be used to provide a basic description of your site to make it easier for search engine spiders to identify your site. These will be added to the headers of each the pages so that they are more identifiable by search engines.

An important option is the Raw Header, which allows an administrator to insert standard JavaScript or anything else into the head tag of the pages on the site. Often, this is used to insert JavaScript for something like Google Analytics into pages. Therefore, if you have some JavaScript that you want to be accessible on every page in the header, you should consider inserting into this text field.

Applications

The Applications menu option allows the different applications on your site to be disabled or enabled. For example, if you do not want to have anything to do with the Reader, you can simply disable it on this page. This removes the links to this application from your site. If you disable Forums, there will no longer be a link that relates to forums on the main page or in the Control Panel.

Post Settings

The Post Settings page is extremely important because it allows an administrator to disable anonymous comments for the entire site. Therefore, if you want to enable anonymous comments on a part of your site, you should enable the anonymous posting setting. This page also records on how a forum should be rated. The choice is either at the thread level or at the post level. In addition, this page controls how many results should be displayed per page for searches.

Date and Time Settings

It is important to set up the settings on this page after you install Community Server. These help determine how dates are stored and how they are displayed to site visitors. After the installation of a new site, the time zone is set to the time that is set on the database server. Changing these default settings can be useful for helping to localize your site. For example, if you have a lot of visitors from around the world, you may want to consider switching the format to a time that makes sense to most of your visitors. While these settings are important to establish initially, it is also important to realize that they can be overridden on a per-user basis. In this way, Community Server allows users to view a site in a way that is most appropriate for them.

Email Settings

By default, email support is disabled for forums. Therefore, if you want to enable users of your forums to be updated via email, then this is a page that you should consult to enable email. In addition, if the SMTP email server requires a login or is on a different server, then this should be established on this page. Whenever you are ready to use email on Community Server, you need to select the Enable Email option on this page and save your changes. In addition, you may need to change some of the other settings on this page to be able to connect to your email server.

For example, if your email server is located at `smtp.email.com` and requires a login and password as well as different port for connecting to the SMTP server, then you will need to change the settings on this page. However, in many situations you can simply enable email and optionally choose the option to use the Windows Integrated Authentication, and you will be fine. You may need to specify that the port to use is port 25. Of course, it is useful not to guess what to put in these settings and instead consult your web host for the appropriate web address and authentication information.

IP Address Tracking

These settings can be helpful for identifying where users of your site live and what ISPs they use. Tracking IP addresses enables you to determine where most of your site's content comes from, as well as what issues are important to certain areas of the world. In addition, you can also use the IP addresses of post contributors to ban them from accessing your site if you need to. This could be useful in a situation where you have identified that a user at an IP address has been spamming your site. With this information, you can ban that person from ever accessing your site again by configuring your web server differently.

Summary

In this chapter, you learned about several of the key pages that are available in the Control Panel. In addition, you learned about the logical layout of these pages so that you are able to easily navigate the options in the Control Panel. You were then presented with several guides for managing the different applications that make up the Community Server platform.

In the next chapter, you will take this knowledge of the Control Panel and apply it to user management. The user management chapter will also extend your exploration of the Control Panel with membership menu options.

7

User Management

After looking at the Control Panel in the previous chapter, you should now be familiar with the underlying layout and organization of its many components. In this chapter, you take another look at the Control Panel and focus on the options that reside under the Membership menu. In addition to the basic options, you will be presented with a more detailed explanation of enforcing username and password requirements through regular expressions, adding new items to these pages, as well as a discussion of the tools that Community Server provides for user management. By the end of this chapter you should be comfortable with the following:

❑   Creating new users

❑   Searching for users using a variety of techniques

❑   Changing new user settings

❑   Controlling how user activity is tracked

Creating a New Member

Under the default settings of Community Server, new users are able to register themselves using the Join link that appears on the top of the page. There is also an option for site administrators to register new users. This is especially useful when you don't want to allow users to register themselves.

To create a new member as a site administrator, log in as an administrator and navigate to the Control Panel. The page for creating a new user is accessible under the Membership menu of the Administration section:

1.   Click Administration.

2.   Click Membership to expand the menu.

3. Click the Create New Account menu option.

4. Type a unique username, a password, and an email address; and select the time zone for the new user, as shown in Figure 7-1.

5. Click the Create User button.

After you click the Create User button, the passwords are checked to make sure that they match. Next, the user store is checked to make sure that this user does not already exist. If all of the preceding checks are successful, the new user account will be created. In addition, depending on whether you have email enabled or not, an email message will be sent to the user to inform them that a new account is available at your site.

For larger sites that allow new users to register themselves, this page will not be as useful as for smaller sites. Creating users can be especially useful whenever you already have a predetermined set of users who will be joining your community. In this situation, an administrator can save the new community members from having to register themselves and perform the task for them. This can be a useful mechanism for announcing your presence to these members because they will be notified via email when their accounts are ready for use.

Figure 7-1: Create New Account Screen

Another use for this page is to help users who experience difficulty with registering. Remember that a system administrator has the permissions to create user accounts manually. Even though this is an easy enough process, it may become tedious if there are a great number of users to add to the system. If this is the situation, you may want to consider doing a batch insert of new users into your user store from a predetermined list of users.

Managing Registration Settings

There are several options available to administrators to control how users are registered as well as who is able to log in to your site. If you want to completely lock down a site so that only administrators are able to log in, there is an option for enabling or disabling login (see Figure 7-2). If you click the Help button next to this option, it says administrators are able to log in even when login is disabled.

The second option allows an administrator to enable or disable banned users from being able to log in. One of the benefits of banning users and not allowing them to log in is that they will not be able to post content to your site. It is important to realize that a user can be banned for a specific length of time and does not always have to be banned permanently; it is up to the administrator.

Whenever you have Show Contact Checkboxes enabled, all of your users will be able to control whether or not they can be contacted by the site or by affiliate sites. These two new options become visible on both the new user registration screen and the profile editing screen for the user. By default, this option is disabled so that users are not able to control whether they are contacted. If you would like to see an example of this setting in use, visit the `http://communityserver.org` web site and create a new account.

The New User Moderation Level setting is important because it dictates whether or not new users have to receive approval on their posts before the posts are published. The default is that they do have to receive approval on posts. However, you should also understand that the users will be moderated whenever the forum that they are posting to is moderated. They would not be moderated, though, if they were administrators. This can be a bit confusing because there are several different scenarios for when a post is moderated or not moderated. Therefore, to help you understand when a post will be moderated, refer to Table 7-1. In the table, the X represents when a post will be moderated, while an empty square represents when a post is not moderated.

Table 7-1: Post Moderation Instances

	Forum Moderated	Form Not Moderated
Administrator		
User Moderated	X	X
User Not Moderated	X	

If you trust the new users who will be registering on your site and do not want to require moderation of their posts, then you should change this level so that the new users are not moderated. It is important to note that you can change this setting on a per-user basis. In order to change this setting, simply find the user and open their profile. On the first tab of the user editing screen, you will see the same drop-down to control to indicate whether the user is moderated or not. In addition, it is also important to realize that this setting really only controls whether a user is moderated on the forums or file gallery. This means that new blog posts are not going to be moderated by keeping this setting at its default.

As an administrator, you are also able to enforce certain naming requirements on new users. This means that you can change the username regular expression to enforce the rule that usernames must contain specific characters. The default username regular expression will, more than likely than not, need to be changed. However, it's possible to create custom rules through regular expressions. For example, if you wanted to enforce the rule that all usernames must be in the form of an email address, you could change it to something like this:

```
^[\w-\.]{1,}\@([\da-zA-Z-]{1,}\.){1,}[\da-zA-Z-]{2,3}$
```

If you would like assistance with creating a regular expression, I advise you to look at the program Regulazy, which has been developed by Roy Osherove. This is a useful tool for taking a text statement and deriving a regular expression that can be used to later validate the original text.

In addition to using only regular expressions, you can also enforce other requirements on usernames. There are two other options for controlling the minimum and maximum lengths of a username that you should be aware of. The default minimum is 3 characters, and the maximum length is 64 characters.

Figure 7-2: New Registration Settings

The account activation setting is useful to control how new users' accounts become active once they are registered. The default setting is that after users register, their account is automatically approved and created. However, you are provided with the option to change this so that new users require an administrator's approval before their account becomes active.

The Password Recovery option is important because it determines the process that will take place whenever users forget their password and attempt to recover it. The default setting is to reset their password whenever they click Forgot Password. In this situation, an email with a new randomly generated password will be sent to the address they have on file. The other option is to send them a link that they need to click to recover their password. Both methods require that the person attempting to recover a password have access to the email account on file with the community site to recover a password.

In addition to the username regular expression, there is also the option to control the format of passwords. While there is no setting for the maximum or minimum lengths of passwords, this can be enforced using a regular expression. This setting can be especially important for heightening the security on your site. By changing this to enforce longer passwords with a variety of characters and numbers, you are making your community more secure. However, it is important to keep usability in mind as well. Make sure that the password requirement is something that is achievable by your community members, as you do not want to deter them from registering with the site.

Searching for Users

There are a couple of ways to find a user in Community Server. The first way is to use the Find People menu option in the Membership menu to search for a user. The other way is to browse through the current users on the Browse People page. Both ways can be equally useful for locating a member.

The Find People page offers a few different predetermined lists that you can browse and will take you to the Browse People page when clicked (see Figure 7-3). These lists are found under the Quick Lists section on the Find People page. Essentially, all that these Quick Lists do is to perform a search on the Browse People page. Here is a list of the preset Quick Lists that are available:

❑ **Top Contributors:** Sorts all members by the number of posts that they have contributed to the site

❑ **Visitors in the last 24 hours:** Displays all visitors for current day, sorted by most recent activity

❑ **Recent Registrations:** Displays all recent users who have joined on current day

❑ **Users Awaiting Approval:** Displays all users waiting to be approved, sorted by username

These are some basic links that should help an administrator to quickly find users. In addition, both the Find People and Browse People pages have a search box that accepts wildcards. Therefore, if you are looking for all of the users who have the letters "ith" at the end of their name, then you can quickly search for "*ith" and you will see these users. The * symbol denotes one or more of anything, while the symbol % denotes zero or more of anything. Therefore, to search for a name that you know has two t's in it somewhere, you could use "%t%t%" and you would get all combinations with at least two t's.

Another important wildcard is the underscore, which denotes an arbitrary character. This could be used in searching for the name Wyatt. Perhaps you want to get all of the words that have one character, followed by the letter y and two t's somewhere else in the word, then you could search for "_y%t%t%"; this would result in Wyatt. You can also append multiple underscores to find the person you are looking for. Thus, if you want to find Wyatt again you could also do "__a__" so that you are looking for any word with two characters, an A, and two more characters.

Aside from the wonderful searching mechanisms on this page, Community Server also makes it easy to find the results by offering various sorting options. In addition, there are also a couple of filtering options for finding a user who either joined in a specific date range or whose last post was between two dates. Both of these options are found in the Filter By Date section.

Similar to the Filter By Date section, there is the option to filter certain user roles and user statuses. For example, if you would like to see all of the banned users on a site, you can simply select the Banned status from the drop-down list and then search for a single asterisk. This same search can be performed to find users with different statuses or in different roles.

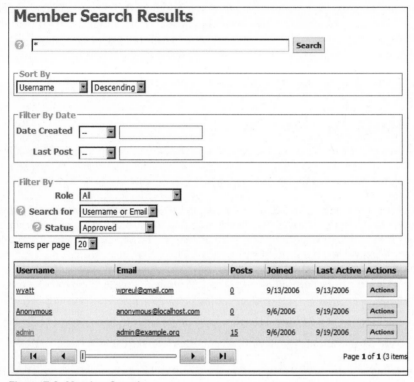

Figure 7-3: Member Search

Once you have found a user, it is a simple matter of selecting the appropriate action that you would like to perform on them. The actions available from the control panel for each user include the following:

❑ Change Username

❑ Reset/Change Password

❑ Add/Remove Roles

❑ Delete User

It is important not to remove the anonymous user account as it is used for visitors who have not logged in to or registered on the site yet.

If you would like to add more options to the Actions menu, you are only required to edit one configuration file. The file is called `MemberSearchContextMenu.config`, and it is located under the `ControlPanel/Membership/` folders. When you open this file, you will notice that it looks similar to other navigation files that have been reviewed in other chapters. It is an `.xml` file that contains a collection of tabs that represents each option in the context menu. Simply add a line here the same way you would when adding a link to the navigation bar. For more information on how to add a link, refer to Chapter 10.

Global Account Profile Settings

Under the Global Account Profile Settings, there are many important settings that can impact how users view your site. The majority of the settings control a user's forum experience; however, the other settings can affect a user's experience on the entire site. To access this page, simply expand the Membership menu in the Administration section of the Control Panel, and click Global Account Profile Settings.

The first few options relate to each other as they impact whether or not users can have a signature attached to their posts and how long the signature can be. The first option determines whether or not users on your site are allowed to create a custom signature. The second option, to enable signatures, is used to show the signatures in forums. If the use of signatures ever becomes a nuisance on your site, you can hide signatures using this option. If you would like to see a good example of a site that is using signatures, then please visit `http://communityserver.org` and look at the posts in the forums.

It is up to an administrator to enable gender to be displayed on a site. However, it is ultimately up to the users to display their gender. It may be important to hide gender on your site if you feel that your community would prefer to keep this information private. Even if users provide their gender, if you disable this option, they are not forced to display it on their posts.

Similarly, an administrator can require that only registered users are able to view other registered users' profiles. This is important if the members of your site do not necessarily want the entire world to see their profile. To enable this, simply change the Require Authentication for Profile Viewing setting to Yes. After you change this setting, when visitors want to view user profiles they will be required to join the community first.

The final setting that is available on this page is the Enable User Theme Selection setting. This is enabled by default and allows users to change their settings so that they view your site using a theme that they select. Under the default installation, there are only a few different themes to choose from. However, if you want to add more, this can be useful for allowing a user to see the community site they would like to see. This would be especially useful if your site had any users that require certain accessibility features. You could alter the default theme so that it met these new requirements and then allow your site members to choose it. Thus, users with special needs could still access and enjoy the site by changing a single setting in their profile.

Cookies

There are different cookies that are used in Community Server to store user settings. The one that is probably used most often is the `CommunityServer-AutoLoginCookie`. This cookie is used to store on the login control the users' preference for whether or not to be logged in automatically the next time they visit the site. This cookie holds a Boolean value representing the value of the automatic login checkbox. This cookie expires after a year; thus, the selection that users make on this checkbox will be remembered for a year or until they delete the cookie. In addition, it is important to understand that the value stored in this cookie can be changed at any time simply by changing whether the checkbox is checked or not.

Another important cookie to take note of is the anonymous user cookie, which is called `CSAnonymous` by default. This cookie is used to track anonymous users by storing a globally unique ID (GUID) as a value in this cookie. Therefore, each user, while technically anonymous, has an identifiable value to distinguish him or her from other users. This is an important concept because through the use of the `CSAnonymous` cookie, Community Server can track and distinguish user activity between different anonymous users on the site.

Once a user is authenticated, another cookie comes into play, named the `CommunityServer-UserCookie`. This cookie's name is appended with the ID of the user so that users of a site can share the same computer and retain their individual preferences and activity in the cookie. This is a useful cookie because it keeps track of the activity of registered users. One of the important pieces of information in this cookie is the last time a registered user visited your site. This can be extremely useful information to keep track of because it helps you recognize whether people are leaving your community site or whether people are registering and staying actively involved. Aside from storing a user's activity, it also can store users' forum preferences as well as other general preferences.

If you would like to disable, rename, or change the expiration time for either the `CommunityServer-UserCookie` or `CSAnonymous` cookies, you can do so using the Cookie and Anonymous Settings Control Panel page. This is accessible from the Membership menu on the Administration page. In most situations, you will not need to change any of the default settings. Regardless, Community Server makes it easy to adjust the settings to match your needs.

Anonymous User Settings

The rights for anonymous users are often controlled using the `Everyone` role in the permissions section of the different applications. Important permissions that relate to anonymous users that you should be aware of are `View` and `Read` rights. Blogs and galleries have the ability to prevent anonymous users from viewing them. To accomplish this, you simply need to change the user permissions on the individual blog or gallery so that the `Everyone` role does not have `View` permissions.

On the forums, `View` is used to allow a user to see that a forum exists. The `Read` right on any role allows a user to see the contents of a forum (including the list of threads within the post). By setting `View` and restricting `Read` to any role, users may see that a forum exists and may see the Thread Subject of the latest post, but if they try to read a thread by clicking a post subject, they will be redirected to the login page. This can be a great way to encourage users to register with a site.

When you prevent anonymous users from viewing or reading a part of your site, you are essentially saying that you also do not want them to be able to read that part of the site using an RSS feed. Community Server takes care of this by disabling the RSS feed because it is not secure. However, if you want registered users to be able to subscribe to content on the site, but prevent anonymous users, then enable Secure Syndication. Enabling this setting makes the RSS links visible to users who have access to read the related content. Additionally, Community Server will use a special unique URL per feed to enable users to view feeds that are not visible to anonymous users. Security is taken very seriously; this is just one of many examples where an administrator has the ability to tighten access to a site.

Avatar Settings

The ability to be identified on a community site in a personalized way can be very important. It is important for people to be able to distinguish themselves among the millions of others that frequent the Internet. For this and many other reasons, the concept of an avatar is extremely useful. Think of an avatar as nothing more than a picture that people use to identify themselves. Avatars are mainly used in the forums; however, they can become useful in other areas of the site.

Community Server allows a site administrator to globally disable avatars on the Avatar Settings screen located under the Membership menu. The screen also allows an administrator to enable the use of remote avatars. By default, Community Server does not allow users to link to an image on an external site for use as an avatar. It is important to realize that these images could be potentially inappropriate or insulting to other community members. Therefore, it is important that you understand your community members and make sure that they are aware of your expectations for appropriateness. Perhaps, it will be beneficial to create a document for community members to agree to that includes discussion of avatars.

The final option on this Control Panel screen is the maximum size that avatars are allowed to be. This size is in pixels and defaults to 80 by 80. If you would like to see what this looks like, simply visit `http://communityserver.org` and look at the forums pages.

Summary

In this chapter, you learned about many of the options that are available in the membership section of the Control Panel. You learned about the different ways to create user accounts as well as some of the different registration options available to these accounts. In addition, you also learned about the different cookies that exist in Community Server. In the next chapter, you will expand on your knowledge of user management by learning about different security options.

8

Managing Security

Now that you have learned about user management, it is time to focus on how to use the Control Panel to manage how users can interact within each of the applications of your community. In this chapter, you will learn about roles, permissions, and context — the core items used by Community Server to manage security.

Overview

Roles are the central foundation on which Community Server's security model is based. Quite simply, a role is a set of users to which permissions are granted or denied. So, instead of assigning a security level or even permissions to an individual user, permissions are assigned to a set of users. Not only does this help streamline security management by decreasing the workload of an administrator, but it also better models the real world. For example, during the "design" phase of a community, you may think about how groups of users will interact with the software. You would ask questions like these: "What types of activities can everyone perform? Which forums should be available for registered users? What additional features should be available to moderators?" These groups of users translate nicely to roles.

Permissions are another key component necessary for managing security. Without them, we just have groups of users. Permissions represent the smallest piece of functionality that can be secured via roles. The users in a role can be allowed or denied permission to a particular action through the Control Panel. For example, administrators can make announcements; registered users can reply to posts; everyone can read posts.

But having roles and permissions isn't quite enough. There's still one thing missing, and that's context. Context defines where the role-permission combination is valid. Sometimes the context is the entire application, such as forums or blogs. But sometimes the needs of the community require that context to be much more granular. For example, one community may choose to allow registered users to reply to posts in all the forums but decide that they are unable to even view posts in the "internal" forums.

So, as seen in Figure 8-1, security is ultimately managed by three things: roles, permissions, and context. Roles define the "who," while permissions define the "what," and context defines the "where."

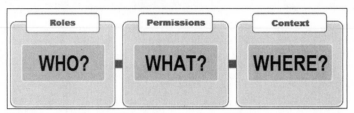

Figure 8-1: Conceptual Diagram of Relationships in Security Model

Roles

As mentioned previously, Community Server does not employ a "security level," nor does it provide a hierarchical security system. Instead it leverages role-based security. Since roles are just simple sets of users, and since a user can belong to multiple roles, the security solution offered by Community Server is extremely flexible.

By default, each time a new user registers, she or he is automatically assigned to both the Everyone and the Registered Users roles. (To change these default role assignments, you can modify the defaultRoles attribute of the communityserver.config file, as discussed in Chapter 10.) Beyond these two default roles, Community Server includes 10 additional built-in roles that can be used out of the box.

Built-in Roles

Each of the built-in roles serves a unique purpose within Community Server. Therefore, none of these roles can be deleted. It's also worthwhile to note that the default "admin" user (created during installation) is a member of all of these roles.

The Everyone role exists primarily to support anonymous access. As such, before any user logs in, she or he is a member of the Everyone role. Since all permission assignments occur at the role level, each user, whether authenticated or not, must belong to at least one role in order for Community Server to determine which permissions are available. The Everyone role serves that purpose. Since Community Server guarantees that all users are members of this role, users should never be removed from this role manually. By default, the system-created "Anonymous" user is a member of only this role.

The Registered Users role functions as a baseline for all authenticated users. Again, once a user is logged in, there needs to be a role assigned to that person so as to distinguish him or her from an unauthenticated user. This role serves that purpose. Community Server guarantees that all registered users are members of this role. As with the Everyone role, users should never be removed from this role manually.

The Moderator and Editor roles are used primarily in the forums, but also have full capabilities, by default, within the Files application. Community Server allows post authors to edit their own posts, but only users in the Editor role are allowed to edit posts created by others. Moderators get this capability, but also are allowed access to the complete moderation menu, including the ability to lock, move, split, join, and delete posts.

The `Owners` role is a special role that is used internally for users who have their own blogs, photos, or file areas. Users should not be added to this role manually as Community Server handles this role's membership behind the scenes.

Each application also has an application-specific administrator role. So, by default, your Community Server site will contain the `BlogAdministrator`, `FileAdministrator`, `ForumsAdministrator`, `GalleryAdministrator`, and `ReaderAdministrator` roles. Each member of these roles has the ability to exercise any and all functionality within the specific application. So a `ForumsAdministrator`, for example, is automatically granted all permissions within the forums application. Similarly, a `BlogAdministrator` has free reign within the blogs portion of Community Server.

The `MembershipAdministrator` role exists for managing users, as discussed in Chapter 7. To create roles, manage role assignments, and create and approve users, you must be a member of this role. One benefit of the `MembershipAdministrator` role is that you can allow people to manage membership-related information without giving them administrator access to all the applications. For larger communities, this is often desirable.

The `SystemAdministrator` role has access to all functionality within Community Server. All permission checks are bypassed for users added to this role. By default, the initially created "admin" user is a member of this role. It is recommended that at least one user be a member of this role at all times in order to guarantee complete access to all areas of a Community Server site.

Managing Roles

While Community Server comes with a large set of roles out of the box, you may still find it helpful to create your own roles to better satisfy the needs of your community. For example, if you were running a community for a local school, you might consider creating roles for `Teacher`, `Parent`, and `Student`. To manage the roles available in your community:

1. Click Control Panel.
2. Click Administration.
3. Open the Membership menu.
4. Click the Manage All Roles menu option.

You will be presented with a simple grid, visible in Figure 8-2, displaying the list of currently available roles. From here you can add a new role, edit a role, or view the list of members belonging to a particular role. To add a new role:

1. Click the Add New Role button.
2. Choose a Name and Description for the new role.
3. Click the Save button.

When adding this new role, you will notice that the Upload Role Icon field is blank. Role icons, used primarily in the forums (and badges), are small images that are used to indicate role membership (see Figure 8-3). On `http://communityserver.org`, for example, you will see a role icon next to forum posts created by users belonging to the `CS Dev` role.

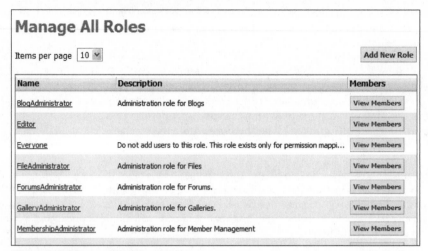

Figure 8-2: Manage All Roles Screen

Figure 8-3: Example of Role Icon

Similarly to the way you add a role, you can edit a role simply by clicking an existing role name in the grid and making any changes necessary, including updating or even deleting the role icon. Deleting a role is available on the Edit Role dialog box, but, as mentioned previously, while custom roles can be deleted, the built-in roles are not removable. Finally, to see which users are currently assigned to a particular role, click the View Members button in the row corresponding to that role.

Role Assignment

Once you are satisfied with the set of roles in your community, it's time to begin assigning users to them. Recall that, by default, every person who registers on your site will be automatically added to the Everyone and Registered Users roles. Unfortunately, Community Server does not provide a way to manage role assignments in bulk. So, the only way to change a user's roles is one at a time.

To add/remove a single user to/from any role, you'll need to first find that user via the Membership Control Panel.

1. Click Control Panel.

2. Click Administration.

3. Open the Membership menu.

4. Click the Find People menu option.

5. Search for the user.

6. Click the Actions button for the selected user (see Figure 8-4).

7. Select the Add/Remove Roles menu item.

Figure 8-4: Finding the Add/Remove Roles Menu Item

After clicking the menu item, you will see the Role Assignment dialog box, shown in Figure 8-5. The roles available to the user are displayed in the list box on the left. The roles that the user is currently a member of are in the list box on the right. To assign the user to a role, just double-click the role on the left side. To remove the user from a role, double-click the role name on the right side. In addition to double-clicking, you can also select a role name and click the appropriate arrow button (> or <) to move it from one side to the other. Finally, if you click the double arrows (>> or <<), you can add a user to all roles or remove him or her from all roles.

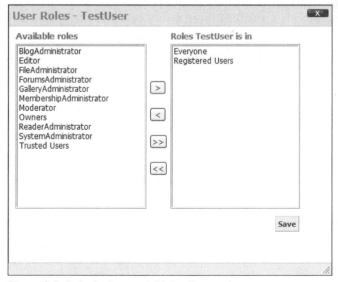

Figure 8-5: Role Assignment Dialog Box

Permissions

Now that roles have been defined, and users have been placed into the appropriate set of roles, our discussion moves to permissions. Recall that permissions refer to the most granular piece of functionality that can be granted or denied from a set of users in a role. Each of the applications has its own set of permissions that can be managed independently from the others. So, while the forums include Sticky and Announce permissions, none of the other applications supports them.

But before diving in to each individual application's specific permission sets, we should discuss how permissions are evaluated. Currently, it is a two-tiered approach. First, each application has a set of global permissions, defining the default behavior for each user within a role. Layered on top of that are section-level permissions, where a section is defined as a forum, blog, file, or photo gallery. If the permissions for a particular role-section combination are not specified, the global permissions are used. If section-level permissions are defined, they take precedence. Therefore, since each application supports global permissions, it is recommended that you set them to work with the most common scenarios. This will guarantee that all newly created sections "inherit" the global permissions, causing less work, since section-level overrides will be less frequent.

As an example, in the forums application the Everyone role is denied post permissions. This means that anonymous users are not allowed to post to the forums. On the other hand, members of the Registered Users role are granted post permissions. Since these are the global permissions, all forums that are created will behave similarly unless overridden. As you can see, this makes it easier for an administrator to set some basic rules for how an application should work and then specify where to allow the rules to be broken.

Managing Blog Permissions

The blog application of Community Server supports seven different permissions, listed and defined in Table 8-1. As you can see from the default global permissions, shown in Figure 8-6, members of the Everyone and Registered Users role can both view and reply to blog posts. Owners, however, are also given the ability to manage content (post, delete) and upload/link to attachments. You may also notice that both Ink and Video support in blogs is off by default across all blogs. As discussed previously, any member of the BlogAdministrator (or SystemAdministrator) role will be able to exercise all blog-related functionality, regardless of the global- or section-level permissions.

Table 8-1: Blog Permission Definitions

Permission	Description
View	Ability to view any content of the blog
Manage Content	Ability to access the Control Panel and post to the blog
Reply	Ability to comment on a post in the blog
Ink	Ability to add ink to a post in the blog
Video	Ability to add a video to a post in the blog
Upload Attachment	Ability to upload an attachment to a post in the blog
Remote Attachment	Ability to link to a remote attachment on a post in the blog

To change the global blog permissions (see Figure 8-6):

1. Click Control Panel.

2. Click Administration.

3. Open the Blogs menu.

4. Click the Global Permissions menu option.

5. Grant/deny permissions per role by checking/unchecking the corresponding role/permission checkbox.

6. Click the Save button.

Name	View	Manange Content	Reply	Ink	Video	Upload Attachment	Remote Attachment
BlogAdministrator	☑	☑	☑	☐	☐	☑	☑
Editor	☐	☐	☐	☐	☐	☐	☐
Everyone	☑	☐	☑	☐	☐	☐	☐
FileAdministrator	☐	☐	☐	☐	☐	☐	☐
ForumsAdministrator	☐	☐	☐	☐	☐	☐	☐
GalleryAdministrator	☐	☐	☐	☐	☐	☐	☐
MembershipAdministrator	☐	☐	☐	☐	☐	☐	☐
Moderator	☐	☐	☐	☐	☐	☐	☐
Owners	☑	☑	☑	☐	☐	☑	☑
ReaderAdministrator	☐	☐	☐	☐	☐	☐	☐
Registered Users	☑	☐	☑	☐	☐	☐	☐
SystemAdministrator	☑	☑	☑	☐	☐	☑	☑
Trusted Users	☐	☐	☐	☐	☐	☐	☐

Figure 8-6: Default Global Blog Permissions

To change a particular blog's permissions:

1. Click Control Panel.

2. Click Administration.

3. Open the Blogs menu.

4. Click the Blogs menu option.

5. Find the blog you are looking for using the filter or search.

6. Click the Edit button.

7. On the Permissions tab, override the global permissions as necessary.

8. Click the Save button.

Managing Photo Gallery Permissions

The photo application of Community Server supports only three different permissions, listed and defined in Table 8-2. As you can see from the default global permissions, shown in Figure 8-7, members of the Everyone and Registered Users role can both view and reply to photo posts. Owners, however, are also given the ability to manage content (i.e., post). As discussed previously, any member of the GalleryAdministrator or SystemAdministrator roles will be able to exercise all gallery-related functionality, regardless of the global- or section-level permissions.

Table 8-2: Photo Gallery Permission Definitions

Permission	Description
View	Ability to view any content of the gallery
Manage Content	Ability to access the Control Panel and post to the gallery
Reply	Ability to comment on a photo in the gallery

To change the global photo gallery permissions (see Figure 8-7):

1. Click Control Panel.

2. Click Administration.

3. Open the Photos menu.

4. Click the Global Permissions menu item.

5. Grant/deny permissions per role by checking/unchecking the corresponding role/permission checkbox.

6. Click the Save button.

Name	View	Reply	Manage Content
BlogAdministrator	☐	☐	☐
Editor	☐	☐	☐
Everyone	☑	☑	☐
FileAdministrator	☐	☐	☐
ForumsAdministrator	☐	☐	☐
GalleryAdministrator	☑	☑	☑
MembershipAdministrator	☐	☐	☐
Moderator	☐	☐	☐
Owners	☑	☑	☑
ReaderAdministrator	☐	☐	☐
Registered Users	☑	☑	☐
SystemAdministrator	☑	☑	☑
Trusted Users	☐	☐	☐

Figure 8-7: Default Global Photo Gallery Permissions

To change a particular photo gallery's permissions:

1. Click Control Panel.

2. Click Administration.

3. Open the Photos menu.

4. Click the Galleries menu option.

5. Find the photo gallery you are looking for using the search capability.

6. Click the Edit button.

7. On the Permissions tab, override the global permissions as necessary.

8. Click the Save button.

Managing File Gallery Permissions

The files application of Community Server supports seven different permissions, listed and defined in Table 8-3. As you can see from the default global permissions, shown in Figure 8-8, members of the Everyone and Registered Users role can view, download, and reply to photo posts. Registered Users are also granted the Vote permission, which is used for rating. You will also notice that in this application, those in the Editor and Moderator roles are given access to the complete file gallery feature set, as are Owners. As discussed previously, any member of the FileAdministrator or SystemAdministrator roles will be able to exercise all file gallery-related functionality, regardless of the global- or section-level permissions.

Table 8-3: File Gallery Permission Definitions

Permission	Description
View	Ability to view, but not download, any content of the folder
Download	Ability to download entries in the folder
Vote	Ability to rate entries in the folder
Reply	Ability to comment on an entry in the folder
Upload	Ability to add entries to the folder
Local Files	Ability to upload a file to an entry in the folder
Remote Files	Ability to link a remote file to an entry in the folder

To change the global file gallery permissions (see Figure 8-8):

1. Click Control Panel.

2. Click Administration.

3. Open the Files menu.

4. Click the Global Permissions menu option.

5. Grant/deny permissions per role by checking/unchecking the corresponding role/permission checkbox.

6. Click the Save button.

Name	View	Download	Vote	Reply	Upload	Local Files	Remote Files
BlogAdministrator	☐	☐	☐	☐	☐	☐	☐
Editor	☑	☑	☑	☑	☑	☑	☑
Everyone	☑	☑	☐	☑	☐	☐	☐
FileAdministrator	☑	☑	☑	☑	☑	☑	☑
ForumsAdministrator	☐	☐	☐	☐	☐	☐	☐
GalleryAdministrator	☐	☐	☐	☐	☐	☐	☐
MembershipAdministrator	☐	☐	☐	☐	☐	☐	☐
Moderator	☑	☑	☑	☑	☑	☑	☑
Owners	☑	☑	☑	☑	☑	☑	☑
ReaderAdministrator	☐	☐	☐	☐	☐	☐	☐
Registered Users	☑	☑	☑	☑	☐	☐	☐
SystemAdministrator	☑	☑	☑	☑	☑	☑	☑
Trusted Users	☐	☐	☐	☐	☐	☐	☐

Figure 8-8: Default Global File Gallery Permissions

To change a particular file gallery's permissions:

1. Click Control Panel.

2. Click Administration.

3. Open the Files menu.

4. Click the Folders menu option.

5. Find the file gallery you are looking for using the search capability.

6. Click the Edit button.

7. On the Permissions tab, override the global permissions as necessary.

8. Click the Save button.

Managing Forum Permissions

The forums application of Community Server supports more permissions than any of the other applications. Each permission is listed and defined in Table 8-4. Since there are so many permissions available in the forums, they have been split across two tabs. Unfortunately, this is the source of confusion for many administrators, as they often forget to check both tabs when bumping up against security "issues."

As discussed previously, any member of the `ForumsAdministrator` or `SystemAdministrator` roles will be able to exercise all forum-related functionality, regardless of the global- or section-level permissions.

Table 8-4: Forum Permission Definitions

Permission	Description
View	Ability to view post information (but not post bodies) in the forum
Read	Ability to view post bodies in the forums
Post	Ability to add a post to the forum (i.e., new thread)
Reply	Ability to reply to a post in the forum (i.e., existing thread)
Vote	Ability to vote in a poll included in a post in the forum
Ink	Ability to add ink to a post in the forum
Video	Ability to add a video to a post in the forum
Local Attach	Ability to upload and attach a file to a post in the forum
Remote Attach	Ability to attach a remote file to a post in the forum
Edit	Ability to edit one's own posts in the forum
Delete	Ability to delete posts from the forum
Create Poll	Ability to add a poll to a post in the forum
Mark as Answer	Ability to mark a post as an answer in the forum
Sticky	Ability to create "Sticky" posts in the forum
Announce	Ability to create "Announcement" posts in the forum
Edit Others	Ability to edit other users' posts in the forum
Moderate	Ability to moderate posts in the forum

To change the global forum permissions (see Figures 8-9 and 8-10):

1. Click Control Panel.
2. Click Administration.
3. Open the Forums menu.
4. Click the Global Permissions menu option.
5. Grant/deny permissions per role by checking/unchecking the corresponding role/permission checkbox.
6. Click the Save button.

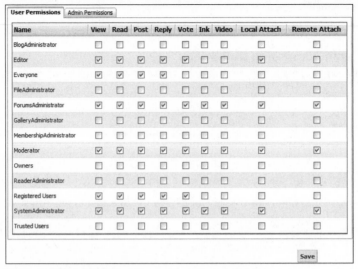

Name	View	Read	Post	Reply	Vote	Ink	Video	Local Attach	Remote Attach
BlogAdministrator	☐	☐	☐	☐	☐	☐	☐	☐	☐
Editor	☑	☑	☑	☑	☑	☐	☐	☑	☐
Everyone	☑	☑	☑	☑	☐	☐	☐	☐	☐
FileAdministrator	☐	☐	☐	☐	☐	☐	☐	☐	☐
ForumsAdministrator	☑	☑	☑	☑	☑	☑	☑	☑	☑
GalleryAdministrator	☐	☐	☐	☐	☐	☐	☐	☐	☐
MembershipAdministrator	☐	☐	☐	☐	☐	☐	☐	☐	☐
Moderator	☑	☑	☑	☑	☑	☑	☑	☑	☑
Owners	☐	☐	☐	☐	☐	☐	☐	☐	☐
ReaderAdministrator	☐	☐	☐	☐	☐	☐	☐	☐	☐
Registered Users	☑	☑	☑	☑	☑	☐	☐	☐	☐
SystemAdministrator	☑	☑	☑	☑	☑	☑	☑	☑	☑
Trusted Users	☐	☐	☐	☐	☐	☐	☐	☐	☐

Save

Figure 8-9: Default Global Forum User Permissions

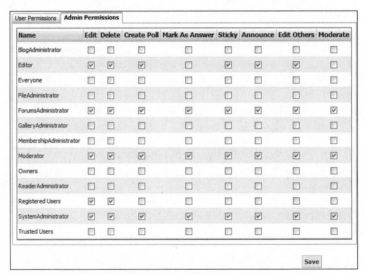

Name	Edit	Delete	Create Poll	Mark As Answer	Sticky	Announce	Edit Others	Moderate
BlogAdministrator	☐	☐	☐	☐	☐	☐	☐	☐
Editor	☑	☑	☑	☐	☑	☑	☑	☐
Everyone	☐	☐	☐	☐	☐	☐	☐	☐
FileAdministrator	☐	☐	☐	☐	☐	☐	☐	☐
ForumsAdministrator	☑	☑	☑	☑	☑	☑	☑	☑
GalleryAdministrator	☐	☐	☐	☐	☐	☐	☐	☐
MembershipAdministrator	☐	☐	☐	☐	☐	☐	☐	☐
Moderator	☑	☑	☑	☑	☑	☑	☑	☑
Owners	☐	☐	☐	☐	☐	☐	☐	☐
ReaderAdministrator	☐	☐	☐	☐	☐	☐	☐	☐
Registered Users	☑	☑	☐	☐	☐	☐	☐	☐
SystemAdministrator	☑	☑	☑	☑	☑	☑	☑	☑
Trusted Users	☐	☐	☐	☐	☐	☐	☐	☐

Save

Figure 8-10: Default Global Forum Admin Permissions

To change a particular forum's permissions:

1. Click Control Panel.
2. Click Administration.

3. Open the Forums menu. This option is displayed as Manage All Forums whenever you are in a Tree View display. If you are in a Grid View display, this option will appear as Forums.

4. Click the Forums menu option.

5. Find the forum you are looking for using the search capability.

6. Click the Edit button.

7. On the Permissions tabs, override the global permissions as necessary.

8. Click the Save button.

Managing Reader Permissions

The Reader is unlike any other application in Community Server, at least from a security viewpoint. Reader doesn't really support permissions. Rather, you can specify which roles will be granted access to the reader application, as shown in Figure 8-11. Either users get access to all of Reader or they do not. Similar to the other applications, any member of the `ReaderAdministrator` or the `SystemAdministator` roles will be given complete access to manage the Reader application from the Control Panel.

To specify which users should have access to the reader application (see Figure 8-11):

1. Click Control Panel.

2. Click Administration.

3. Open the Reader menu.

4. Click the Manage Access menu option.

5. Select which roles should be granted access to the Reader.

6. Click the Save button.

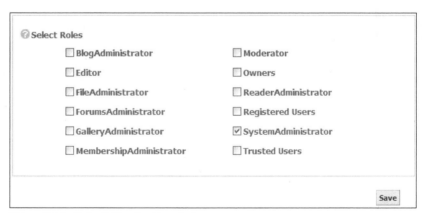

Figure 8-11: Default Reader Permissions

Summary

In this chapter, you learned about the various permissions that exist in Community Server. These allow you to control the access to different parts of each application. You explored how to change these permissions for the blogs, photo galleries, file galleries, forums, and Reader applications. In the next chapter, you will extend your knowledge of how to control the various aspects of this platform and learn many advanced configuration options that are a part of Community Server.

9

Reporting Capabilities

There are several different reports available with Community Server that include, but are not limited to, blog activity, page views, user activity, and forum post activity. As a result, a site administrator is provided with several easy ways to gather statistics about each Community Server site. In addition, many of the reports are easily exported to a .csv file that can be loaded into Microsoft Excel. Although there are several reports that are installed with Community Server, only the Exceptions Report and Jobs Report are available with the Express Edition. If you are interested in additional reporting capabilities, you should purchase the Standard Edition or higher Community Server package. For more information on how to purchase Community Server, refer to Chapter 1.

While Community Server contains several built-in reports, it also maintains more statistics and data that are not revealed through a report. You can get even more data out of Community Server using tools such as Microsoft Reporting Services.

Exceptions Report

Community Server refers to the errors that occur on a site as exceptions, which is the same way that .NET refers to them. As a result, any exceptions that you encounter in the Exceptions Report (see Figure 9-1) will be the same as what you would encounter when programming with the Community Server application program interface (API). Therefore, the Exceptions Report is a good starting point for anyone who is interested in learning more about developing for Community Server. It provides a convenient place to see a listing of the different types of exceptions that are a part of Community Server.

Again, an exception is nothing more than a way to describe a specific type of issue that arises on your site. To help you understand how these issues relate to your community site, I will describe a few of the various exceptions in more detail. It is important to note that this is not an exhaustive list of all of the possible exceptions that Community Server offers; it is merely some of the more common exceptions that you may experience. As a result, it may be helpful to look at the titles of the other exceptions that are available; sometimes the title is descriptive enough to enable you to understand the issue. It's also important to understand that some exceptions are a normal occurrence; there are cases where errors are handled internally to Community Server such as requests for pages that do not exist.

To see the list of exceptions that I am referring to, complete the following steps to access the exceptions report in the Control Panel:

1.   Log in to your site using an administrator account.

2.   Click Control Panel.

3.   Click Administration.

4.   Click Reports, then on Exceptions Report.

Whenever you are viewing the exceptions report, you will notice that you are presented with a few drop-down lists to help narrow the list of displayed exceptions. If your site has been operational for a while, or if you have had any exceptions, you should see them listed in this report.

The first column of the report displays the type of exception that occurred. Meanwhile, the last part of the report entry displays the message that represents each particular exception; usually this is the stack trace. Another important column to note is the one for the number of occurrences, which displays the total number of times that this particular type of exception has occurred. It is also important to note that the exceptions are not grouped by the type, but by the actual exception occurrence. Therefore, you can have a specific type of exception displayed more than once in the report and occurring more than once for each entry displayed.

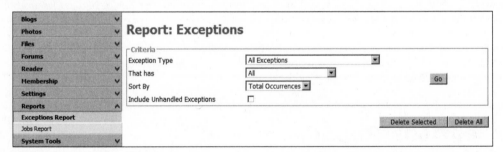

Figure 9-1: Exceptions Report

Now that you are logged in to your site's Exception Report, we can examine the various types of exceptions that you may encounter. Let me reiterate that this is not an exhaustive list of every type of exception; therefore you may want to look at the exception type drop-down list or even the CSExceptionType enumerator. To view the CSExceptionType enumerator, load the Community Server Components project, navigate to the Enumerations folder, and open the ForumExceptionsType.cs file. Even though the file is called the Forum Exceptions Type, it is actually an enumerator of the root Community Server Exceptions. Another tip for learning about how a particular exception is used is to do a global solution search for an exception type in the list. As a result, you will be presented with the actual code that calls the exception you searched. Here are a few of the many types of exceptions that are a part of Community Server.

❑ *Access Denied* occurs whenever a user does not have the appropriate permissions to perform an action but attempts to perform the action anyway. For example, this may occur whenever a user with limited access tries to edit content that only administers have access to edit.

❑ *Email Unable to Send* occurs whenever an attempt to send an email to a recipient fails. This could be a result of an error with your email server.

❑ *Section Not Found* occurs whenever a blog, forum, or gallery cannot be found. This can be the result of a user tampering with the querystring and trying to access different sections.

❑ *File Not Found* occurs whenever a requested file cannot be found on the web server. This could be a result of a file being deleted or moved and the link to it not being updated.

❑ *Invalid User Credentials* occurs whenever a user tries to log in with either an invalid username or password.

❑ *Unknown Error* can be just about any exception; generally this will be the result of a programming error. It could be anything from trying to access a null object to an error from an individual control such as a drop-down list complaining about multiple items being selected.

❑ *Skin Not Found* occurs whenever a skin file is missing that was requested by a user.

To view many of the Unknown Error exceptions, you may need to check the Include Unhandled Exceptions box and click the Go button. This will likely display more exceptions than you originally were viewing with the default report.

Managing Exceptions

It is important to keep a handle on the types of exceptions occurring on your site; therefore, you will want to visit this report often. Exceptions can be an annoying experience for your site visitors, especially the unhandled exceptions. The reason unhandled exceptions are more troublesome from a user's perspective is that they will receive a generic message that may give them little idea of what they can do to resolve the error. Usually, visitors will do their part to resolve an issue on their own, especially if the error message gives them clear instructions on how to do so. Take, for example, the invalid credentials message; if a user receives this message, they will more than likely attempt to log in again with the correct credentials. However, if users receive a very generic message that an error was encountered, they may give up hope and leave your site. This is something that you will want to try to avoid; therefore, you should take care to eliminate all possible unhandled exceptions.

One of the ways that you can help provide useful information to your visitors when an exception does occur is to make sure that the exception messages being displayed are easily understood by your visitors. For example, if you have a site visited primarily by computer novices, then you may want your exception messages to be as straightforward as possible to help mitigate future occurrences of exceptions.

Community Server provides an easy way to change exception messages simply by editing the `Messages.xml` resource file. `Messages.xml` is located in the `Languages/en-US/` directory and can be edited with Notepad. There can also be different messages files, depending on how your site is localized, which you will learn about in Chapter 15.

Make sure that you are editing only the title and body section of the message, and not the ID. If you open the `ForumExceptionType.cs` file, you will notice that the IDs in the `Messages.xml` file correspond to value of the exception type that they will be displayed as. For example, the message ID for the `Unknown Error` is 999, and the `CSExceptionType` enumeration value for the `UnknownError` is also 999. You should not change these IDs unless you are doing so intentionally.

Aside from managing the exception messages, you should also become accustomed to managing the Exceptions Report itself. This is a straightforward task that only involves the removal of exceptions from the list. However, before you go about removing exceptions that have already been fixed, you may want to consider if it would be useful to have a history of all of the exceptions on your site. To keep a backup of the issues log before deleting the exceptions, either export the `cs_Exceptions` table in your Community Server database or to copy the exceptions from the report before you remove them. Either way, you should still develop a process for handling the exceptions that appear in the report so that they do not occur again. If you are managing a large site with several developers, it may be helpful to export the exceptions to an issue-tracking system.

Jobs Report

Community Server runs a number of tasks as background jobs. The Jobs Report is a static report that displays current statistics about the jobs that are configured to run. As a result of its static nature, there is really no way to interact with the report other than clicking Refresh on the browser to get the most recent statistics. It does, however, help identify when a job last ran or if it is currently running. This can be helpful for identifying the root cause of an exception that may have occurred. As a result of having the jobs information while diagnosing an issue you are able to have more of a complete look at your site's activity.

You access the Jobs Report simply by completing the following steps, which are similar to those you use to access the Exceptions Report.

1. Log in to your site using an administration account.
2. Click Control Panel.
3. Click Administration.
4. Click Reports, then on Jobs Report.

Now that you have access to the Jobs Report, let's take a look at the specific information provided. Again, it should be noted that, like the Exceptions Report, there is no convenient Export button to export the job details into any external document format. Therefore, to export the report you must copy and paste the data into an external file, such as a Microsoft Word file.

At the top of the report are overall statistics about all of the jobs installed on your site. The Jobs Service Statistics section relates to when the jobs were installed and the last time they were run. In addition, you will see if they are currently running and how much time has elapsed between running the jobs. From this information you should be able to predict the next time that the jobs will run. For example, if they were last run at 5:00 pm, and 15 minutes exist between running the jobs, then you can safely predict that they will be run again at 5:15 pm. Furthermore, if you wait 15 minutes, you can test your prediction by refreshing the report and seeing if the statistics were updated to reflect this latest execution time.

Aside from the statistics that are provided at the top of the report, there are statistics that are provided for each job. These jobs are conveniently divided by whether they are sharing a thread or whether they are run in their own thread. By default, the majority of your jobs will share a thread; only the Feed Updater and Email Jobs are on their own thread. When looking at the type of thread, you will notice that it is the full namespace to the job. This can be helpful in locating the code that is executing for a particular job by searching for this namespace and class name in the Community Server SDK. You are also presented with information about whether the job is enabled and whether it is currently running. In addition, you can to view the timestamp showing when each job was last run along with the time it ended successfully. You will probably notice that most of the jobs finish in less than a second; therefore, the times when they began and ended are the same.

Site Reports

There are several reports that are used to display statistics about the site as a whole. These are important because they can help gauge the overall activity of the community. In addition, these reports are useful for determining what pages are gaining the most traction and attracting the most users.

Page Views

The Page Views Report is a convenient way to learn about what pages on your site are the most popular. It is quite straightforward, providing the URL of each page that has visits along with the number of visits received for that page. In addition, you are provided with a button to export your report to a Microsoft Excel spreadsheet. This can be a useful way to track visitor trends on your site. For example, if you want to track what pages are viewed the most often on Monday versus Friday, then you can change your date range to include each day and then generate the report for Monday and Friday. After you have generated the report, you can export them both to an Excel file and compare the results side by side and see what pages were the most popular on each day.

To access the Page Views Report, you will need to at least have the Standard Edition of Community Server installed and then complete the following steps (see Figure 9-2):

1. Log in to your site using an administrator account.
2. Click Control Panel.
3. Click Reporting.
4. Expand the Site menu and click Page Views.

Figure 9-2: Page Views Report

One of the ways that you can use the information from this report to improve your site is to fine-tune the pages with the most activity. If there are only a couple of pages on your site receiving all of the traffic, then you may want to fine-tune the site so that these pages are delivered faster. Perhaps you could try to cut down on any unnecessary bandwidth that is used to generate these pages — trim the graphics on these pages or fine-tune the markup on the pages. In addition, you may also want to look for ways to make the content on your site more targeted now that you know what content your visitors are looking for. What you do with the information from this report is up to you; simply knowing how to generate the report for different dates is enough to get you started.

User Activity

The User Activity Report displays information regarding how many visitors your site has had, along with information on how many pages each user viewed. The first piece of information, how many users visited your site, is always important to know. It allows you to know how many users are registering on your site versus only viewing it anonymously. This can help an administrator know when a community is growing with active users and not only users who visit the site once.

In addition, it also informs you of whether or not site visitors are simply loading a couple of pages and leaving. This can be helpful information for knowing whether or not visitors continue to browse your site or if they leave only after viewing a couple of pages. In addition, the results of this report can be exported in the same way that other reports' results are.

Overview Report

The Overview Report displays basic information regarding how many new users have registered at your site, how many new threads were created, and how many new posts were created. It is important to understand that the posts can include forum posts, blog posts, new photos, and files as well as post comments. In addition, the Overview Report can be exported to an Excel spreadsheet. Generating this report can help you to identify whether your site is drawing new users who are registering or whether the numbers are declining.

Blog Reports

There are a few different reports that are targeted at generating statistics that relate to blogs. These will allow an administrator to determine the topics that are most popular based on different criteria. As a result, these reports are useful for gauging what posts your visitors are reading the most.

Blog Activity

The Blog Activity Report (see Figure 9-3) is divided into a couple of sections for displaying information regarding all of the blogs on your site. This information is most useful for a site that has multiple blogs where new users are able to register and create a new blog. The summary statistics display how many new blogs were created, how many were enabled or disabled, and how many were activated in the specified date range. This summary information can be a nice overview of how the current month compares to previous months in terms of new blogs or blogs being disbanded and disabled. However you decide to use this information, you should consider looking at sets of data for trends in the blog activity.

Figure 9-3: Blog Activity Report

In addition to the blog activity summary, details about each blog on your site are also provided. The blog details consist of the blog name and the number of blog posts, articles, views, comments, and trackbacks. All of these details can be sorted simply by clicking the column title. Thus, you can get an ordered list with the blog with the most comments appearing at the top of the list. Once you have the list ordered in the way you would like it to be displayed, you can easily export it to Excel by clicking the Export button.

Popular Topics by Views

The Popular Topics by Views Report is a report that you can generate in order to see the top 25 most-viewed blog posts. What is nice about this report is that it spans all of the available blogs on your site and is sorted from the most-popular post to the least-popular post. As a result, you are able to see what people are looking at the most on your site and who is drawing the most traffic. Another use for this report would be to generate a list of the top 25 topics every week and then display them to your visitors. This can be an easy way to draw attention to posts that everyone is interested in.

Popular Topics by Comments

The Popular Topics by Comments Report is very similar to the Popular Topics by Views Report, except that the list is ordered from the most-commented topic to the least-commented topic. Again, this report contains the top 25 most-commented topics that exist in all of the available blogs on your site. The information gathered from this report can be useful to help identify the most-talked-about topics. It can also be helpful for letting your visitors know what is getting the most talk time so that they can read what everyone else is talking about. Therefore, you may want to display the results of this report to your users by exporting it or manually adding it somewhere on your site.

Forum Reports

The forum reports are similar to the blog reports in that they generate statistics about a specific application on your site. Like the blog reports, they show the activity as well as the topics that are the most popular. Furthermore, the forum reports are the last of the application-specific reports that are included with Community Server.

Forum Post Activity

The Forum Post Activity Report is similar to the Blog Activity Report in that it simply provides an overview of the overall posts and number of visitors accessing the forums. The report is divided into two sections; at the top is a basic summary with the number of active forums that exist. Below that, the activity report displays information about each forum, such as the name, number of replies in the forum, number of threads, and number of active users in the forum.

The details of this report can be helpful for identifying a forum that may have a lot of active users but does not have any active replies or threads. With this information, you can deduce that the users are not contributing to the forum. In addition, you can also use this report to see what forums have the greatest number of active users. However you decide to use this report, remember that you can always export it for whatever date range that you generate the report for.

Popular Topics by Views

The Popular Topics by Views Report is a convenient place to determine what topics are receiving the most traffic. You can see a listing of the top 25 most popular topics, and it can be useful for determining what users of your site are most interested in reading about. Another important thing to realize is that the topics span forums; therefore, you are able to get a broad view of all of your forum posts.

Popular Topics by Replies

The Popular Topics by Replies Report is similar to the Popular Topics by Views Report, and shows a listing of the top 25 reports that contain the most number of replies. This is a good resource for gauging what topics are generating the most discussion. In addition, this report spans all of the forums in your site; therefore, it provides a broad look at your forum topics. One possible use for this information is to compare it to the Popular Topics by Views Report and look at whether or not both reports have the same items as being the most popular.

Custom Reports

Community Server provides a nice framework that you can use to build your own custom reports. In addition, the source code is freely available to you, so you can see how the report's front-end code is structured. However, the `CommunityServer.Reporting` project is not included with the SDK, so you are unable to view the code that actually generates the reports. Therefore, you will probably want to create your own separate project for your custom reports. For the purpose of understanding how to create a custom report, we will go through the code necessary to create a simple File Gallery Activity Report. The purpose of the report is to display basic statistics about all of the folders on a Community Server site. A large part of this report code is the basic code from the provided reports. Therefore, we can thank Telligent for providing the basic blueprint for how a report can be structured. Note that this is not the only way to go about creating a report for Community Server, but it is one that is closely in line with the reports that are provided. If you have many reports that you need to add to Community Server, you may be interested in exploring the Microsoft Report Builder that is a part of SQL Reporting Services. However, you should note that one of these reports will require a somewhat different approach to integrate it with your site's reporting Control Panel.

The Community Server Custom Report that we are building will gather the following information about all of the File Gallery folders on your site: date the folder was created, total number of files, total disk space being used, and the name of the folder. This is relatively simple information but can be helpful for identifying the overall disk space being used by a site's file gallery.

To help visualize the data that you want to display in the report, it is helpful to start by looking at the database and the data that you are aggregating. Therefore, you should spend some time studying the basic structure of the tables that you want to use in your report. For the purposes of this example, we will only using the cs_Sections and cs_Groups tables. If you want to show file gallery statistics for each individual file, you could incorporate the cs_Posts table where the individual file post is stored.

Community Server reports rely on stored procedures to aggregate the data that is being displayed. In this example, we will use a stored procedure to collect the data that we want to display. The stored procedure will allow the inputting of both a record range and a date range. Here is the stored procedure that you can add to your Community Server database to add support for the new report:

```
CREATE PROCEDURE [dbo].[cs_FileGalleryActivityReport_Get] (
  @nRecordNumberStart INT,
  @nRecordNumberEnd INT,
  @BegReportDate DateTime,
  @EndReportDate DateTime
)

AS BEGIN
  DECLARE @totalRecords INT

  DECLARE @tblTempData TABLE (
      nId INT IDENTITY, SectionId INT, GroupId INT,
      [Name] VARCHAR (100), DateCreated DATETIME,
          TotalPosts INT, TotalThreads INT, DiskUsage INT
  )

  INSERT INTO @tblTempData (
    SectionId, GroupId,
    [Name], DateCreated,
    TotalPosts, TotalThreads, DiskUsage
  )
  SELECT [cs_Sections].[SectionID], [cs_Sections].[GroupID]
      ,[cs_Sections].[Name], [cs_Sections].[DateCreated]
      ,[cs_Sections].[TotalPosts], [cs_Sections].[TotalThreads]
      ,[cs_Sections].[DiskUsage]  FROM [cs_Sections]
  INNER JOIN [cs_Groups] ON [cs_Groups].[GroupID] = [cs_Sections].[GroupID] AND
    [cs_Groups].[ApplicationType] = 6
  WHERE [cs_Sections].[IsActive] = 1 AND
    [cs_Sections].[DateCreated] BETWEEN @BegReportDate AND @EndReportDate
  ORDER BY [cs_Sections].[DateCreated]

  SET @totalRecords = @@rowcount
  -------------------------------------------------------------------------------
  SELECT [SectionID], [GroupID], [Name],
    [DateCreated], [TotalPosts],
    [TotalThreads], [DiskUsage]
```

```
        FROM @tblTempData
        WHERE nId BETWEEN
            @nRecordNumberStart AND @nRecordNumberEnd
        ORDER BY nId ASC

        SELECT @totalRecords
    END
```

In the preceding stored procedure, the application type is hard-coded to 6, which is the application type for the file gallery. If you look in the `cs_ApplicationType` table, you can see all of the types of applications available in Community Server. In addition, you will also notice that the data is placed in a temporary table, and then the final values that are returned are selected from this temporary table. The reason for this is to make it easier to provide paging support to the front-end user. This solution provides a higher level of performance than many others because it decreases the amount of data being sent to the web server to only what is required by the client. Once you have created this stored procedure, you should test it using the SQL Management Studio or Query Analyzer to make sure that it returns the appropriate data. Here is a sample of the SQL you can run to execute this stored procedure and get up to 20 records back:

SQL to test cs_FileGalleryActivityReport_Get Stored Procedure

```
DECLARE    @return_value int

EXEC   @return_value = [dbo].[cs_FileGalleryActivityReport_Get]
        @nRecordNumberStart = 1,
        @nRecordNumberEnd = 20,
        @BegReportDate = N'1-1-01',
        @EndReportDate = N'1-1-08'
```

1. To begin with, you should create a new web application project and name it `CommunityServer.CustomReports`.

2. Now, create an empty class file for each of the following classes:

   `FileGalleryActivityResultSet.cs`

   `CustomReportsSqlProvider.cs`

   `FileGalleryActivityResult.cs`

3. Open your `FileGalleryActivityResult.cs` file, and add the following code:

```
private string _name;
private int _groupId;
private DateTime _dateCreated;
private int _totalPosts;
private int _totalThreads;
private int _diskUsage;

public FileGalleryActivityResult() {
    _name = string.Empty;
    _groupId = -1;
    _dateCreated = DateTime.MinValue;
    _totalPosts = -1;
    _totalThreads = -1;
    _diskUsage = -1;
```

```
    }

    public string Name {
        get { return _name; }
        set { _name = value; }
    }

    public int GroupId {
        get { return _groupId; }
        set { _groupId = value; }
    }

    public DateTime DateCreated {
        get { return _dateCreated; }
        set { _dateCreated = value; }
    }

    public int TotalPosts {
        get { return _totalPosts; }
        set { _totalPosts = value; }
    }

    public int TotalThreads {
        get { return _totalThreads; }
        set { _totalThreads = value; }
    }

    public int DiskUsage {
        get { return _diskUsage; }
        set { _diskUsage = value; }
    }
```

This class is to be used to contain each row of data that we get back and will be used to populate a table of statistics about each individual folder. You can think of this class as being similar to a business object in some respects.

4. Now, we will add the code for the result set class that will contain a collection of the `FileGalleryActivityResult` objects. Add the following code to the `FileGalleryActivityResultSet` class. The collection of result objects will be stored in the `_records` ArrayList. Also, as displayed in the following code, the constructor creates a new `ArrayList` to avoid a null object exception.

```
private ArrayList _records;
private int _totalRecords;
private int _totalStorage;
private int _totalFiles;

public FileGalleryActivityResultSet() {
    _records = new ArrayList();
}

public ArrayList Records {
    get { return _records; }
    set { _records = value; }
```

```
    }

    public int TotalRecords {
        get { return _totalRecords; }
        set { _totalRecords = value; }
    }

    public int TotalStorage {
        get { return _totalStorage; }
        set { _totalStorage = value; }
    }

    public int TotalFiles {
        get { return _totalFiles; }
        set { _totalFiles = value; }
    }
```

5. Let's create the code to call the stored procedure and populate the results. You will get the connection string from the site's `Web.config` `SiteSqlServer` application-setting entry. Then you will call the stored procedure, passing in the values from the web form for the date range and item count range. Once you have the results, you will populate the Records ArrayList with each one for use in populating the web form that you will create. Therefore, open the `CustomReportsSqlProvider.cs` file and add the following code. Also, you should note that this is a sealed class and that the methods are static (be sure to make the `FileGalleryActivityResultSet` class public as well).

```
public sealed class CustomReportsSqlProvider {

    private static string _connectionString;

    private CustomReportsSqlProvider() { }

    static CustomReportsSqlProvider() {
        CustomReportsSqlProvider._connectionString =
            ConfigurationManager.AppSettings["SiteSqlServer"];
    }

    private static SqlConnection GetSqlConnection() {
        return new SqlConnection(CustomReportsSqlProvider._connectionString);
    }

    public static FileGalleryActivityResultSet GetFileGalleryActivityResults(int
            recordNumberStart, int recordNumberEnd, string reportDateStart,
            string reportDateEnd) {
        using (SqlConnection sqlConnection =
                CustomReportsSqlProvider.GetSqlConnection()) {
            SqlCommand sqlCommand = new
                SqlCommand("dbo.cs_FileGalleryActivityReport_Get", sqlConnection);
            FileGalleryActivityResultSet results = new FileGalleryActivityResultSet();
            sqlCommand.CommandType = CommandType.StoredProcedure;
```

```
sqlCommand.Parameters.Add("@nRecordNumberStart", SqlDbType.Int).Value =
    recordNumberStart;
sqlCommand.Parameters.Add("@nRecordNumberEnd", SqlDbType.Int).Value =
    recordNumberEnd;
sqlCommand.Parameters.Add("@BegReportDate", SqlDbType.DateTime).Value =
    reportDateStart;
sqlCommand.Parameters.Add("@EndReportDate", SqlDbType.DateTime).Value =
    reportDateEnd;
sqlConnection.Open();
using (SqlDataReader sqlReader =
    sqlCommand.ExecuteReader(CommandBehavior.CloseConnection)) {
  while (sqlReader.Read()) {
    FileGalleryActivityResult result = new FileGalleryActivityResult();
    result.DateCreated = (DateTime)sqlReader["DateCreated"];
    result.DiskUsage = (int)sqlReader["DiskUsage"];
    result.GroupId = (int)sqlReader["GroupID"];
    result.Name = sqlReader["Name"] as string;
    result.TotalPosts = (int)sqlReader["TotalPosts"];
    result.TotalThreads = (int)sqlReader["TotalThreads"];
    results.TotalFiles += result.TotalPosts;
    results.TotalStorage += result.DiskUsage;
    results.Records.Add(result);
    }
  sqlReader.NextResult();
  sqlReader.Read();
  results.TotalRecords = (int)sqlReader[0];
  sqlReader.Close();
  }
sqlCommand.Dispose();
sqlConnection.Close();
return results;
      }
    }
  }
```

At this point, you should be able to compile the project and have it build successfully. If you encounter any build errors, make sure that you have updated your `using` statements and have the appropriate references in the project. All that is left is to create a front-end web form page that you can use to get the report data and display it to the user.

Integrating a Custom Report

Now that you have a project created and a custom report in it ready to go, you can build a page that will display the report to the user. Please keep in mind that a lot of the code for this page came from the `BlogActivityReport.aspx` page that comes with Community Server. The reason for using this existing page is so that a consistent look can be maintained for all reports. You will notice that the page uses a `ComponentArt` control as well as a custom Community Server control. Therefore, ensure that your project references are updated to point to the Community Server web project and the `ComponentArt.Web.UI` library.

To integrate the report into the structure of the other reports, you will want to create a new web form page and copy it to the `ControlPanel/Reporting` directory. Additionally, you should add an entry to the `NavBar.config` file inside your Reporting folder to create a navigational link to the new report page. You can begin by creating a new web form in the `CommunityServer.CustomReports` project and calling it `FileGalleryActivityReport.aspx`.

1. Add the following in the `NavBar.config` file inside the Tabs section, which is located in your `ControlPanel/Reporting` folder (see Figure 9-4):

```
<Tab text="File Gallery" name="FileReports">
   <SubTabs>
      <Tab text="Activity Report"
         href="~/ControlPanel/Reporting/FileGalleryActivityReport.aspx"
         name="FileGalleryActivityReport" />
   </SubTabs>
</Tab>
```

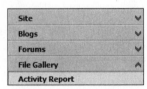

Figure 9-4 Activity Report Added to NavBar.config

2. Add the following code to the `FileGalleryActivityReport.aspx.cs` file. Also, if you need an example of other reports' code behind, you should look at the other pages in your reporting folder.

Be sure to include the following namespaces in your code behind:

```
using System.Web.UI.HtmlControls;

using CommunityServer.Components;

using CommunityServer.ControlPanel.UI;

using CommunityServer.ControlPanel.Tools.Reports;

using CA = ComponentArt.Web.UI;

public partial class FileActivityReport : BaseToolsPage {
    protected CA.Grid Grid1;
    protected ActivityQueryControl FileGalleryActivityQueryControl1;
    protected Label lblTotalFiles;
    protected Label lblTotalGalleries;
    protected Label lblTotalStorage;
    int _recordCount = 0;

    protected void Page_Load(object sender, EventArgs e) {
```

```
            if (!Page.IsPostBack && !this.IsCallBack)
                Bind();
    }

    private void Bind() {
        FileGalleryActivityResultSet results = BuildReportData();
        Grid1.DataSource = results.Records;
        _recordCount = results.TotalRecords;
        lblTotalFiles.Text = results.TotalFiles.ToString("#,###");
        lblTotalStorage.Text = results.TotalStorage.ToString("#,###");
        lblTotalGalleries.Text = results.TotalRecords.ToString("#,###");
        Grid1.DataBind();
        Grid1.RecordCount = _recordCount;
    }

    private FileGalleryActivityResultSet BuildReportData() {
        CSContext context = CSContext.Current;
        string begReportDate = "1/1/1900";
        string endReportDate = "1/1/1900";
        int startRecord;
        int endRecord;
        Grid1.PageSize = 20;

        startRecord = (Grid1.CurrentPageIndex * Grid1.PageSize) + 1;
        endRecord = ((Grid1.CurrentPageIndex + 1) * Grid1.PageSize);

        if (Globals.IsDate(context.QueryString["brd"])) {
            begReportDate = context.QueryString["brd"];
            FileGalleryActivityQueryControl1.BegSearchReportDatePicker =
                DateTime.Parse(begReportDate);
            FileGalleryActivityQueryControl1.BegSearchReportDateCalendar =
                DateTime.Parse(begReportDate);
        }
        if (Globals.IsDate(context.QueryString["erd"])) {
            endReportDate = context.QueryString["erd"];
            FileGalleryActivityQueryControl1.EndSearchReportDatePicker =
                DateTime.Parse(endReportDate);
            FileGalleryActivityQueryControl1.BegSearchReportDateCalendar =
                DateTime.Parse(endReportDate);
        }

        return CustomReportsSqlProvider.GetFileGalleryActivityResults(startRecord,
            endRecord, begReportDate, endReportDate);
    }

    protected override void OnInit(EventArgs e) {
        Grid1.PageIndexChanged += new
      ComponentArt.Web.UI.Grid.PageIndexChangedEventHandler(Grid1_PageIndexChanged);
        Grid1.NeedDataSource += new
            ComponentArt.Web.UI.Grid.NeedDataSourceEventHandler(Grid1_NeedDataSource);
```

```
        Grid1.NeedRebind += new
            ComponentArt.Web.UI.Grid.NeedRebindEventHandler(Grid1_NeedRebind);
        this.Load += new EventHandler(this.Page_Load);
        base.OnInit(e);
    }

    void Grid1_NeedRebind(object sender, EventArgs e) {
        Grid1.DataBind();
        Grid1.RecordCount = _recordCount;
        lblTotalGalleries.Text = _recordCount.ToString();
    }

    void Grid1_NeedDataSource(object sender, EventArgs e) {
        FileGalleryActivityResultSet results = BuildReportData();
        Grid1.DataSource = results.Records;
        _recordCount = results.TotalRecords;
        lblTotalGalleries.Text = _recordCount.ToString();
    }

    void Grid1_PageIndexChanged(object sender, CA.GridPageIndexChangedEventArgs
        args) {
        Grid1.CurrentPageIndex = args.NewIndex;
    }
}
```

To get the preceding code to work correctly, you will also need to add the appropriate controls to your HTML code. These controls should consist of a `ComponentArt` grid control and a few labels to display the overall statistics of the report. To get a good idea of what this front-end code should look like, refer to the code on the `BlogActivityReport` page. The important thing is to replace the columns with the ones for the file gallery. Here is what these columns should look like in your HTML code so that they bind to the correct data field:

```
<columns>
    <CA:gridcolumn width="150" datafield="Name" headingtext="Gallery Name" />
     <CA:gridcolumn width="150" datafield="TotalPosts" headingtext="Total Files"
        FormatString="#,###" />
     <CA:gridcolumn width="150" datafield="DiskUsage" headingtext="Disk Usage"
        FormatString="#,###"/>
</columns>
```

Once you have the page ready, you simply need to copy it to the `ControlPanel/Reporting` folder and run it in the web browser by clicking the new reporting menu link to File Gallery. You can follow the same process to create other reports in the future using Community Server. In addition, you may not always be required to create your own stored procedure because there are existing statistics that you can gather about different areas of Community Server. There is a great potential for new reports to be created for Community Server; currently only a small portion of a site is covered by the provided reports.

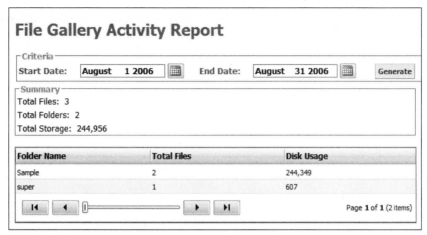

Figure 9-5: A Generated File Gallery Activity Report

Summary

In this chapter, you learned about the different reports that are available in Community Server. Specifically, you learned about the general site, blogs, and forums reports. All of these reports, as you have observed, combine to create a useful perspective on a community site for any administrator. In addition, you have also learned how to create your own report and extend Community Server's reporting capabilities. This knowledge will be useful whenever you need to look at your community site from a different perspective by creating a new report.

In the next chapter, you will learn about the different configuration options that are available in Community Server, including the various configuration files and how to change them.

10

Core Configuration Options

The configuration files found in the Community Server install directory are useful for changing a site's core functionality without having to alter any source code. In addition to a `web.config` file, which is installed with every ASP.NET application, Community Server also includes the `CommunityServer.config` and `SiteURLs.config` files. These files are simply configuration files that allow users to set some application-wide options such as the database connection string. Thus, both ASP.NET and Community Server utilize XML configuration files that are editable in any text editor.

The Community Server configuration files are well documented and a great resource for learning more about the various configuration options available. If you read through the documentation in these files, you should obtain a good understanding of what can be configured. If you would like to learn more about a particular configuration option beyond what is available in this chapter, you should read the documentation inside each configuration file or visit the online documentation at `http://docs.communityserver.org`.

ASP.NET Configuration

ASP.NET provides a configuration system that allows for machine-wide settings to be overridden with more specific site- or even directory-level settings. All settings are configured either at machine level, web application level, or directory level.

The base level, known as machine-level configuration, is defined in a file called `machine.config`. There is a single instance of `machine.config` for each .NET Framework version installed on the server. There is also an optional `web.config` file for configuring all web applications running on a particular system. The `web.config` file is placed in the root of a given web application and overrides settings specified in `machine.config` file. Beyond the application-level `web.config` file, there is another optional `web.config` file that exists on a per-directory basis and can be placed in each directory within a web application. Directory-level `web.config` files are useful for securing files in a specific directory; however, directory-level web configuration has a limited number of settings that can be specified. At runtime, an application uses a merged view of all configuration settings to determine the runtime configuration settings of the web application.

Often, these default settings will be modified and extended to meet the requirements of the respective application. Some of these common configuration sections include the ability to define connection strings, error-handling behavior, security, and HTTP modules or handlers, just to name a few items. If you need to go beyond this high-level overview, then it may be helpful to consult the MSDN documentation that is available from Microsoft.

In addition, it is also useful to understand that making changes to a `web.config` file causes the web server to refresh a running web application. Whenever you *touch* the `web.config` file, which simply means that the modified timestamp on the file changes, the web application utilizing the configuration file will be restarted or refreshed.

While modifying the `web.config` in version 1.0 and 1.1 of ASP.NET did cause the entire web application to reset, the ASP.NET team is doing work to only cause application-level resets when necessary. Modifications to an ASP.NET 2.0 application's `web.config` file only cause application resets for changes to specific configuration elements. Consult the MSDN documentation for more details.

ASP.NET Configuration and Community Server

Community Server uses the `web.config` file in a way that is common to any standard ASP.NET application. Community Server uses the provider pattern for handling a user's profile, role management, site membership, and handling anonymous user. These custom providers are defined in the `web.config` file in the root of the web site. In addition, Community Server uses the main `web.config` file to contain the connection string that it uses to connect to the database. Note that this file also contains the specific providers for logging a user in to the site; improper alterations of this file can result in dire consequences to your site, so be careful whenever you make any changes to it. To help protect your site, it is important to make a backup of the `web.config` file before you make changes to it. If you have a running backup, then you will be able to easily roll back to a stable version of the `web.config` file.

That being said, you should still look at the `web.config` file in the Community Server's root directory to get a better grasp of its usefulness. To do this, I recommend either using Visual Studio or Notepad as an editor. However, before you open the `web.config` file, make sure that you make a backup copy of it, just in case you accidentally remove an important setting. Now that you have made your backup copy, it is safe to open the `web.config` file using your editor of choice.

Common ASP.NET Sections

Most `web.config` files have several configuration sections; Community Server defines several custom configuration sections as well. To do each section justice, we will go through them one at a time, looking at what they are used for, along with some optional parameters that you can use to change their default settings.

Membership Section

Description	Use this section to define custom providers and to alter the Community Server provider in order to control where and how user accounts are stored.
userIsOnlineTimeWindow	The amount of time that a session remains active after a user becomes inactive. This value is in minutes; the default is 15 minutes.
hashAlgorithmType	The name of the algorithm to use for hashing data. The default is SHA1.
defaultProvider	The name of the default provider to use; if you have more than one provider available, then you should specify a default provider.

Community Server SQL Membership Provider

Description	This provider is used to connect to the database for storing membership data for users. The source code for this provider can be found under the MemberRole project as the CSMembershipProvider class. You will find that it is amazingly simple, inheriting most of its functionality from SqlMembershipProvider.
connectionStringName	The name of the connection string in the connection section to use.
enablePasswordRetrieval	A Boolean value indicating if password retrieval is enabled.
enablePasswordReset	A Boolean value indicating whether or not a user a user's password can be reset.
requiresQuestionAndAnswer	Specifies whether or not to require that a user account have a question and secret answer before the user account is created.
requiresUniqueEmail	Specifies if a unique email address is required for each account for the account to be considered valid. Enabling this is a good way to alleviate duplicate user accounts.
passwordFormat	The default value is Hashed; specifies how the password will be stored.
applicationName	The name of your installation environment.
description	A short description of your provider; this is a standard attribute of all of the providers.
maxInvalidPasswordAttempts	The number of failed password attempts before an account is locked.
passwordAttemptWindow	The timeout in minutes before a login request is cancelled.

Table continued on following page

minRequiredPasswordLength	The minimum number of characters that are required for a password to be considered valid.
minRequiredNonalphanumericCharacters	The minimum number of characters that are neither digits nor alphabetic characters that must be included in a password before a password is considered valid.

In .NET 2.0, it is possible to specify custom profile information within an application's configuration file and have that information accessible in a strongly typed way from the application itself. You are now able to define custom profile properties in the web.config file that are exposed as properties on the ProfileCommon class. As a result of this new feature, you are able to easily extend and capture custom information about a user during the registration process quite easily in Community Server. Before we go over how to define custom profile properties, it will be helpful to look at the default configuration of the profile section in the web.config file.

Profile Section

Description	Use this section to define what profile properties you would like to capture for each user. Usually, profiles consist of at least the user's first and last name, but additional information may be captured to help identify each user.
Enabled	Boolean value to determine if the entire profile section is turned on.
automaticSaveEnabled	Whether of not the profile should be automatically saved whenever a change is made.
defaultProvider	The name of the provider that will be used if no other provider is explicitly stated.

Community Server SQL Profile Provider

Description	Used to define where the profile data will be stored for your site members.
connectionStringName	The unique name of your connection string entry; this will help identify it in code.
applicationName	The name of the application; this property is inherited for Community Server providers.

Role Manager Section

Description	Use this section to specify how user roles should be handled. A role can be any useful title applied to one or more application privileges. For example, a role might be Admin, which provides access to every aspect of an application.
cacheRolesInCookie	A Boolean used to determine if the roles should be stored in a cookie for faster access from the client.

cookieName	A unique name used to describe your cookie; it will be used to name the cookie.
cookieTimeout	The length of time, in minutes, before a cookie is removed after not being accessed for an extended amount of time.
cookiePath	The default value is the root path, or "/" used for describing the path that the cookie will be stored in.
cookieRequireSSL	Whether or not SSL is required for a cookie to function correctly. The default value is false; turn this on if you have SSL enabled on your server and functioning appropriately throughout your application.
cookieSlidingExpiration	A Boolean value indicating whether or not to use a sliding expiration time. If it is enabled, which it is by default, the cookie timeout will be set from the last time that a cookie was accessed. If the timeout is 15 minutes, the cookie's life will end only 15 minutes after the last time that a cookie was accessed. Otherwise, it would simply be 15 minutes from when the cookie was created.
createPersistentCookie	A Boolean value to determine whether or not a cookie will remain alive long after a user is done using your site.
cookieProtection	Determines the type of protection to place on your cookie to prevent it from being tampered with. The default is All; however, you can optionally change this to None, Validation, or Encryption.
maxCachedResults	The maximum number of roles to cache in a cookie; the default is 1000.
defaultProvider	The name of the provider to use as the default whenever none are explicitly stated.
domain	Used to add a domain property to the cookie.

Community Server SQL Role Provider

Description	Defines how the roles used for determining a user's permissions will be stored and handled. For example, the ASP.NET membership classes provide a default way to retrieve information about the roles that a particular user has.
connectionStringName	The name of the connection string to use for a provider. The corresponding connection string should exist in the connection string section of the configuration file.
applicationName	The name of the application instance; the default is dev. This property is created by Community Server and is not a part of the inherited .NET properties.

In addition to the common sections listed previously, there are also several other sections that are important to recognize. These other sections vary from providing security to assisting in the debugging of an application. Instead of going into depth about each one, I will simply offer a brief description of each. If you would like to learn more about a specific section, then I highly encourage you to look at Microsoft's MSDN documentation.

Standard Web Configuration Sections

compilation	Offers a way to specify the language of the application, such as C#. In addition, you can specify whether it should be compiled in debug mode.
pages	Allows you to define settings for all of the pages in your application. These settings are usually found in the page directives of pages, such as autoEventWireup.
trace	Defines whether custom trace statements are generated when accessing your application either internally or externally.
sessionState	Allows you to specify a location for state data if it is enabled, including the connection to the server.
customErrors	Offers a way to handle unhandled exceptions. Usually a page is redirected to, and the exception is displayed to those accessing the site locally (remoteOnly).
httpModules	Defines custom HTTP modules for a site that respond to events that occur throughout a request.
httpHandlers	Defines custom HTTP handlers for controlling how specific pages or file types are presented.
authentication	Allows you to specify Forms or Windows authentication for a site, as well as how to store this authentication data (usually a cookie).

appSettings Section

The appSettings section is useful for providing a key value collection of configurable items specific to an application. Compared to many ASP.NET applications, Community Server just barely scratches the surface with respect to this section, but there are a few settings because of the CommunityServer .config and SiteUrls.config files. The appSettings section can be useful if you decide to extend Community Server, because it provides a convenient place to add custom configuration options.

Community Server Standard Application Settings

SiteSqlServer	The database connection string; usually contains a user ID, password, database name, and database server. This is required for Community Server to connect to the database.
SiteSqlServerOwner	The database owner for the Community Server database; usually it is dbo.
MachineValidationMode	An entry used to describe the type of hash used to create the machine keys. The default value is SHA1; however, you should not change this unless you know exactly what you are doing.
ClientScriptLocation	The relative path to the ComponentArt client.

CommunityServer.config

The `CommunityServer.config` file is the core configuration file for many of the Community Server–specific components. There is a special class that was designed just for handling this file. The class is `CSConfiguration` and it controls how the `CommunityServer.config` file is read and stored in the cache. The `CommunityServer.config` file contains the registration details for many of the providers that are used by Community Server. In addition, it also contains core configuration options, the paths to specific applications, the details for installed modules, and application-specific options for everything from blogs to galleries. Therefore, this configuration file plays a critical role in the usefulness of Community Server.

Core Options

The `CommunityServer.config` file wraps all of the various configuration options inside of the `<CommunityServer>` tag. The first entries you will find inside of this tag are the attributes that compose the `<Core>` tag. The file itself does a good job of explaining what each of the attributes allows you to do. Therefore, I will quickly present a couple of situations when you might want to change these attributes. After these examples, you will find the list of all of the available attributes and a short description of the purpose of each.

Suppose that you have translated Community Server to the Danish language and are planning for new users to all speak Danish as their primary language. Therefore, you would like to enable Community Server to default to the Danish language for all new users. A simple way to accomplish this task would be to change the entry for `defaultLanguage` to equal the language key of `da-DK`. This key can be found in the `languages.xml` file located in the `Languages` directory.

Now, suppose that you want to conserve all of the available bandwidth on your server so that it is used only to deliver content to site visitors. It would be desirable to remove any calls to other sources that do not provide content to your visitors. One of the calls that you can remove is `enableLatestVersionCheck`, which makes a call to an outside service to determine what the latest version of Community Server is. As a result, you decide to change the default value of this setting to false to eliminate this extra call.

CommunityServer.config Core Configuration Options

Name	Description
defaultLanguage	The code used to represent the default language that you will be using on your site; the default value is `en-US`. If you have installed another language that you would like to use throughout your site, then this is the place to tell Community Server to change languages.
disableEmail	Boolean value to tell Community Server whether or not to disable all email processing on the installation containing the respective configuration file; the default is `false`.

Table continued on following page

Name	Description
disableIndexing	Boolean value to disable all indexing of the .NET cache. The default is false, which you should really never change.
disableThreading	Boolean value used to force Community Server to use a single thread only. The default is false and should really never change. If you set this to true, then you will most likely notice performance degradation.
smtpServerConnectionLimit	The maximum number of connections to make when sending email to the SMTP server. The default is -1, which means that no limit is imposed.
enableLatestVersionCheck	Boolean value to determine if your installation should check whether or not your site is up to date with the most current Community Server version; the default is true.
systemType	The type of system that is running; the options are Self, DNN, and SharePoint. The default is Self.
backwardsCompatiblePasswswords	A Boolean value used to determine whether or not to try to upgrade an older account to the new password format before failing. The default value is false.
textEditorType	A reference to the assembly and main type for the text editors.
ssl	Determines what types of pages to require SSL. The default is Ignore, which means that it does not matter what pages use SSL. You can optionally set it to Password, which means to use SSL on pages that are passing passwords. The final option is to use All, which requires SSL on all pages.
defaultRoles	The default roles to accept for users accessing the site if none are provided. The default is to allow Everyone and Registered Users.
wwwStatus	Determines how to validate a site if a www begins the site's URL. The default is Ignore to ignore if a www exists; you can optionally change this to Require, which means that a www must begin the URL. Finally, this can be Remove, which means that a www cannot begin the URL.
enableVirtualization	The default value is false; however, this property is not really used. You could actually remove the entry from the configuration and be fine doing so.
enableProductListing	Boolean value indicating whether or not to query the products available at the Telligent store and display them on the manage licenses page; the default is true.

Name	Description
enableUsersOnline	Boolean value used to override whether or not to display the users that are currently online. The default is `true`.
announcementRssUrl	The URL to the RSS feed that is displayed on the administration dashboard main page.

Understanding the Markup Section

The purpose of the `markup` section inside of the `CommunityServer.config` file is to provide a location for specifying HTML tags that are allowed in posts. Anything that is not listed in this section will be removed from post content.

One of the big motivations for stripping away tags from posts is to help safeguard your site from malicious users. If a malicious user is able to post JavaScript, then he or she would be able to create all kinds of nasty things that your site visitors would be infected with. The thing to realize is that a post becomes part of the underlying code that executes when a user visits that particular page. Therefore, being able to add JavaScript or form fields to a page can mislead users into inadvertently providing private information to these malicious users. Fortunately, the `markup` section is available to take care of filtering out these potentially hazardous tags. It is important to note that the content editor for ads does not restrict JavaScript. The average user on your site, however, is not going to be accessing the ad content editor, so you should feel safe about its allowing JavaScript. You should also realize that most ad services, such as Google AdSense, require JavaScript support for their ads to be placed on your site.

The `markup` section supports both tags and attributes. If you would like to allow support for the `hreflang` attribute of an anchor tag, then your resulting anchor tag entry would look like the following (note that the `hreflang` attribute was added to the end of the list of the attributes already enabled):

```
<a href="true" title="true" name="true" target="true" rel="true" hreflang="true" />
```

If you do not want to include an attribute or a tag, you simply need to remove it from the `markup` section or set the value on that attribute to `"false"`. Anything marked `true` will be allowed and anything marked `false` will be removed. Any attributes not listed will be removed. Another important thing to recognize is that the tags are organized inside an `<html>` tag. This is telling Community Server that all of the allowed tags must reside inside of an `<html>` tag to be considered valid. Therefore, an anchor tag appearing outside of an `<html>` tag will be removed from a post. This is important as it helps to keep the resulting code valid.

Gallery Options

The `gallery` section appears toward the beginning of all of the feature-specific sections and is used to configure the photo gallery. Reading the documentation that is provided at the top of the `gallery` section in the `communityserver.config` file is a good place to learn more about each of the options. As a result of the wealth of documentation already provided, I will simply list out a table, similar to the previous ones, with the name of the option and a short description about each.

Community Server Photo Gallery Options

allowEncodedUnicodeCharsInMetadata	Boolean value indicating whether or not metadata should be configured to allow encoded Unicode characters. The default is true and, unless you are using SQL Server 2000 SP4 or a recent version of SQL Server 2005, you should leave it alone.
enableFileSystemStorage	Indicates if you would like images to be stored on a file system in addition to or in replacement of a database. The default value is true, which is usually fine to leave.
fileSystemStorageLocation	A path to the location where images should be stored if the enableFilesSystemStorage option is true.
enableDataStoreStorage	Indicates whether or not to store images in the database. If you would like to prevent attachment images from being stored in the database and file system, then you may consider switching this to false for attachment images. However, if you notice degradation in performance, you will more than likely want to change this back to true.
enableDirectLinks	Indicates whether or not users have direct access to images stored on the file system regardless of their security level. The default is false because true would bypass the permissions of images.
Extensions	A case-sensitive list of valid image extensions that can be uploaded and handled by the photo gallery. The default is all, meaning that any file is valid.

Weblog Options

There are several core configuration options that are available in the weblog section. In addition it is important to note that many of these options are configurable in the blog administration pages. Therefore, you should not feel as though the configuration files are the only places that you can change many of these settings. For example, the aggregate post count is an option on the general options administration page as well as being an option in the weblog section of the communityserver.config file.

❏   defaultTheme — Specifies the name of the theme to use for blogs. This will be used when a blog theme that a user chooses is missing a skin or view that needs to be displayed. The default value for this option is the default theme. This option is useful in the example where a user chooses the default2 theme for their blog and then proceeds to add a feature that is not a part of the default2 theme pack. In this situation, Community Server will look at the defaultTheme setting to find the missing skin files.

❏   enableSkinCache — Indicates whether or not to cache the blog skin files on the server or reload them per request. The default value for this option is true.

❑ `enableThemes` — Indicates if you would like users to be able to change the theme of their blog. The default for this option is `true`, and unless you are required to have a uniform look across all blogs, then you should leave this setting at `true`.

❑ `aggregatePostSize` — The maximum number of characters to display when a post is aggregated. The default is 250, which is enough of a size to allow a user to read a couple of the beginning sentences of a post. If you would like to display more of a post's content whenever it is aggregated, then you could increase this number.

❑ `createDirectories` — A Boolean value indicating whether or not to create a new directory for each blog that is created. The default value is `true`, which means that each blog on a site will get its own directory from the perspective of someone accessing the site.

❑ `enableCommentRedirects` — A Boolean value indicating whether or not to redirect users to a new page whenever viewing a blogs comments; the default value is `true`.

❑ `servicePostCountLimit` — The maximum number of posts that are returned from a call to one of the blog services. This will most commonly be used when looking at your post history using the MetaBlog API. The default value is 25.

❑ `aggregatePostCount` — The maximum number of posts returned from requesting an aggregate list of posts. This is useful for controlling how many posts will be displayed on the main blog page. The default value is 25.

❑ `individualPostCount` — The maximum number of posts that will be displayed on a users main blog aggregate page, as well as the number that will be returned to feed aggregators subscribing to a blog. The default value is 15.

The preceding list contains the main configuration options for the `weblog` section in the `communityserver.config` file. There are more options, however, that are listed under the `<AttachmentSettings>` tag under the `weblog` section. These other options are similar to the photo gallery settings in that they indicate the valid file types and storage location of attachments to posts. Therefore, refer to the "Photo Gallery" section for more specific information about the options available to weblog file attachments.

Forum Options

The forum has an `<AttachmentSettings>` tag for configuring how file attachments will be handled that is similar to that of the weblog and photo gallery. To learn more about the specific options, refer to the photo gallery table describing what is available for configuring a forum file attachment. Also, you should realize that under most configurations many users do not have access to attach files to forum posts. Therefore, this should factor in any changes that you make to this section. The documentation that is provided in the `communityserver.config` file above the `forum` section is a great place to learn more about the various configuration options for file attachments.

File Gallery Options

Because file configuration options have already been covered in the `AttachmentSettings` tags described in other sections, I will not go into any further depth about what they are here. If you would like to learn more about what options are available, refer to the photo gallery discussion of the `<AttachmentSettings>` tag. However, I will explain some considerations for the way you might want to change this section of the file gallery.

If you are planning to upload many large files and you have a relatively small maximum database size, then you may want to set the `enableDataStoreStorage` property to `false`. This will prevent the files that you upload into the file gallery from being stored in your database. You should note, however, that the main purpose of having both modes of storage is so that you can have an easily accessible backup of your files. This is useful in a scenario where files are no longer accessible in a database but are still available on the file system. Therefore, you should consider this when disabling either of these modes of storage.

Reader Options

The options that are configurable under the `reader` section affect not only the Reader but also the blog roller because the two are almost one component. Therefore, keep in mind the implications of any changes that you make to the reader because this will impact the blog roller. Now that you are aware of the implications, take a look at the following list of available configuration options:

❑ `LastModifiedInterval` — Perhaps the most important option is this one as it indicates how current the information that your roller and Reader will be. This is a numeric value that determines how many minutes to wait between updating the feeds that you have subscribed to. The default value is 60; therefore, your feeds will be updated every hour. However, if you are running a news site or any other site that requires up-to-the-minute information you may want to decrease this number. Conversely, if you are running a site that does not require this information to be updated as frequently, or if the sources you subscribe to are not updated often, consider increasing this number so that the job will not be run as often.

❑ `Roles` — Indicates the user roles that have access to the reader. The default values are for `SystemAdministrator` and the `FeedReaderAdministrator` to be able to access a Reader.

❑ `TruncationLength` — This is the maximum number of characters to display on the roller page. The default value is 500, which is configurable in the `settings` section of the administration menu.

Understanding the CSModules Section

The `CSModules` section is where you would control what modules to use on your site. It is really nothing more than a name value collection of module names and the assemblies to find the module. As you would expect with a collection, you are provided with add and remove options for each module.

❑ `add` — Indicates that the following name and value should be added to the `CSModules` collection. The new entry will be added to the end of the collection.

❑ `remove` — Indicates that the entry that follows in the `CSModules` collection should be removed if it exists. In most situations, this is not that useful as you can generally simply delete an entry from the `CSModules` section and do not have to explicitly remove it using the `remove` keyword.

The syntax for adding a new module to Community Server is to specify a unique name that will identify the module internally. Second, you need to set the type to the fully qualified name of the module, add the namespace plus module class name, and then place a comma and insert the name of the assembly that contains the module. The assembly should be placed in the `bin` folder of your Community Server installation; otherwise, the assembly will not be able to be initialized correctly.

For further information regarding the modules, refer to Chapter 11. This chapter is a great place to learn about how to create your own module and also how to install or uninstall a module.

Understanding the Jobs Section

The `jobs` section is similar to the `CSModules` section in that it is also nothing more than a name-value collection of available jobs to run. Also, it is important to understand that a job is quite simply a function or set of functions that runs in the background of your site. For example, the feed updater, which updates the aggregated feeds on the main page, runs every minute. This is something that a site administrator does not have to start; instead, Community Server manages the job and knows when to run it.

In addition to the standard `add` and `remove` options, `job` entries also allow more advanced configuration options to control each particular job. Here is a listing of these available options; to see them in action simply refer to the `jobs` section of the `communityserver.config` file.

❏ `minutes` — The number of minutes to wait between running jobs. You can override this value on a per-job basis, meaning that you can make a job run more frequently or less frequently.

❏ `singleThread` — Boolean value that determines whether or not to run the jobs on a single thread. If a particular job requires more than one thread you can add a `singleThread` attribute and set it to `false`.

❏ `enabled` — Boolean value that determines whether or not a particular job is enabled. If you would like to uninstall a job and leave its entry in the configuration file, set its enabled value to `false`.

The `SiteUrls.config` file plays a key role in helping Community Server be usable. Without the `SiteUrls.config` file, Community Server would have to have a lot of hard-coded URLs throughout its source code and would lack any real flexibility for adding new pages. Because of the `SiteUrls.config` file, Community Server is knows where to find the pages that make up the application. You can think of the `SiteUrls.config` file as a place that provides all of the application paths for an installation, from where to navigate when someone clicks a link in the navigation menu to where to look when someone subscribes to a blog RSS feed. Thus, the accuracy of the `SiteUrls.config` file is critical for avoiding broken links and making your site's links function as they should. You should always have a backup copy of your current `SiteUrls.config` file.

Common Sections

One of the most useful sections of any of the configuration files is the `navigation` section of the `SiteUrls.config` file. It allows you to add links to your navigation menu, as well as control which users will be able to see them. In addition, you are able to specify whether the text and resulting link are read from a resource file or are defined directly in the configuration file. For example, the link text and navigational URL for the `blog` menu item is read from the `Resources.xml` file located under the appropriate language subfolder of the root `Languages` folder. Let's examine the entry in the `SiteUrls.config` file for this navigational item in the `navigation` section.

```
<link name="blog" resourceUrl="webloghome" resourceName="weblogs" roles="Everyone"
    applicationType = "Weblog" />
```

The name attribute defines a key label for this entry; it is also how this link will be selected when a user is viewing a page that is part of the blog link. If you look at the BlogMaster.ascx master page, you can see that the blog menu item is selected whenever a page uses this master page because of the following line:

BlogMaster.ascx
```
<CS:SelectedNavigation Selected = "blog" runat="Server" />
```

Next, there is resourceUrl, which controls where users will be redirected whenever they click the blog menu item. You are not required to use a resourceUrl. Instead, you are free to define a URL using the navigateUrl attribute. If you were to define the navigateUrl for the blog link, it would look like navigateUrl="/blogs/default.aspx". Moreover, by using navigateUrl, you are able to more easily link to external resources. For example, if you wanted to add a link to MSDN, you could make navigateUrl equal http://msdn.microsoft.com.

In the blog example, the link is found with the combination of the webloghome entry inside the URL section and the weblogs entry inside of the location section of SiteUrls.config. Let's consider an abbreviated version of these other sections to understand how they are compounded together. As you can see, the resourceUrl points to the webloghome entry inside of <urls>, which then points to the weblogs entry inside of <location>, which results in the /blogs/default.aspx path:

```
<urls>
    <url name="webloghome" location="weblogs" path="default.aspx" />
</urls>

<locations>
    <location name="weblogs" path="/blogs/" />
</locations>
```

If you wanted to specify the actual text that is displayed in the navigation menu, then you would either use text or resourceName. Whenever you use resourceName, Community Server looks in the Resources.xml file located in your Languages directory for an appropriate entry. In the following example, Blogs will be used as the link text. However, you are free to change this text to a different value, depending on what you would like displayed.

Resources.xml
```
<resource name="weblogs">Blogs</resource>
```

In addition to being able to change the text displayed, you are also able to control whether or not a link appears for a particular user. You can list the roles that you would like the link to be visible for. For example, if you specify SystemAdmin as a role, and a user with the SystemAdmin role logs in, then he or she will be able to see the link. If you do not specify any role at all, the link defaults to Everyone.

Configuration Changes

When making any configuration changes to the SiteUrls.config file, it is important to remember that you should first make a backup copy. This will help ensure that if you do make a mistake in one of your changes, you will at least be able to fall back to a previous, more stable version. In addition, you should always try to test your changes locally before pushing them to your production environment. To test your changes locally, you must first have a local installation of Community Server. You should also try to mirror your production installation. You should also be aware that making changes to the Community

Server–specific configuration files will likely require the application to be manually restarted. If you follow these simple guidelines, you will be sure to avoid some of the potential issues associated with changing your site's configuration.

It is also important that before you do make these changes, you always get the latest copy of your configuration file. Do not assume that you have the latest version; always FTP and download the latest copy. There is always room for error, and the last thing you want to do is overwrite your production environment's `SiteUrls.config` file with an outdated version.

Adding Custom Pages

Whenever you plan to extend the functionality or simply add a new static page to Community Server, you will probably want to provide a link for users to click to get to the new functionality. One of the easiest, and most appropriate, ways is to add a new entry for your page in the `navigation` section of the `SiteUrls.config` file. When you use this method, a new link is displayed in the navigation menu for your entire site. Therefore, on any page that a user may navigate to on your main site, a link will persist for the new page that you are adding.

There are a couple of routes that you can take when you are adding a new page. If you plan on localizing your site in a different language, then you will want to place the text that will be displayed for your link inside of a resource file and then reference it from your new entry. The other option is to include the text directly in the new entry.

In our example, we will be adding a new page that has a copy of your résumé. Because this is your current résumé, we will assume that the page will simply contain static content. However, it really does not matter if the content on the page is dynamic, as we only care about its location and the text to display for the link.

Before completing the following steps, make a copy of your `SiteUrls.config` file and also place a static `resume.htm` file at the root of your site.

1. Open your `SiteUrls.config` file using Notepad or Visual Studio.

2. Locate the `navigation` section, which will be around line 50.

3. Add the following entry between the links where you want the résumé link to be displayed:

```
<link name="resume" navigateUrl="resume.htm" text="Résumé"
   roles="Everyone" />
```

4. Save `SiteUrls.config` and recycle your site to test that the link was added correctly (the `SiteUrls.config` file is only read when the application is restarted).

Once you have loaded the site after making the previous changes, you will notice a new link named Resume appear in your navigation bar. Note that we used the second option to provide a link name. We could have created an entry in the `resources.xml` file. If you would like to reorder the location of this link, all you need to do is reorder the list of navigation links inside your `SiteUrls.config` file. The last thing to mention is that the `roles` property is set to `Everyone`. This is important to change if you plan to restrict a link so that it is only visible to users with a certain role. In addition, you should note that it is not a required property; if you do not supply anything, your link will be available to everyone.

Modifying the Navigation Bar

Being able to change the text and target of an existing page link is important. Next is a short example of how you would change the Blogs link to read My Thoughts and point to your blog. For the purposes of this demonstration, I will be using the link http://myblogaddress to represent your blog's URL.

1. Open your SiteUrls.config file using Notepad or Visual Studio.

2. Locate the navigation section, which will be around line 50.

3. Change the line with the name blog to the following:

```
<link name="blog" navigateUrl="http://myblogaddress" text="My
    Thoughts"  roles="Everyone" applicationType = "Weblog" />
```

4. Save the changes to the SiteUrls.config file and open your site in a browser to test your changes.

Advanced Configuration Options

There are a few advanced options that you should know about when editing the SiteUrls.config file. These options mainly center on the URL entries in the URLs section. The more-useful options that you should know about are the pattern and vanity properties. These properties allow you to change the way a URL is displayed to a user without changing the function of the link. You can add a descriptive URL to your link without changing system functionality.

For example, if you want to have a URL that points to a page called displayblog.aspx and it accepts a variable as a querystring of the blogid, you could hide the actual querystring variable from the user. The entry that you would use to do this would have the following pattern and vanity:

```
pattern="(\d+)/displayblog.aspx" vanity="displayblog.aspx?blodid=$1"
```

In the preceding example, the pattern has the regular expression to accept any characters in the URL and follows the URL with a path to displayblog. In addition, the vanity entry with the symbol of $1 means that the first querystring value will be passed in as the blogid.

ApplicationConfiguration

If you are interested in creating your own configuration section, you can do so by extending the ApplicationConfiguration base class so that your new section is stored in the database. To implement your own custom configuration section that is stored in the cs_ApplicationConfigurationSettings table, you can extend the base ApplicationConfiguration class. This class provides you with an easy way to extend Community Server and provide custom configuration options that do not require any change to be made to the configuration files. Generally, this would be used in a situation where you were creating a brand-new core application that would be combined with the other Community Server applications. Currently, the blog, file gallery, forum, Reader, and photo gallery all use the cs_ ApplicationConfigurationSettings table to store their core settings.

Extending ApplicationConfiguration

It is quite easy to actually extend the `ApplicationConfiguration` class and add a new entry to the `cs_ApplicationConfigurationSettings` table. The difficult part comes when you want to read back the information from the table; however, this is still not a difficult task thanks to the .NET `System.Xml` namespace. In the following example, we are considering a situation where you are creating a new application that needs to store some core configuration data in the database. There are only two entries that need to be stored: a Boolean `IsActive` field and an integer `MaxEntries` field. The following code is the complete class that you could create to accomplish this task:

```
public class ExampleConfiguration : ApplicationConfiguration
{

    protected override string ConfigSection
    {
        get { return "CommunityServer/Example"; }
    }

    public override ApplicationType ApplicationType
    {
        get { return ApplicationType.Admin; }
    }

    private static readonly Type thisType = typeof(ExampleConfiguration);

    public static ExampleConfiguration Instance()
    {
        return Instance(true);
    }

    public static ExampleConfiguration Instance(bool useCache)
    {
        return Instance(thisType, useCache) as ExampleConfiguration;
    }

    private int _maxEntries = 2;
    public int MaxEntries
    {
        get { return _maxEntries; }
        set { _maxEntries = value; }
    }

    private bool _isActive = false;
    public bool IsActive
    {
        get { return _isActive; }
        set { _isActive = value; }
    }

    protected override void Initialize(System.Xml.XmlNode node)
    {
```

```
    base.Initialize(node);
    if (node != null)
    {
        XmlAttribute maxEntries = node.Attributes["MaxEntries"];
        if (maxEntries != null)
            this.MaxEntries = Int32.Parse(maxEntries.Value);

        XmlAttribute isActive = node.Attributes["IsActive"];
        if (isActive != null)
            this.isActive = Boolean.Parse(isActive.Value);
    }
  }
}
```

Extending the `ApplicationConfiguration` class only requires that you override the `Initialize` method. In our example, we used this method to read the configuration details from our entry in the table. It is important to understand that the configuration settings are stored in Extensible Markup Language (XML) format. Therefore, whenever you are reading back the settings, it is very logical that you would look for specific attributes of the `XmlNode`. In the example, you first check to make sure that the attribute is not null, then you try to read each configuration option as an `XmlAttribute`. If you are successful with reading the specific attribute, then you can parse it out to a specific field. The reason you will want to check for nulls is to avoid exceptions that would be caused when your configuration class initializes without the appropriate configuration details being stored in the database. An exceptional (pardon the pun) situation like this would occur the first time you run your code and have not assigned any values to be stored in the database.

Aside from overriding the `Initialize` method, you will also want to make sure that you have local properties to store your configuration settings. These properties will be used to write your various settings to the database. Therefore, the property names should be accurate and match the names of the attributes that you are reading in the `Initialize` method.

The `ConfigSection` is important because it specifies how your XML configuration will be formatted under Community Server. If your configuration settings relate to Community Server, as they should, you should specify that the `ConfigSection` getter returns a section name that starts with `CommunityServer`. Finally, the `ApplicationType` is also an important property that you should specify. In the `cs_ApplicationConfigurationSettings` table there is a column that corresponds to an enumerator called `ApplicationType`. This entry in the database should really be unique as it does not make sense to have two separate entries for configurations that relate to the same application. If you are unsure about what type of application you are creating, there is an entry for an unknown application type.

Additional Configuration Files

In addition to the core configuration files, there are also several other configuration files that you can use to manipulate specific areas of a site. These configurations files range from other `web.config` files to files that control the navigation options on a site.

Directory-Level web.config Files

Beyond the root web.config file, there are several more that are located throughout various subdirectories within Community Server. These files provide specific configuration options for the directory and subdirectories in which they reside. In addition, these directories will inherit configuration details from parent directories.

To help gain an understanding of the additional web.config files that you will find in Community Server, let's look at a specific example. Inside of the ControlPanel directory you will find the BlogAdmin subdirectory, which contains a web.config file. If you open this configuration file, you will find the following code:

```
BlogAdmin web.config file
<configuration>
    <system.web>
  <authorization>
        <allow roles="SystemAdministrator,blogadministrator" />
        <deny users="*" />
  </authorization>
    </system.web>
</configuration>
```

The <authorization> section indicates who will be able to view the pages in this directory and any subdirectories. In addition, the absence of any other specific section details also indicates that any of the settings in the parent web.config will be acceptable for this directory. For example, the root web.config file has the <customErrors> mode set to RemoteOnly; therefore, the web.config in the BlogAdmin directory will inherent this same setting. However, if the BlogAdmin web.config specifies a different mode, then the files in the BlogAdmin directory will take on this new error-handling setting.

All of the different web.config files mainly specify certain roles that have the ability to access the files in its respective directory and subdirectories. Therefore, if you want to tighten or loosen the access to the Control Panel, then you can edit these files and add or remove roles. In addition, you can also override the default inherited settings by specifying your own in these additional web.config files. However, I would advise leaving the default settings alone as you do not want to create a security hole in your site.

Tabs.config

The Tabs.config file located in the ControlPanel directory is used to control what links are displayed in the main Control Panel navigation bar. Therefore, you can use this file to add additional navigational links in your Control Panel. By default, the text of all of the different links is gathered from the resource files. In addition, for the specific applications, such as a blog or forum, whether or not to display the link is determined from the specific validation class. Each of the validation classes returns a Boolean indicating whether or not the respective application is enabled. Thus, if the blog application is disabled, the link to administer blogs will not be displayed.

To add your own link that will appear on the Control Panel navigation bar, you would add one line to the `Tabs.config` file. Let's assume that you want to add a link to the `email.aspx` file and have the text for the link say `Email`. You could easily add the following line to `Tabs.config`:

```
<Tab text="Email" href="email.aspx" />
```

When you refresh your Control Panel, you will now see a link that says `Email` (Figure 10-1) that navigates to `email.aspx` when clicked.

Figure 10-1: Navigation Tabs with Email Tab added

SetupNavBar.config

If you are interested in configuring the navigation menu of the administration section of the Control Panel, then you will want to edit the `SetupNavBar.config` file. Open the file with Notepad and you will notice that it is divided into same structure of the menu in your Control Panel. At the root level, you have a `TabsCollection`, which contains one or more `tab` sections. Each `tab` section has a collection of `SubTabs` that contain tabs. The root tab serves as the title that represents the links that expand outward from it. Take, for example, the Blogs tab, which expands to include options for creating a new blog and managing groups. This blogs menu is represented by the following tab entry in the `SetupNavBar.config` file:

Snippet of SetupNavBar.config Blogs Menu
```
<Tab resourcename="CP_BlogAdmin_NavBar_Blogs" name="Blogs" roles =
    "systemadministrator;blogadministrator">
  <SubTabs>
      <Tab resourcename="CP_BlogAdmin_CreateNewBlog"
        urlname="blog_ControlPanel_AdminSectionEdit" name="BlogCreate"
        iTabType="CommunityServer.ControlPanel.Controls.GridItemValidator,
        CommunityServer.Web" />
      <Tab resourcename="CP_BlogAdmin_BlogGroups"
        urlname="blog_ControlPanel_AdminGroups" name="BlogGroups"
        iTabType="CommunityServer.ControlPanel.Controls.GridItemValidator,
        CommunityServer.Web" />
  </SubTabs>
</Tab>
```

The previous code results in the first two entries in the blog admin menu. If you wanted to add a new menu item to the blog administration menu, then you would add a new tab entry in the `<SubTabs>` section. For example, if you wanted to add a new entry for managing your favorite blogs (Figure 10-2), then you could add the following code inside the `<SubTabs>` section:

```
<Tab name="FavoriteBlogs" text="Favorite Blogs" href="favoriteblogs.aspx" />
```

Figure 10-2: Blogs Menu with Added Favorite Blogs Entry

Summary

In this chapter, you learned about the different configuration files that exist in Community Server. Furthermore, you learned which settings each of these files contains as well as how to alter these settings. In addition, this chapter prepared you to create your own configuration section for any custom applications that will need them.

In the next chapter, you will learn about Community Server modules. You will learn how to create your own module as well as how to distribute your newly created module.

Part IV

Extending Community Server

11

Modules

Community Server is an extensible platform that allows developers to easily create and deploy new features. One of the ways that developers are able to extend Community Server is through the use of Community Server modules, or CSModules. You can think of a module as a compiled assembly that you simply plug in to Community Server and that then participates in Community Server events. For example, you could find a module that provides you with an easy way to receive notifications whenever an exception occurs on your site. You would then be able to drop this module into Community Server and receive the benefits of the new feature immediately. In this way, modules allow you to easily extend your site without having to have been the original developer of the module. In fact, they are easy enough to install that you don't even have be a developer to be able to install them. Even more important, they allow sites to receive the benefits of new functionality without requiring them to alter any of the Community Server source code. Modules are the recommended way to extend Community Server.

In this chapter, you will explore modules and learn how to create them. This chapter covers the following:

- ❏ Module benefits
- ❏ Module architecture
- ❏ Module events
- ❏ Installing a module
- ❏ A sample module

Module Benefits

If you are a developer, then you will be happy to know that using modules allows you to extend Community Server without requiring an intricate knowledge of the underlying application code.

The modules do not have to be complicated to create; yet they can be extremely powerful. They are also flexible enough so that more experienced programmers are able to create even more advanced modules. Therefore, the framework for creating Community Server modules actually allows for developers to have varying degrees of development knowledge. In the later parts of this chapter, we will look at a module that requires very few lines of code and that is not complicated but still has big rewards, just to give you a taste of what is possible with basic .NET programming abilities.

A nice benefit of modules is that they enable custom solutions to be developed to meet very specific needs. Perhaps a client that you are working with requests a feature that is not currently a part of the Community Server installation they are using. A very valuable solution would be to create a module that could hook into their existing Community Server installation. Another nice ability of using modules is that they are easily uninstalled or disabled. This is helpful if a new feature is only required as a short-term solution. Another situation in which this ability is useful is if a module that you created was included as a core component of the next release of Community Server. Fortunately, Telligent is very good at announcing new features to the public so that you can plan for a situation such as this one. Regardless, it is important to recognize that the ability to disable a module is provided. Again, another purpose of the module could be to provide a short-term placeholder for an upcoming feature of Community Server.

There is another important purpose of modules in Community Server, which is that they allow enterprise-ready modules to be created and sold to clients. There are a few of these modules that are available for purchase directly from Telligent; however, others are able to sell their own modules if they would like. In this way, Community Server is able to reach a larger market, providing a wider range of editions and installation options. Enterprises are able to deploy modules that enable different types of user authentication, provide better searching capabilities, and offer more robust reporting capabilities.

Module Architecture

Quite simply, modules hook into the Community Server event pipeline and provide new functionality. There are several events that are possible to subscribe to, which I will discuss in the next section. You may be asking yourself what it means to subscribe to an event. If you subscribe into the error event, this means that when an error occurs on your site, the error event would be raised and then the method that you "subscribed to" into this event would be executed.

In order for a module to run correctly, it must first be installed and configured properly. The basic process for doing this is to copy the assembly containing your module into the `bin` folder of your site. Next, you should configure Community Server so that it knows to include your module when running events. You can do this by editing the `communityserver.config` file and adding a new tag for your module in the module section. If, for example, you have a module named `ExceptionNotification` that is located in the `WyattPreul.CS.Modules` namespace within the `WyattPreul` assembly, then you would reference it using the following code:

Reference to ExceptionNotification Module in communityserver.config

```
<CSModules>
    <add name="ExceptionNotification"
        type="WyattPreul.CS.Modules.ExceptionNotification, WyattPreul" />
</CSModules>
```

The previous code informs Community Server to look in the `WyattPreul` assembly for the `ExceptionNotification` class, which implements the `ICSModule` interface and initializes it. Once Community Server initializes this module, the methods that subscribe to the application events will be invoked when each event fires.

It is important to understand the order of execution for all of the steps that are to take place. We will consider what happens when an error occurs on your site and you have a module that subscribes to the `CSException` event. Keep in mind that this is a somewhat high-level explanation that does not account for situations in which a `Global.asax` class or `HttpModule` is used to intercept an exception.

1.   An exception occurs on the site.

2.   The `CSExceptionHandler` delegate is notified.

3.   Your module's method that subscribes to the `CSException` event responds.

As you can see from this explanation, the process is actually not complicated. Now, to better understand how this exception method actually functions, you can take a look at the code required to subscribe to exception event:

The Method Required to Implement ICSModule

```
public void Init(CSApplication csa, XmlNode node)
{
    csa.CSException += new CSExceptionHandler(csa_CSException);
}
```

The Method That Will Be Called Whenever the CSException Event Occurs

```
void csa_CSException(CSException csEx, CSEventArgs e)
{
    throw new Exception("An exception occurred before this one.");
}
```

According to the preceding code, whenever an exception occurs on the site that this module is installed on, another exception is raised with the resulting message of "An exception occurred before this one." This is definitely not a module that you should be installing on your site; however, it is a good demonstration of the underlying code of a module. We will be going into much more depth with how to code a module later in this chapter.

Community Server Events

There are several events that you can subscribe to whenever you are constructing a module; these events are all accessible from the `CSApplication` object. These events are the heart of your module; they are what a module uses to be able to perform different activities. To learn what events you are able to subscribe to, refer to the following table. Also, be aware that this is a general overview for these events; to truly understand how they operate, I encourage you to experiment with them and build sample modules that use them. In addition, you should think of an event as the entry point for your entire module.

Event Name	Description
AuthorizePost	Executes after a post is authorized to occur for a given user. The content of the post has not actually been posted, but the user is authorized to post the content. The sender is a User object, and the arguments are the CSEventsArgs class.
CSException	Executes after an exception occurs. It can be used to intercept Community Server–specific exceptions and handle how they are processed. The CSException object is passed in as a parameter to a subscribing method. A result is that you have access to the details of the exception.
Favorite	Occurs whenever an item is marked as a favorite. You can use this to perform reporting on items that are marked as favorites or to do anything else you can imagine with a new favorite item.
PostConfigurationInitialized	Executes after the configuration files for the site have been read and are initialized. It uses a generic EventHandler; therefore, do not expect any Community Server–specific object to be passed into your subscribing method.
PostPostAttachmentUpdate	Executes after an attachment was updated on an existing post. This can be useful for controlling details about post attachments. The PostAttachment object is passed in, providing you direct access to the updated attachment.
PostPostUpdate	Occurs after any post was updated; usually this would be after the content of a post changes. The interface for the content of the post is sent into your subscribing method, giving you access to the body of the updated post.
PostSearch	Generic event that occurs after a search was made on the site. This could be useful for learning more about what users are searching for.
PostSectionGroupUpdate	Occurs after a section group changes. A section group can be a gallery group, a forum group, a blog group, or a folder group. This event would occur after a group was changed and updated. You should also notice that a group contains one or more sections. The Group object is passed in as a parameter.
PostSectionUpdate	Occurs after a section was updated. Also note that a section can contain subsections. The Section object is passed in as a parameter.
PostUserInvitationUpdate	Occurs after a user's invitation was updated. The Invitation object is passed into the subscribing methods.
PostUserUpdate	Occurs after a user has been updated in some way. Most likely this will be a result of a user updating profile information. The User object is passed in as a parameter to the subscribing methods.

Event Name	Description
PrePostAttachmentUpdate	Occurs before an attachment is officially added to a post. This can be useful for intercepting files before they are actually attached to posts. The content of post is passed in as well as the Attachment object.

Event Name	Description
PrePostUpdate	Occurs whenever a post is about to be updated, but the post has not yet been updated. The content of the post is passed in as a parameter using the IContent interface, providing access to what the post will be updated to.
PreProcessPost	Occurs when a post is about to be processed. The content of the post is passed in as a parameter to the subscribing method.
PreRenderPost	Occurs when a post is about to be rendered and displayed. This can be useful for intercepting the content of a post at the last minute, before it is actually displayed.
PreSearch	Occurs when a search is submitted but has not yet taken place. The handler is the generic EventHandler; therefore, there are not any Community Server–specific objects passed in as parameters.
PreSectionGroupUpdate	Occurs before a section group is updated.
PreSectionUpdate	Occurs just before a section, such as a blog, is going to be updated. The Section object is passed in as one of the parameters.
PreUserInvitationUpdate	Occurs just before an invitation, which is used to invite users, is updated in some way. The UserInvitation object is passed in.
PreUserUpdate	Occurs just before a user is updated in some way. Generally, this would be a result of profile information changing. The User object is passed in as a parameter.
Rate	Occurs when a rating is changed. Remember that ratings are usually applied to posts, such as a blog post.
UserInvitationAccepted	Occurs after a user has accepted an invitation to join the site. The UserInvitation object is passed in as a parameter, which gives you access to the user, the invitation, and time that they accepted.
UserKnown	Occurs after an unknown user has been identified and is now known. This would generally occur after a user signs in and is validated. The User object is passed in as a parameter.
UserRemove	Occurs when a user is being removed from the site. This can be a result of an administrator deleting the user or the user deciding to be removed. The User object is passed in as a parameter.
UserValidated	Occurs after a user signs in successfully.

Where to Get Modules

There are many modules that are available for free for Community Server. Deciding which modules are appropriate for your site can be a daunting task. To help you identify the appropriate modules and enhancements to install, I have a few basic suggestions that revolve around the acronym N.A.R.E. The acronym stands for "No Alpha or Reported Errors" when it comes to choosing an enhancement for your site.

Alpha releases are those releases that are not yet ready to be considered beta. These are generally the first builds, which have not had much testing. Alpha releases are generally an attempt by the developer to get something pushed out to the public to receive more testing. Unless you want to be one of these testers, I would advise against installing an alpha release of a module on your production Community Server installation. I would recommend installing alpha software only on your development environment or test machine. Configuring a development or test machine is easy to do, especially since Community Server is offered in an easy-to-install Microsoft Installer (MSI) package. An explanation on how to set up your development environment will be provided in Chapter 13.

The second part of the acronym refers to not installing a module with reported errors on your production installation. Keep in mind that different developers follow different release processes. Many developers will not release an alpha or beta version of their modules. Additionally, while a developer may claim to be using a module on their site, they may have a different configuration and may not have fully tested every way their module could interact with your system. Fortunately, users and developers are generally good at reporting errors on sites such as http://communityserver.org. Therefore, you should search for errors related to the prospective module and if there are any, determine whether the errors have any impact on your site.

Many of the modules that you will find are located on personal blog sites of developers who use Community Server. A listing of some of these sites is found in Appendix B. In addition to the blog sites, http://communityserver.org also provides many modules that you can download and use.

Installation Considerations

Every module should be tested in your test environment before being deployed to production. If you do not have a local installation of Community Server and do not have the appropriate software installed to have one any time soon, then when you do install the new module in your production environment, you should monitor it heavily initially.

Another important thing to keep in mind is the time of the day that you decide to install a new module. Try to avoid installing it during the time when you have the most traffic on your site. I would advise you to install it a few hours before your site has its peak usage. If you do this, you will quickly become aware of any impact the new module has on your site.

Additional points to consider when choosing a module to install include "Who is the publisher?" and "Are they likely to continue to support the module?" You should avoid situations where it appears that a developer is not going to actively support a module in the future or has already discontinued their support of it. One way to predict this is to look at the release cycle of the developer's work. If the developer has not published anything in months, then that likely means that they will not actively support a module.

There are situations where it is acceptable to install modules that are no longer supported by the original developer(s). If you are comfortable with programming, and the source code for the module is freely available, then you may decide to install this module. The important thing to take note of is that you are more than likely going to be the person responsible for fixing any errors that you might encounter while using the module.

Another situation in which it would be acceptable to install an unsupported module is if the module is widely accepted among Community Server users and has passed a great deal of scrutiny. In a situation like this, many people have already installed and are using the module. It's less likely that you will run into issues that someone else has not already experienced, and if you need support that the original developer can no longer provide, you can at least contact other users of the module for assistance.

Installing a CSModule

Once you have downloaded the module file, you may have to extract it to a temporary local directory. Often, modules are packaged with a `readme` file in a compressed archive. Therefore, if you do extract your module, you should navigate to the directory where the files were extracted from and read the `readme` file if it exists. If a `readme` file does exist, then you will more than likely find instructions on how to install the module. There are situations in which additional configuration changes are required for the module to function correctly. Regardless, you can complete the following basic steps for installing a module inside a Community Server installation. For the purposes of the following instructions, I am assuming that you have access to the Community Server configuration files on the server hosting your site. In addition, you should make a backup copy of your `communityserver.config` file, located under the main web folder, before proceeding with the following steps:

1. Copy the module assembly to your site's installation `bin` directory. The module assembly is the file in your downloaded package with the extension of `.dll`. The `bin` directory is usually found under `web\bin`.

2. Open the `communityserver.config` file located in your root installation folder, using Notepad or any other text editor, including Visual Studio.

3. Locate the section in your `config` file called `<CSModules>`.

4. At the end of the section, before the closing `</CSModules>` tag, create a new line and type the following:

```
<add name="YourModulesName" type="YourModulesNamespace, YourModulesAssemblyName" />
```

   The name is the unique name of your assembly, such as `ExceptionNotification`. The text for `YourModulesNamespace` is generally the name of your assembly plus a period, then the name of your module. For example, if your assembly is called `WyattPreul` and your module is `ExceptionNotification`, `YourModulesNamespace` would be `WyattPreul.ExceptionNotification`. The text representing `YourModulesAssemblyName` should simply be replaced with the name of your assembly, which in our example is `WyattPreul`.

5. Save the changes you made to `communityserver.config` and recycle your web application.

Try to access a part of the site that causes the newly installed module to execute. Hopefully, at this point everything is running correctly for you. However, if you still are experiencing issues, then you should seek help from the developer of the module that you are installing. Make sure to include a detailed description of your server's configuration.

Test First, Use Later

It is important when you are developing or using a module that you understand the importance of testing the module before you assume that everything is ready for you to start using it in production. The initial mindset that you should take when you first install a module is that of a tester. You should be looking at the module from a wide range of angles, trying to identify possible issues that you may experience with it. You can think of "test first, use later" as two separate personas that you take on throughout the lifecycle of your experience with a module.

The test first persona can be thought of as one you would adopt if you were testing software that you were developing yourself. The reason that you should test first is because of the costs associated with finding a bug and trying to identify it later in your usage of a module. For example, if you simply install a module and believe that everything is running correctly on your site, and then a month later an issue comes up that is associated with the module that you installed, it will be difficult to identity the module as the culprit. Furthermore, it will be much more time-consuming to fix the bug later in your usage because it is no longer fresh in your mind. Therefore, it is best to test a newly installed module up front before you decide to start using it in production.

At this point, I have been talking about testing a module at a very high level; now I will talk about the specifics of how you can actually test your module. One of the most useful ways to test your module is by actually running the module in a development environment and checking that it runs correctly. This can be a good way to test that everything is functioning appropriately before deploying it to a production environment. You can also perform a load test on it. A load test is nothing more than running your module in an environment with a varying degree of traffic load. The question that is being answered by performing a load test is whether or not your module runs correctly in an environment with a few users or a very large number of users. Another type of testing would be to perform unit tests on your module. This can be accomplished if you have access to the source code for the module and have a unit-testing framework such as NUnit.

Maintaining Your New Module

When using third-party modules, it is important to keep tabs on the publisher. Be aware of new releases for your version of Community Server. One way to do this is to frequent the site where you originally downloaded the module. Another way is to either subscribe to an RSS feed on the originating site or join a mailing list to receive updates.

To help maintain your module, pay attention to user feedback in community forums. For example, if you created a module and users are complaining about a bug in it, you should pay attention to these comments and fix the bug. In addition, if you do not have access to the code, but users of the module are commenting about a configuration change that can be made to boost the performance of the module, perhaps you should investigate making this change.

Building Your First Module

In the following sections, you will be looking at a simple module that you can create and deploy that will notify you when an unhandled exception occurs on your site. Currently, Community Server offers a very useful exception report; however it requires that you be signed in as an admin to view the report and look for exceptions that may signal potentially serious issues.

To build the following module, you should have a copy of Visual Studio 2005. An Express version of Visual Studio is available from Microsoft. Another requirement is to have a local copy of the `CommunityServer.Components` assembly, which is available in the `bin` directory of your Community Server installation.

Exception Notification Module Example

1. Open Microsoft Visual Studio 2005 and press Ctrl-Shift-N to open the New Project dialog box.

2. Select Visual C# as the language and Class Library as the type of project. For the project name type: **CS.Modules** and click the OK button to create the project.

3. A blank class will be created in your new project; rename Class1 to **ExceptionNotification**, both in the editor and as the name of the physical file. If you rename the file first, the change will be carried into the class declaration.

4. Right-click your project in the Solution Explorer and select Add Reference.

5. In the Add Reference dialog box, select the Browse tab and locate the `CommunityServer.Components` assembly.

6. Add the following `using` statements to the top of your class file, below the existing `using` statements. This reference is used for implementing the `ICSModule` and sending email.

```
using CommunityServer.Components;
using System.Net.Mail;
```

7. Add the following after your class declaration so that you are implementing the `ICSModule`:

```
public class ExceptionNotification : ICSModule
```

8. Now that you have declared that the class will implement the `ICSModule` interface, you must actually implement it. Add the following required method so that you don't break your contract:

```
public void Init(CSApplication csa, System.Xml.XmlNode node)
{
}
```

9. Technically speaking, you already have all of the code necessary for this to be your first module. You could compile the assembly and install it in Community Server, and you would have a new module; of course, it would not actually do anything. Therefore, let's add the code to subscribe to the `CSException` event, and then you will add the method to send the notification. The first thing you will do is add the following line in the `Init` method to subscribe to the `CSException` event:

```
csa.CSException += new CSExceptionHandler(csa_CSException);
```

10. Now add the following code to handle sending the notification. This method will be using a hard-coded recipient email address and will not format the message of the exception. In addition, it also requires that a new `using` statement be added to the top of your document; therefore add the new `using` statement and then the method:

```
void csa_CSException(CSException csEx, CSEventArgs e)
{
    MailMessage message = new MailMessage("errors@yoursite.com", "you@yoursite.com",
        "CS Exception", csEx.Message);
    SmtpClient client = new SmtpClient();
    client.Send(message);
}
```

11. Everything is ready to be compiled now; therefore, right-click your project in the Solution Explorer and select the Build option.

12. Assuming that everything was built successfully, you can now install your module in your Community Server installation. The assembly will be in your project's `bin\debug` folder, which you can copy to your site's `bin` folder. After you have copied everything, simply follow the steps outlined in the previous section on making the necessary `communityserver.config` changes.

As you can see from the Exception Notification example, creating a module for Community Server is a fairly simple process. The Community Server team has done a wonderful job of making their product extensible through the use of modules. If you want to learn more about modules, feel free to begin reading Chapter 13, which offers a much more in-depth look at creating custom modules.

Summary

Modules enable a site to gain new functionality without your having to alter any of the physical code that is running the site. They work by subscribing to events that can occur on a site and adding functionality when the events do occur. Modules are also simple to distribute and install on an existing site, as they require only a minor configuration file change.

In the next chapter, you will learn how to alter the core code that is running inside Community Server. This provides you with a solution when a module will not work. Additionally, the next chapter will also provide you with information regarding ways you can extend Community Server using the Provider Pattern so that you do not have to touch any core code.

12

Modifying Community Server Code

This chapter provides an overview of the implied responsibilities associated with open source projects in particular and software development in general. It provides a detailed example of modifying core Community Server code and also gives you a good overview of how to use the Provider Pattern in Community Server to avoid changing core Community Server assemblies. By the end of this chapter, you should feel comfortable changing Community Server code and will know how to extend Community Server more easily.

The following items are covered throughout this chapter:

- ❑ Responsibilities of open source development
- ❑ Working with the development community
- ❑ Improving existing features
- ❑ Bug handling
- ❑ Implementing the provider pattern
- ❑ Sharing improvements

Recommendations

It is important to understand and identify what Community Server core code is. This code is really any of the code that is a part of the SDK and that ships in the assemblies packaged with Community Server. The SDK includes most of the projects that build the assemblies located in the web project's `bin` directory. Therefore, the code that operates Community Server that you need to be concerned with is available in this SDK.

In order to change any of the Community Server code you first need to have a copy of it. Download the SDK of the version of Community Server that you plan to modify. Before you change any of the core code that makes up Community Server, first think of any way that you can avoid changing the code in the core assemblies. The main issue that arises from changing core assemblies is that whenever a service pack or upgrade is released there is the potential that your modification will be lost. The reason for this is usually not tracking your changes in the code itself. If you do change code in Community Server, it can be helpful to keep a log of what files and lines in that file you changed. This is an important issue to consider before changing any of the core code. Also, as a side note, whenever you do decide to change core code, it is helpful to compile your final code using the Release configuration in Visual Studio.

One of the ways that you can easily track your changes is to use a source control application. The core Community Server development team uses subversion for its source control application. As a result of using a source control application, you can easily perform a difference and see what changes have been made to the original SDK that you checked in. This is useful whenever you need to know what assemblies will need to be updated again after applying a service pack so that you do not lose any changes that you have made to the code. Additionally, source controls allow you to roll back any changes that you have made to a state.

Dutiful Open Source Development

The Community Server team fosters an open community and encourages everyone to leave feedback about the project. Since the Community Server source code is available, feedback is not limited to high-level feature requests, but may also include new features being developed and also coding suggestions for what is already implemented.

One of the unspoken assumptions behind open source software is that the community will, in some capacity, contribute to the growth of the software product itself. This can be through a simple suggestion or through feature development by community members. Therefore, whenever you download Community Server or are looking through the code, you should feel a sense of responsibility to help improve the product and further the growth of the community itself.

There are several things that you can do to help improve Community Server. One of the most popular is contributing to the knowledge base of the community. This is often done by answering questions in the forums located at `http://communityserver.org` and also by writing about Community Server on your blog. Another popular contribution that you can make is by creating new enhancements to the product itself. This can be through modules or tasks or even by integrating a completely separate application with Community Server. There are numerous possibilities for how you can contribute to Community Server; therefore, you should not feel limited.

Another aspect of an open community is the responsibility of its members to report any bugs that they discover. You can report these in the forums. Reporting bugs is discussed in greater detail later in the chapter. Additionally, there is also a sense of responsibility that members share to provide any feedback or general thoughts on Community Server in much of the same way that they report bugs. After all, one of the purposes of an open community is to help the overall project grow. Because you are in many ways a stakeholder, it is important that you provide these thoughts and feedback so that the project can thrive and be even more successful.

Working with the Development Community

The Community Server development team is relatively small, which makes it easy to get in contact with them. The core development team and the development community on the whole are heavily interactive. If you are interested in contributing your thoughts and becoming a part of this development community, your expertise will also be warmly welcomed.

To join the development community, you really only need to create a free account on `http://communityserver.org` so that you are recognized in the community. Once you create this account, explore the different forum groups and check out the areas that you are most interested in. The different forums are well organized, so it's easy to find the appropriate forum to discuss the topic you're looking for. For example, if you have any feedback that you want to provide in regard to the Community Server source code, then you should provide that in the Coding with Community Server forum. Similarly, if you are interested in discussing different setup options, then look in the Setup & Installation forum.

Your expertise is especially welcomed in response to other members' inquiries, which you should feel inclined to answer if you know the solution to a problem. In addition, you will collect points as a result of your contributions, and these can also be gratifying and potentially rewarding. One of the important aspects of contributing to Community Server is that you have the potential to be recognized as a Community Server MVP. This is an honor that is bestowed upon community members for their participation and dedication to Community Server. This does not mean that you should try to accumulate as many points as possible, because MVPs are not only recognized for their participation in the forums but also can be recognized for their source contributions as well as any other unique contribution that they provide. The MVP program at this point is also a rewarding honor because the members receive an Enterprise Edition license for Community Server.

Bug Handling

An important part of the overall development and success of Community Server is eliminating the bugs that exist. It is an undeniable fact that software will have bugs in it; the important thing is to eliminate as many bugs as possible. The Community Server team does an amazing job of fixing the bugs that are discovered, but there are likely bugs that have not been discovered or reported. As mentioned earlier, an important part of furthering the success of Community Server is to report any bugs and possibly fix the bugs that you find.

Identifying Bugs

Perhaps the most challenging part of bug tracking is deciding what is, in fact, a bug. Occasionally, a behavior in software that one person believes to be a bug is the same thing that another person believes to be a feature.

An example of a feature and a bug getting confused can be found in the Exceptions Report of Community Server. In this report there is a Delete All button at the bottom of the page that will delete and remove all exceptions when clicked. The confusing part is that whenever users filter out a subset of exceptions and click the Delete All button, they may believe that they are only deleting the exceptions that were filtered.

Thus, this button can be observed as being a bug on the one hand as it does not behave as expected for many users, while on the other hand, it does do exactly what it says. Therefore, before you report a bug it can be useful to consider any situations where it may be the expected behavior. If you cannot think of any reasonable situations where the behavior would be expected, then you should report it as a bug so that it can be corrected.

There are several different routes you can take for identifying bugs in Community Server. The simplest and most straightforward approach is to simply use the product and then identify anything that you notice that misbehaves or is displayed improperly. The other method is to build test cases around the software and actively go about testing it for bugs. In order to understand both of these processes let's take a look at two scenarios.

The first scenario is a bug that can only be caught by actually running a Community Server site. The bug was on every other line in the tags management page of a blog; the Delete Confirmation window did not appear after the Delete button was pressed. This was a bug that was discovered by browsing the site and paying close attention to the different links and their button behavior. It was identified as being a bug because the Delete buttons on the same page for the same types of items did not have the same behavior.

The second scenario for identifying bugs is to actually write test cases that can identify bugs. In Community Server, there are several email templates that are used to generate an email to be sent to site users for different situations. Therefore, one way that you can potentially find bugs in the email system is to write a test that sends one of these emails and then reads in the email that was sent to compare it to the expected email. If the expected email is different from the email that is sent, then you will know there is a bug somewhere in the email system.

Telligent is already doing a lot of testing around Community Server; therefore it is not necessary for everyone to test Community Server through code. However, if you are interested, you can always write your own test cases to look for bugs in particular areas that concern you the most. The approach that Telligent is taking is to create web application in ruby (WATIR) tests that target the user experience of Community Server. WATIR tests allow for the user interface of Community Server and user experience to be fully tested. In addition, there are also forms of integration tests that are created to test and locate any potential bugs in the Community Server code. Of course, there are many other reasons why testing is already in place for Community Server; the important thing for you to realize is that it is a viable option for helping to locate and identify bugs.

Again, the main question that you should ask yourself in order to identify if something is a bug or not is this: Is this behaving the way I expect it to? How you answer this question is ultimately how you determine whether something is a bug or not. Once you identify something as a bug, it is important to determine if the steps you used to the find the bug are reproducible. This means that you should try to reproduce the bug to determine if it was a fluke that you observed or if it is definitely a bug.

Reporting Bugs

The process of reporting a bug found in Community Server is fairly straightforward. Simply log in to the account that you created on `http://communityserver.org` and navigate to the forums section of the web site. Under this section, you will find a forum called Bugs & Issues where you can post your bug report.

Whenever you report a new bug it is important to include a detailed description of the bug itself as well as other details to help reproduce it. In addition, you should also search the forums before you post a bug report to make sure that someone else has not already reported it. If the bug is already described somewhere else in the forums, then you should feel inclined to contribute to the discussion and provide your thoughts on how to reproduce the bug and any other ideas that you may have. To help make sure that you have included all of the necessary details in your bug report, include as many of the items on the following checklist as possible:

❑   A subject that describes the type of bug and where it occurs

❑   In the body, the steps to reproduce the bug

❑   The frequency of the bug — if it occurs every time an action occurs or only some of the time

❑   Where in Community Server the bug occurs

❑   The version of Community Server that you are running

❑   The environment that the bug occurs in; the version of Windows, SQL Server, and web browser

❑   The load or traffic volume on the server when the bug occurs

All of the information that you can supply when reporting a bug will be helpful for identifying the root cause of the bug. Any and all information will be helpful; therefore, you should not be deterred from reporting a bug if you are missing some of the information included in the preceding checklist. It is merely a template for what basic information will be most helpful to include for resolving the issue posed by the bug.

After you have reported your bug on the Community Server forums, you may want to subscribe to be notified by email whenever someone replies to your post. This can be easily done in your user preferences, which is accessible by clicking your username in the upper-right corner of the site.

Fixing Bugs

Aside from finding and reporting bugs, you also have the opportunity to fix them. If you believe that you know how a bug can be fixed, you can report this in the forums. In order to fix a bug, you should make sure that you have a working copy of the Community Server SDK available.

Before you go down the route of finding and fixing the bug, you should first make sure that no one else is already working on it. One of the last things that you want to happen is to spend an hour fixing a bug only to find out that someone else has already fixed it. Therefore, you should spend some time upfront researching to make sure that the bug has not already been resolved and also that someone is not already working on it. If no one is working on it or if a solution has not been found, then you should feel welcome to fix the bug.

In order to correct a bug, it is usually helpful to identify where the bug is coming from and what is causing it to occur. Once you have identified the root cause of a bug, it is not too difficult to also identify a possible solution. It helps to spend a little time upfront thinking out the scenario and thinking through the various solutions. There are usually a couple of ways to resolve issues; identifying the best possible solution before attempting to code will be helpful for cutting down the time it will take to fix the bug. The next step that you should take is to try out an idea for how to fix the bug and test it to see if it indeed does correct the issue.

Once you believe that you have a solution for the bug, you should try to reproduce it and make sure that you have indeed corrected the issue. When you feel confident in your solution, you should then report your fix in the forums. It will be most helpful if you post your fix in a reply to the original bug. In addition, you should also contact a Community Server team member to inform them of your fix. These individuals are easily identified by their Community Server Team Member icon, which is visible under their name in the forums.

Improving Existing Features

There are times when you or a client will need a feature that is not already available in Community Server. Perhaps there is a plan to include the feature in a future release, but it is currently not available and you cannot wait. At a time like this, you can extend Community Server in some capacity to include your new feature.

It is important that if you are going to create a new feature or improve what is already available, you try to implement your code in a way that will not modify existing assemblies. The reason that you want to avoid modifying these assemblies is so that whenever a service pack or new version of Community Server is available, you do not lose your feature.

For example, if you modify the rating system in Community Server and do so inside one of the core assemblies, then whenever that assembly gets updated you will lose your rating system. For this reason, you should avoid placing your improvements inside the existing assemblies.

Community Server does a good job at allowing a developer to place improved code in separate assemblies and still have it function. One of the ways that these improvements can be achieved is by creating custom providers. Because Community Server uses the Provider Pattern for its data retrieval, it is easy to control where and how data is retrieved without touching any of the core assemblies. You will learn how to create custom gallery providers later in this section as an example of using the Provider Pattern.

Modifying Core Code

There are some important things that you should keep in mind in order to keep your fix intact whenever a newer version of Community Server is available.

First and foremost, it is important that you record somewhere what your modifications are and where they exist. If you forget to write this information down, it will become much more difficult to make the same change again when a new version of Community Server is released. In the event that you did forget where your modification was made, you can use a comparison tool such as WinMerge or Beyond Compare to locate what files were modified in the SDK and then finally what files were modified because of your changes. Once you have located the appropriate changes that need to be reapplied to the newer version, you can simply make the changes and overwrite the appropriate assemblies with your change.

It is also important to realize that if your fix or new feature is not included in a new version, you will need to make the change to the code again. As a result, you will need a copy of the SDK, which is not always available at the same release time as the new version. Therefore, you may end up waiting for the newest SDK in order to make your changes. Of course, these changes are only necessary if you plan to upgrade to newer versions of Community Server. There is nothing that forces you to upgrade your site to the latest version. However, do realize that if you decide not to upgrade, you are potentially missing out on bug fixes and usually new features.

Core Code Modification Scenario

For the purposes of understanding how to modify core Community Server code, the following scenario may be helpful. Imagine that you created a Community Server implementation for an important client. The client has discovered a bug that no one has caught before because it is caused by some obscure behavior. Following are the steps that the client describes to you to replicate the error:

1. Sign out of the site.

2. Click the login link on the top right multiple times.

3. Log in and you will encounter an error trying to redirect you to the returning URL.

The client insists that you fix this issue immediately. You look through the forums on http://communityserver.org for a solution and you ask the other community members for help. Fortunately, someone does reply to you quickly on the forums and they point out that the URL is getting re-encoded every time the client clicks the login link. As a result, this causes the URL to be incorrect whenever the login page tries to redirect the user to it. In addition to all of the previous information, the user on the forum also points out the code to fix the issue.

Improvements by Changing Core Code

A quick fix for the issue that the client is complaining about will require a change to the SiteUrls class located in one of the core assemblies. Because of the urgency to resolve this issue and make your client happy again, you go about making the code change yourself. You open the SDK solution of the Community Server version that is installed on the client's site. Next, you navigate to the SiteUrls.cs file and then find the Login property. Once you have added code indicating that the returnUrl will be decoded before being encoded, your resulting code looks like this:

```
public virtual string Login
{
    get
    {
        string currentPath = CSContext.Current.Context.Request.Url.PathAndQuery;
        string returnUrl = null;
        returnUrl = ExtractQueryParams(currentPath)["ReturnUrl"];
        if (Globals.IsNullorEmpty(returnUrl))
            returnUrl = CSContext.Current.RawUrl;

        returnUrl = Globals.UrlDecode(returnUrl);
        returnUrl = Globals.UrlEncode(returnUrl);

        return urlData.FormatUrl("login", returnUrl);
    }
}
```

The line that was added to fix the issue was the line that reads `returnUrl = Globals.UrlDecode (returnUrl)`. This will force any encoded URL to be decoded before being encoded and appended to the querystring. As a result, a `returnUrl` will never be re-encoded every time that the login link is clicked. After you have made this change, you compile the project and test the results to make sure that the issue is indeed fixed. Once your results have been verified, you upload the assembly to the web server for the client to approve before it makes its way into production. The previous process worked for alleviating the headache that your client was having and also was quick at resolving the problem. This change required a core code change because you had to touch the code in the SDK and essentially alter the assembly where its compiled form resides.

Improvement by Extending Core Code

While the previous change fixes the problem, it is possible to fix this bug without having to alter the core assemblies. This is done through the use of a custom provider for the `SiteUrls`. As Rob Howard explains it, "The theory behind the [Provider] Pattern is that it allows us to define a well-documented, easy-to-understand API but at the same time give developers complete control over the internals of what occurs when those APIs are called" (`http://msdn.microsoft.com/library/default.asp?url= /library/en-us/dnaspnet/html/asp02182004.asp`). Because the development team implemented this code using the Provider Pattern, you can tap into the core code and add or override the functionality as needed without rewriting everything in the `SiteUrls` class. By design, the `SiteUrls` class is inherited, and the properties are `virtual`, so you can override them. In addition, whenever the `SiteUrls` class is created, it looks for a provider to take care of its services. Therefore, by making your own custom `SiteUrls` type class, you can fix the previous bug without having to recompile any of the core assemblies.

To begin creating a custom `SiteUrlsProvider` class, you first want to have a new project that you can compile the resulting code into so that you do not have to touch an existing project. You can create a new project in Visual Studio called `CustomProviders` that is a class library. Once you have the project created, you want to add a new class that will contain our `SiteUrlsProvider`; therefore, you should call it `SiteUrlsProvider`. Once you have the class created, you should add the following code to it. The entire code will be provided here and then explored and utilized in the remainder of this section:

```
using System;
using System.Collections.Generic;
using System.Text;
using CommunityServer.Components;
using System.Web;

namespace CustomProviders
{
    class SiteUrlsProvider : SiteUrls
    {
        public SiteUrlsProvider(SiteUrlsData data) : base(data) { }

        public override string Login
        {
            get
            {
                string currentPath =
                    CSContext.Current.Context.Request.Url.PathAndQuery;
                string returnUrl = null;

                returnUrl = ExtractQueryParams(currentPath)["ReturnUrl"];
```

```
        if (Globals.IsNullorEmpty(returnUrl))
            returnUrl = CSContext.Current.RawUrl;

        returnUrl = Globals.UrlDecode(returnUrl);
        returnUrl = Globals.UrlEncode(returnUrl);

        return this.UrlData.FormatUrl("login", returnUrl);
      }
    }
  }
}
```

One of the first things to notice about the previous code is that it is relatively short and straightforward. Also notice that the System.Web using statement was added to the default list of using statements. In addition, a reference in the project is required for this and the Community Server assemblies. Whenever you are working with Community Server from an external project, it is imperative that you reference the assemblies that you will be using. In this case, CommunityServer.Components will be used; therefore a reference was added to include this assembly in the project.

On the line that declares the class, you can see that it inherits from the SiteUrls class. As a result of this inheritance, this class will not need to reinvent the wheel by re-creating the methods and properties found in the SiteUrls class. Instead, this class can go along its way and optionally override and add new methods or properties to the existing structure. This can be extremely useful whenever you want to integrate a new application so that you can notify Community Server where key components of the application are located. In addition, if you want to change how any of the URLs are generated, you can easily do that with your new provider.

The next section of code is the constructor for the custom provider. This is where your class will be created, and it is also where you will pass the required SiteUrlsData object to the base constructor found in the original SiteUrls class. The SiteUrls class only has one constructor that requires this SiteUrlsData object, which is why it must be included in the constructor of the custom provider.

After the constructor is the location where the actual bug fix is located. This is where the Login property is overridden and the fix to decode the URL is put into place. The code should look familiar because it is the same code that was used previously in the core code change example. The only difference is the override keyword. This means that whenever the address for the login page is requested, this custom property will be deferred to over the base property. As a result, the person making the request will not experience the bug that is found in the base SiteUrls class.

Finally, after you have examined the previous code and have it placed in the CustomProviders project, you should try building the project. If you experience any issues, make sure that you have included all of the appropriate references. Once you have a successful build, you should navigate to your CustomProviders output directory, which is probably under the bin\Debug folder. In this folder, you will find the assembly that was generated from the build, which you should copy into the bin folder of your Community Server web project. Make sure that you are performing these steps in a development or test environment. The last thing you want to do is to bring down a production site with a faulty assembly or configuration.

Once you have the assembly copied to the `bin` folder, you should proceed to open the `communityserver.config` file located in the web projects root directory. The `communityserver.config` file contains all of the custom providers that Community Server uses to perform a lot of its functionality. Inside the `<providers>` section of the configuration file, you can add the following code, which will reference the custom provider that was just copied:

```
<add name = "SiteUrlsProvider"
     type = "CustomProviders.SiteUrlsProvider, CustomProviders, Version=1.0.0.0,
             Culture=neutral, PublicKeyToken=null"
/>
```

When you have added the previous code to the `communityserver.config` file, you should save your changes. Before testing your results, it may be helpful to understand why the previous code was added to the configuration file in the first place. If you look at the `SiteUrls` class, you will notice that it looks for a provider with a key of `SiteUrlsProvider`, which it will instantiate if found. Since the name of the provider in the `providers` collection is `SiteUrlsProvider`, `SiteUrls` will attempt to create it. In order to create the class at runtime, it relies on the location of the assembly and the namespace to find the `SiteUrlsProvider` class. With this information, it tries to get the type and then activate an instance of that type using the `System.Activator.CreateInstance` method. Once the instance is created, it can rely on your overridden version of the `Login` property to handle the navigation to that particular page.

Now that the `SiteUrlsProvider` has been built, and your Community Server site has been configured, you should test your results. In order to test this, you can try the same steps that you used to find the bug. These include clicking the Sign In link multiple times and then trying to log in. You should find that you are redirected to the appropriate page after logging in. To make sure that the bug is there whenever the `SiteUrlsProvider` is not; you can simply delete the provider entry that was added to the `communityserver.config` file and try again. If after removing the provider you experience the issue again, then you know that this provider fixed the `SiteUrls` code.

Again, the important thing to realize with using the approach described here is that you did not have to touch any of the core code. Even though you did not change any of the core code or assemblies, you were able to modify how Community Server behaves by using the custom provider. As a result, you have learned that it is possible, and sometimes quite easy, to fix core Community Server code without touching the core code itself.

Gallery Provider

Aside from the global `SiteUrls` you can also create a provider for individual features, such as the blog or gallery. These serve as a way to control how data is read and transformed into the paths that are a part of each individual feature. The construction of a custom `GalleryUrlsProvider` is very similar to that of the `SiteUrlsProvider`. To provide a more rounded overview of some of the available providers in Community Server, this section will also look at creating a `GalleryDataProvider`.

With the `GalleryUrlsProvider`, you can literally control the URLs for all aspects of a photo gallery. In addition, you can do all of this with code, bypassing the usage of the `SiteUrls.config` file for gallery URLs. The best part about using a custom provider is that you can easily pick and choose which URLs you want to control through code and which ones you want to control through the configuration file. If you would like to see a list of the all available gallery URLs that you can alter, simply look at the appropriately named `GalleryUrls.cs` file in the `Gallery.Components` namespace.

Similar to the previous example, the GalleryUrlsProvider class will reside in a new project called CustomProviders. Therefore, if this project has not already been created, you should do so before proceeding. Once you have the project created, simply create a new class file called GalleryUrlsProvider and copy the following code into that class file. This class will require a reference to CommunityServer .Galleries.Components as well as to the CSGalleries project that is in the SDK solution.

```
namespace CustomProviders
{
    class GalleryUrlsProvider : GalleryUrls
    {
        public static readonly string GalleryUrlsProviderName =
            "GalleryUrlsProvider";

        private static GalleryUrlsProvider _defaultInstance = null;

        private static GalleryUrlsProvider()
        {
            if (_defaultInstance == null)
                _defaultInstance = new GalleryUrlsProvider();
        }

        public static GalleryUrlsProvider Instance()
    {
      return _defaultInstance;
    }

        public override string ViewPicture(string applicationKey, int categoryID,
            GalleryPost galleryPost)
        {
            return galleryPost.TitleUrl;
        }
    }
}
```

The GalleryUrlsProvider class functions by inheriting from the GalleryUrls class. The GalleryUrls class controls what the URLs in the gallery will look like. In this example, the GalleryUrlsProvider class overrides the URL for the ViewPicture link. This is the address that pictures link to whenever they are clicked in the various gallery controls. Using this custom code, the link will simply point to the address stored in the TitleUrl property of a gallery post. The importance of the custom provider is that it allows an instance of the class to be created using the Instance method. This is different from the previous example. In the GalleryUrlsProvider, the instance of the class is created by the System .Activator calling the Instance method because the constructor is private. The only thing needed to get the previous code to work with an installation of Community Server is to copy the assembly into the bin folder of your Community Server installation and add the following entry into the providers section of the communityserver.config file. Once this entry is added, whenever you access your photo gallery and click a picture, you will be directed to the TitleUrl of the selected photo.

```
<add
    name = "GalleryUrlsProvider"
    type = "CustomProviders.GalleryUrlsProvider, CustomProviders,
    Version=1.0.0.0, Culture=neutral, PublicKeyToken=null"
/>
```

Another custom provider that can be created is the `GalleryDataProvider`. This provider allows for custom control of how information used in the photo gallery will be stored and accessed. If you are planning to extend the functionality of the existing provider, then you can always inherit from the `GallerySqlDataProvider` class. However, for the purposes of this demonstration, the provider that will be created can be used as a starting point for creating a way to access and store photos in a flickr account using Community Server. To begin with, you can create a new class file in the `CustomProviders` project and call it `GalleryFlickrProvider`.

At this point, it is important to point out that the class name of your provider can be anything. However, the entry in the `providers` section of the `communityserver.config` file must be given the same name as one of the available providers. The reason for this is that Community Server looks for specific key names in the provider's collection to find an appropriate provider. Therefore, if you rename the `GalleryUrlsProvider` to `PhotoGalleryUrlsProvider`, it will not be used as the URL's provider because its name is not recognized.

Inside the `GalleryFlickrProvider`, place the following code snippet. While the code will not implement all of the methods required by the `GalleryDataProvider`, it does give a good introduction to how you implement some of the methods to work with a flickr account. Also, it is important to note that the following code uses the `FlickrNet` API to connect to the flickr service. Therefore, if you are going to attempt creating a complete flickr provider for Community Server, then you will want to get a copy of this freely available API.

```
using System;
using System.Collections.Generic;
using System.Text;
using FlickrNet;
using CommunityServer.Components;
using CommunityServer.Galleries.Components;

namespace CustomProviders
{

    public class GalleryFlickrProvider : GalleryDataProvider
    {
        private Flickr _flickr;
        private string _userId;
        private string userId;

        public GalleryFlickrProvider(string apiKey, string userId)
         {
            _apiKey = apiKey;
            _userId = userId;
        }

        public Flickr flickr
        {
            get {
                if (_flickr == null)
```

```
            _flickr = new Flickr(_apiKey);

            return _flickr;
        }
        set { _flickr = value; }
    }

    public override ThreadSet GetPictures(GalleryThreadQuery query)
    {
        ThreadSet ts = new ThreadSet();
        PhotoSearchOptions search = new PhotoSearchOptions(_userId);
        search.PerPage = SQLHelper.GetSafeSqlInt(query.PageSize);
        search.Page = query.PageIndex;

        Photos photos = flickr.PhotosSearch(search);

        if (photos != null && photos.PhotoCollection != null)
            foreach(Photo photo in photos.PhotoCollection)
                ts.Threads.Add(PopulateGalleryPostFromFlickrPhoto(photo));

        ts.TotalRecords = Convert.ToInt32(photos.TotalPhotos);

        return ts;
    }

    public static GalleryPost PopulateGalleryPostFromFlickrPhoto(Photo photo)
    {
        GalleryPost post = new GalleryPost();

        post.SectionID = -1;
        post.PostID = Convert.ToInt32(photo.PhotoId);
        post.Subject = photo.Title;
        post.Body = photo.Title;
        post.Username = photo.OwnerName;
        post.IsApproved = true;
        post.PostConfig = GalleryPostConfig.IsCommunityAggregated;
        post.GalleryPostType = GalleryPostType.Image;
        post.Name = photo.Title;
        post.TitleUrl = photo.ThumbnailUrl;
         post.AttachmentFilename = photo.Title;

        PostAttachmentMetaData meta = new PostAttachmentMetaData();
        meta.IsRemote = true;
        meta.ContentType = "image";
        post.Attachment = meta;

        return post;
    }
}
}
```

In the previous example, the `GalleryFlickrProvider` class inherits from the `GalleryDataProvider`; however, it does not implement all of its members. For this to be a fully functioning provider, it would need to implement many more methods required by the photo gallery. The one method that is created is `GetPictures`, which accepts as a parameter a query used to search for specific pictures. In this example, it populates the available flickr search properties; then requests the available photos from flickr that match the search criteria. In addition, there is also a useful method listed previously called `PopulateGalleryPostFromFlickrPhoto`. This method will take a flickr photo object and convert it into a Community Server post object that can be used by the photo gallery. As a result, if you do plan on extending this idea for a flickr provider, then this method can be especially useful for converting from the way that a photo is stored in flickr to the way it is stored in Community Server.

It is also important to look at the constructor for the previous class because it accepts a couple of parameters. These parameters can be passed into the class from its entry in the `providers` section of the `communityserver.config` file. Whenever the previous provider is used by Community Server, the photos from the photo gallery will be retrieved from the flickr account specified by the `_userId` field. Therefore, the preceding code is a good example of how a provider can control the way that photos are stored and accessed in Community Server. Like the other provider examples, this one also does not require that any of Community Server's core source code be touched or changed in any way.

Available Providers

To give you a better understanding of what can be created using a custom provider, a list of available providers follows. There is a wealth of possibilities when you consider that each of these providers can control a wide range of Community Server functionality. Again, these are simply the key names that Community Server looks for in the `providers` collection created from the `communityserver.config` file:

ForumsUrlProvider

ForumDataProvider

ForumEmailsProvider

GalleryUrlsProvider

GalleryDataProvider

GalleryEmailsProvider

FeedReaderDataProvider

FileGalleryUrlsProvider

FileGalleryDataProvider

FilesEmailsProvider

BlogRelevantPostScoringProvider

BlogUrlsProvider

WeblogDataProvider

```
WeblogEmailsProvider

SiteUrlsProvider

SiteUrlsDataProvider

ApplicationKeyProvider

CommonDataProvider

CommonEmailsProvider

SearchProvider

UrlReWriteProvider

MemberRoleProfileProvider

RollerBlogsDataProvider

RssCtrlDataProvider

EmailTemplateProvider
```

Sharing Your Knowledge

Any time that you resolve a bug in Community Server it is helpful to everyone in the community if you share your solution. In addition, whenever you create new functionality, it can also be beneficial to share this knowledge. While it is not mandatory that you do share your solutions and creations with the community, it is your contribution that will help you to be better recognized among the community.

There are several ways that you can contribute your knowledge to the Community Server community. One of the more popular is to simply provide your findings in the forums at `http://communityserver.org`. Another popular method is to start a blog where you discuss or share your Community Server knowledge. The more knowledge that everyone provides, the better Community Server will become.

Summary

The Community Server community is an open one and encourages participation from its members in many forms. As a result, community members have a responsibility to report any bugs and general thoughts that they have. Community Server can also be easily altered either by changing core source code or by using the Provider Pattern to replace core code with custom code.

In the next chapter, you will learn more about creating modules. You will also learn about how to create your own tasks that can be run by Community Server periodically.

13

Writing Custom Modules

Many people think they need to work directly with the Community Server database in order to extend it or write their own modules. The truth is that working this way can actually make things harder and lengthen the development process.

Telligent employees and Community Server folks say "Community Server is a platform." This means that Community Server is built on rich APIs (which stand for application programming interfaces) that allow you to change its behavior to work for your own needs without changing the database or even writing one line of code to retrieve data from the database. If you search the Web, you may be surprised by which web sites are powered by Community Server. Developers are able to modify the platform to such an extent that it's not always obvious what was developed through Community Server.

In some cases, you may need to actually extend the database to accomplish a certain task (this doesn't happen frequently). If you find yourself in this situation, extending the database is covered in full detail in Chapter 14.

The primary goal of this chapter is to show you all of the fundamentals that you need to extend your Community Server site with APIs. It is an important chapter for every developer who wants to develop for Community Server. You will learn about common Community Server APIs that are frequently used. This chapter also discusses three straightforward ways to extend Community Server, which are pretty easy to develop: `CSModule`, `CSJob`, and Spam Rule. We'll see real world examples for each of these concepts and how each can solve many of the needs that site owners commonly have.

After reading this chapter, you'll be well equipped to write custom modules for Community Server with a few lines of code.

Community Server APIs

Community Server APIs are where you'll see the power of this great platform. They're the "behind-the-scenes" part of Community Server. You may use this application every day and not need to know anything about its APIs, but if one day you decide to extend it for your requirements, you need to learn about them or hire someone who does.

You don't need to have the Community Server source code to be able to start development for it. Using the Community Server assemblies, you'll be able to work with APIs and do whatever you want. This is the reason why many Community Server folks can release their modules before Telligent releases final versions.

Community Server 2.1 for ASP.NET 2.0 has several default assemblies, but they're not all useful for you in your development. Source code for some of these assemblies is available but is private for others. Whether you have source code or not, you can add appropriate assemblies as references to your projects and start development.

The most common DLLs for Community Server development, which we will use in this chapter, are as follows:

- ❑ CommunityServer.Components.DLL
- ❑ CommunityServer.Spam.DLL
- ❑ CommunityServer.Blogs.DLL
- ❑ CommunityServer.Discussions.DLL
- ❑ CommunityServer.Galleries.DLL
- ❑ CommunityServer.Files.DLL

ApplicationKey and SectionID

Community Server is made up of five applications that work off the base platform. The applications are forums, blogs, photo galleries, file galleries, and the Reader. There are two common ways to identify a section in a Community Server application, via two different identifiers: ApplicationKey and SectionID.

ApplicationKey is a string value that the site administrator chooses for a section when he or she creates it. For example, an ApplicationKey for each blog is the value that you see in the address bar or the name of folder in file gallery that you see. This string value is unique and can help you to identify a section.

SectionID is an integer value that the system assigns to a section automatically when it's being created. This number is unique and is another way to identify a section. SectionID is equal to the primary key value of a corresponding row in the cs_Sections table in the database.

You should know that having one of these two identifiers is sufficient. All Community Server methods have different overloads to get an ApplicationKey or SectionID as their parameter.

CSContext

CommunityServer.Components.CSContext is one of most common namespaces in Community Server APIs. The CSContext.Current object contains various properties that give useful information about the current request and application. You can compare this object with a combination of Page.Request and Server.Application in ASP.NET.

It is important to understand all of the common properties of the CSContext object. You will frequently use these properties in your Community Server development, so it's worth knowing the purpose of each property. Table 13-1 lists all common properties of the CSContext object with a short description about them.

Table 13-1 CSContext Common Properties

Property	Description
AnonymousUserID	Globally unique identifier (GUID) of an identifier that is assigned to an anonymous user.
ApplicationKey	String value of ApplicationKey for current section.
ApplicationType	An enumerator value of ApplicationType, which represents the type of application that current code is running for.
AuthenticationType	String of AuthenticationType, which represents the type of authentication in the current application.
BlogGroupID	Integer value of the current blog group ID.
CategoryID	Integer value of the current category ID.
Config	An instance of the CSConfiguration object that contains useful configuration information about current application.
Context	An instance of the HTTPContext object for current request.
CurrentUri	An Uri object for current request's URI.
Group	An instance of the Group object for the current group.
GroupID	Integer value of the current group ID.
HostPath	String value of HostPath for the current request.
IsAuthenticated	Boolean value to check if user is authenticated.
IsEmpty	Boolean value to check if the current CSContext is empty.
IsUrlReWritten	Boolean value to check if the current URL is rewritten.
IsUserTokenRequest	Boolean value to check if the current request is a user token request.
IsWebRequest	Boolean value to check if the current request is a web request.

Property	Description
MessageID	If a message is being shown to end user, this returns the ID of that Message object. You will learn more about messages in Chapter 15.
PageIndex	If the user is viewing a list of indexed items, this returns the integer value of the current index.
Post	Returns an instance of Post object for the post that is being viewed. It can be null if user is viewing a page that doesn't contain an individual post.
PostID	Integer value of the current post ID.
PostName	String value of the current post's name.
QueryString	NameValueCollection of current querystring keys and values.
QueryText	String value of current querystring.
RawUrl	String value of current Raw URL.
RequestStartTime	DateTime value for when current request is started.
RoleID	GUID of the current Role ID.
Section	An instance of the Section object for current section.
SectionID	Integer value of the current section ID.
SettingsID	Integer value of the current settings ID. If multiple sites are hosted in same database, their SettingsID is different, so SettingsID is a way to recognize individual Community Server site instances.
SiteSettings	An instance of the SiteSettings object that has useful information about current application settings.
SiteUrls	String value of the current site URL (domain only).
Statistics	An instance of the SiteStatistics object, which has statistical information about current site.
Tags	An array of strings that contains all tags that are available in the current request.
ThreadID	Integer value of the current thread ID.
Url	String value of the current request's URL.
User	An instance of the User object for the current user who is viewing the site.
UserID	Integer value of the current user's ID.
UserName	String value of the current user's name.

In addition to these important properties, CSContext has some important methods, which are listed in Table 13-2.

Table 13-2 CSContext Methods

Method	Description
GetGuidFromQueryString	Returns a GUID from querystring by getting a string key as its parameter.
GetIntFromQueryString	Returns an integer value from querystring by getting a string key. It also gets a default integer value to return if there wasn't any value available for specific key.
MapPath	Similar to Server.MapPath in ASP.NET. Returns the physical path that corresponds to the virtual path that is passed to it.
PhysicalPath	Similar to HttpRequest.PhysicalPath in ASP.NET. Returns the physical file path corresponding to the URL that is passed to it.

Not every property listed previously should have a value wherever you try to use them. Sometimes, you'll get an object null exception (object reference not set to an instance of an object) if you try to use some properties in your code because they're only available in certain pages. For example, you can't retrieve the ApplicationKey or SectionID for a section in the Control Panel via the CSContext object. Instead, there are some other alternatives that you will see later. As another example, you can't retrieve a BlogGroupID when you're calling your code in a forum page.

> **Don't call** CSContext.Current **many times to get your desired properties. It has a huge performance effect on your code. It's strongly recommended to create an instance of the** CSContext **object and set it to** CSContext.Current **for one time; then get anything you want from this object. This is an important performance tip for your code.**

Later in this chapter, you will see several examples of different usages of CSContext properties to understand how important this object is.

Post

The second most important and commonly used class in Community Server APIs is CommunityServer.Components.Post. Some other classes such as WeblogPost, ForumPost, and GalleryPost derive from this class and share most of its properties and methods. Object instances of these classes are a part of the Community Server foundation.

Generally, you will use Post objects when you want to retrieve general information about posts via one of several set objects (the Query/Set model will be discussed later in this chapter), but will use its derived classes when you need an individual post type for an application or want to update or add a new post. Note that this is a general statement, and you will see it in the examples in this chapter.

Most data in Community Server will be stored in a single table in the database, named cs_Posts. Every blog post, forum post, file gallery post, and gallery photo item (information, not the photo itself) will be saved in this table. Their difference is only in the application type that will be used and the values that will be stored for their columns.

Some of the first things that you need to learn about `Post` are its important properties and methods as well as their usages. Table 13-3 lists common properties for the `Post` object. Not all properties are listed because the purpose of some properties is obvious from their names.

Table 13-3 Post Properties

Property	Description
Attachment	An instance of the `PostAttachmentMetaData` object, which represents information about `Post`'s attachment.
AttachmentFileName	String value of attachment's file name.
Body	String value of `Post` body.
EmoticonID	Integer value of emoticon ID that is assigned to this post.
Excerpt	String value of `Post` excerpt. A short description about each post.
ExtendedAttributesCount	Integer value of extended attributes count. Extended properties will be discussed in next section.
HasAttachment	Boolean value to check if post has an attachment.
HasExcerpt	Boolean value to check if post has an excerpt.
HasInk	Boolean value to check if post has ink content.
HasPoll	Boolean value to check if post has `Poll`.
HasVideo	Boolean value to check if post has a video.
InkID	Integer value of ink ID that is assigned to the post.
IsApproved	Boolean value to check if post is approved.
IsLocked	Boolean value to check if post is locked. If a post is locked, others can't send any reply to it. You can see this in forums.
Name	String value of post name. This is different from subject.
ParentID	Integer value of parent post ID. Usually each post has a parent. For example, a blog post is the parent of its comments or trackbacks, and a forum post is the parent of all replies to it.
PollDescription	String value of `Poll` description.
PollExpirationDate	`DateTime` value for expiration date of `Poll`.
PollTitle	String value of `Poll` title.
PostDate	`DateTime` value of the date and time when post is sent. This value is calculated based on the server time that administrator has chosen for site.
PostID	Integer value of `Post` ID.
PostLevel	Integer value of `Post` level.

Property	Description
PostStatus	A PostStatus enumerator value that represents the status of post (Approved, Ham, Spam).
PostType	A PostType enumerator value that represents the post type (SinglePost or StalePoints).
RatingAverage	Double value of ratings average for a post.
Replies	Integer value of number of replies to post.
Section	An instance of the Section object where this post is being used.
SectionID	Integer value of the section ID where post is being used.
SortOrder	Integer value that specifies the sort order for post.
SpamScore	Integer value of summation of points that are assigned to post by spam blocker rules.
SpamStatus	A SpamStatus enumerator value that represents the spam status of post (Clean, NotProcessed, Spam, Suspect).
Subject	String value of post subject.
ThreadDate	DateTime value of the date and time when the parent thread for post is stored.
ThreadID	Integer value of parent thread ID.
User	An instance of User object that has sent the post.
UserHostAddress	String value of user's host address.
UserID	Integer value of user's ID.
UserName	String value of user's name.
UserTime	DateTime value of the date and time when this post is sent but on basis of user Time Zone.
Views	Integer value of the number of views for post.

Table 13-4 represents common methods for Post object.

Table 13-4 Common Methods for the Post Object

Method	Description
AddPollItem	Gets a PollItem object and adds it to collection of PollItems for current post.
ClearPollItems	Clears all PollItems for current post.
GetExtendedAttribute	Gets a string name for an extended attribute and returns its string value. Extended properties will be discussed in next section.

Table continued on following page

Method	Description
RemovePollItem	Gets a PollItem object and removes it from collection of PollItems for current post.
SetExtendedAttribute	Gets a string key and value for an extended property and adds it to extended properties. Extended properties will be discussed in next section.
SetPostMedia	Gets a PostMedia enumerator value and sets the type of PostMedia for post (Audio, Empty, Image, Poll, Video).
UpdatePollItem	Gets a PollItem object and updates that item in collection of PollItems for current post.

The following code snippet shows the usage of the Post object in action. This listing is a simple function that gets a set of Post objects via a BlogThreadQuery, and PostSet then iterates through them and returns the PostID of the most popular post (post with more views) for the current blog that is being viewed. The Query/Set model will be discussed later in this chapter.

```
int GetPopularPostID()
{

    CSContext context = CSContext.Current;

    BlogThreadQuery query;
    query.SectionID = context.SectionID;
    query.BlogPostType = BlogPostType.Post;

    PostSet set = WeblogPosts.GetPosts(query, false);

    // Find most popular post
    int views = 0;
    int popularPostID = 0;

    foreach (Post post in set.Posts)
    {
        if (post.Views > views)
        {
            views = post.Views;
            popularPostID = post.PostID;
        }
    }

    return popularPostID;
}
```

Extended Properties

Extended properties are very nice and helpful features in Community Server APIs. Assume that you want to store and retrieve some data that can't be stored in default Community Server database columns. One solution is to write your own code to extend the database and save your data in your new structures. For a small amount of data there is a better solution.

Using extended properties, you can store your data in and retrieve it from the database without changing its structure. Community Server team members have created the necessary columns in various tables to store this data and also the appropriate APIs so that it is easy for you to work with them.

Many objects in Community Server APIs support extended properties such as `Post` and its children (`WeblogPost`, `ForumPost`, `GalleryPost`), `Section`, and `User`. The way to use these APIs for all objects is similar. Community Server provides some helper methods to set and get different types of data for extended properties, but all of them use two core methods: `GetExtendedProperty` and `SetExtendedProperty`. `GetExtendedProperty` gets a string name for extended property and returns its value. `SetExtendedProperty` gets a string name and a string value and saves an extended property for them.

By default, common data is stored as extended properties in Community Server. For example, all information about blog feedback authors and URLs are stored as extended properties on the `WeblogPost` object. The following list contains some of the properties that are stored as extended attributes in the database for this object:

❑ The commenter's name will be stored as the `SubmittedUserName` extended property.

❑ The trackback name will be stored as the `trackbackName` extended property.

❑ The trackback URL will be stored as the `TitleUrl` extended property.

Thankfully, Community Server provides normal properties for all default information that it stores as extended properties, so you don't need to be aware of their extended property name. One good application for extended properties is storing extra information about registered users. You can save some information, such as the phone number and security code, as extended properties for the `User` object. Later in this chapter, you'll see some examples of extended attributes.

Query/Set Model

The Query/Set model is one of the essential principles in Community Server development. To get data from APIs and manipulate them, you need to use a process that consists of two important steps:

❑ **Define a Query object** — Community Server provides several types of `Query` objects, which are very similar. These objects are responsible to define a query to fetch data from database.

❑ **Use a Set object** — After defining a `Query` object, you need to use a `Set` object to keep your data.

You're probably familiar with .NET development, where you write a SQL query to select specific data then save them into one of the data objects such as a `DataSet`.

Community Server implements the same model, but makes it simpler and saves you from having to work directly with the database. Instead of using a SQL query, which can be complicated with the Community Server database, you will use a `Query` object, which is very simple and easy to use. You will also use a `Set` object rather than a `DataSet` because `Set` objects provide the appropriate properties and methods to simplify Community Server development.

Now that you understand the concept of the Query/Set model in Community Server development, we can talk about different `Query` and `Set` objects that play a role in this model.

`ThreadQuery` is the base class for all `Query` classes. You can use it to select a collection of threads or `Post` objects. `BlogThreadQuery`, `ForumThreadQuery`, and `GalleryThreadQuery` classes are derived from this base class and can be used to select a collection of `WeblogPost`, `ForumPost`, or `GalleryPost` objects. In addition to these `Query` classes, there is a `UserQuery` class, which isn't derived from `ThreadQuery` and will be discussed in the `User` section later in this chapter.

There are two general `Set` classes in Community Server APIs: `ThreadSet` and `PostSet`. `ThreadSet` can be used as a container for a set of threads, and `PostSet` can be used as a container for a set of posts.

Obviously, you can convert a `Post` object to one of the `WeblogPost`, `ForumPost`, or `GalleryPost` objects, so there is no need to have a separate `Set` class for each of these classes and you can use `PostSet` instead.

`Query` objects let you select data based on several parameters. They also allow you to sort or filter them based on different parameters. These parameters will be presented on basis of a `Query` object type so you should choose the appropriate `Query` object for the application that you're going to develop against.

`Set` objects help you select a collection of different types of post objects, but you need to use another mechanism to select a single post. Each application provides a namespace that contains several static methods to let you select a single post, a set of posts from a query, add a post, update a post, and finally remove a post. Steps to use these namespaces and their static methods are similar for all applications, and you just have to use appropriate namespace and class names.

The following code provides an example of `WeblogPosts` static methods. This is a method that gets current post in a blog as `WeblogPost` object, updates its subject to "Hello World!", and saves all changes. It uses `CommunityServer.Blogs.Components.WeblogPosts` namespace static methods to accomplish these tasks.

```
void ChangeSubject()
{
    CSContext context = CSContext.Current;

    WeblogPost post = WeblogPosts.GetPost(context.PostID, true, true, false);
    post.Subject = "Hello World!";

    WeblogPosts.Update(post);
}
```

The following examples help to clarify the concept of `Query` classes.

The next listing is a code snippet of `BlogThreadQuery` usage, which selects recent published blog posts and sorts them in descending order. Its page size is 20, and its page index is 0, so it will return the first page of 20 selected posts.

```
BlogThreadQuery query = new BlogThreadQuery();
query.BlogPostType = BlogPostType.Post;
query.PublishedFilter = BlogPostPublishedFilter.Published;
query.SortBy = BlogThreadSortBy.MostRecent;
query.SortOrder = SortOrder.Descending;
query.PageSize = 20;
query.PageIndex = 0;
```

Now, take a look at a code snippet of ForumThreadQuery usage that selects forum threads for the current forum and sorts them in descending order based on total replies, while ignoring sticky posts. It will return the second page of results, where each page has 15 threads.

```
ForumThreadQuery query = new ForumThreadQuery();
query.SectionID = CSContext.Current.SectionID;
query.SortBy = SortThreadsBy.TotalReplies;
query.SortOrder = SortOrder.Descending;
query.IgnoreStickyPosts = true;
query.PageSize = 15;
query.PageIndex = 1;
```

The following is a code snippet of GalleryThreadQuery usage that selects the first page of photo gallery items that are approved and sorts them in descending order by ratings.

```
GalleryThreadQuery query = new GalleryThreadQuery();
query.PostStatus = PostStatus.Approved;
query.SortBy = GalleryThreadSortBy.Rating;
query.SortOrder = SortOrder.Descending;
query.PageSize = 25;
query.PageIndex = 0;
```

Blog Recent Feedback Control

So far in this chapter, you've discovered some important concepts in Community Server development through code snippets. Here is a real-world example that uses most of these concepts to help you understand the usage in the previous sections.

This example is a custom control that can be used to list recent feedback comments for individual blogs in their sidebar with some details. It's also customizable to show any number of recent feedback comments and to select local comments or trackbacks only.

This control is implemented as a single ASP.NET user control with code inline model. Thanks to Visual Studio 2005, you can use IntelliSense for your development. Implementing this control as a single-user control makes it easy to deploy.

Start with a new user control and use a Repeater server control in order to display recent feedback comments and their details. Bind it to a DataSet, which is returned from a function in the code and contains some information about recent feedback comments like post subject, author, type, URL, and date. Put this user control in /Themes/Blogs/default/Skins because you want to add it to the default blog theme sidebar and start your development.

The main body for the code consists of a function named getFeedbacks, which takes five parameters and returns a DataSet of recent feedback comments with their information. Its parameters are listed here:

❑ SectionID — Integer value of blog SectionID.

❑ Count — Integer value of the number of recent feedbacks that will be shown to visitors.

❑ HasComment — Boolean value to check if recent comments must be listed.

❑ HasTrackback — Boolean value to check if recent trackbacks must be listed.

❑ Excerpt — Boolean value to check if a part of post title must be listed.

Logic for the `getFeedbacks` function is simple and is presented in this code example:

```
private DataSet getFeedbacks(int sectionID, int count, bool hasComment,
    bool hasTrackBack, bool excerpt)
{
    BlogThreadQuery query = new BlogThreadQuery();

    ThreadSet feedbacks = new ThreadSet();

    if ((hasComment == false) && (hasTrackBack == false))
        return null;
    if (hasComment == true)
        query.BlogPostType = BlogPostType.Comment;
    if (hasTrackBack == true)
        query.BlogPostType = BlogPostType.Trackback;
    if ((hasComment == true) && (hasTrackBack == true))
        query.BlogPostType = (BlogPostType.Comment | BlogPostType.Trackback);
    query.SortBy = BlogThreadSortBy.MostRecent;
    query.SortOrder = SortOrder.Descending;
    query.PublishedFilter = BlogPostPublishedFilter.Published;
    query.PageSize = count;
    query.SectionID = sectionID;


    feedbacks = WeblogPosts.GetBlogThreads(query, false);

    DataSet ds = new DataSet();
    DataTable dt = new DataTable();

    dt.Columns.Add("ID");
    dt.Columns.Add("Date");
    dt.Columns.Add("UserName");
    dt.Columns.Add("Url");
    dt.Columns.Add("Subject");
    dt.Columns.Add("PostUrl");
    dt.Columns.Add("FeedbackType");
    dt.Columns.Add("BlogName");
    dt.Columns.Add("BlogUrl");

    ds.Tables.Add(dt);

    foreach (Post feedback in feedbacks.Threads)
    {
        WeblogPost post = WeblogPosts.GetPost(feedback.PostID, false, true, false);
        WeblogPost parentPost = WeblogPosts.GetPost(feedback.ParentID, false, true,
            false);

        DataRow Row = ds.Tables[0].NewRow();

        Row["ID"] = feedback.PostID;

        if ((feedback.GetExtendedAttribute("SubmittedUserName") != null) &&
            (feedback.GetExtendedAttribute("SubmittedUserName") != string.Empty))
        {
            Row["UserName"] = feedback.GetExtendedAttribute("SubmittedUserName");
```

```
                    Row["FeedbackType"] = "Comment";
            }
            else
            {
                Row["Username"] = feedback.Username;
                Row["FeedbackType"] = "Comment";
            }

            if (feedback.GetExtendedAttribute("trackbackName") != null &&
                feedback.GetExtendedAttribute("trackbackName") != string.Empty)
            {
                Row["UserName"] = feedback.GetExtendedAttribute("trackbackName");
                Row["FeedbackType"] = "TrackBack";
            }
            Row["Url"] =
                SiteUrls.Instance().Redirect(post.GetExtendedAttribute("TitleUrl"));
            Row["Date"] = post.PostDate;
            Row["Subject"] = post.Subject;
            Row["BlogName"] = post.Section.Name;
            Row["BlogUrl"] = post.Section.Url;
            Row["PostUrl"] = BlogUrls.Instance().Post(parentPost);

            ds.Tables[0].Rows.Add(Row);
    }

    return ds;
}
```

After getting recent feedbacks via this function, you can pass required parameters to it and bind results to a `Repeater` control, `RecentFeedbacksList`, in the page's load event (see the following):

```
private void Page_Load(object sender, System.EventArgs e)
{
    CSContext context = CSContext.Current;

    DataSet ds = new DataSet();
    ds = getFeedbacks(context.SectionID, 10, true, true, true);

    RecentFeedbacksList.DataSource = ds;
    RecentFeedbacksList.DataBind();
}
```

So, your final code should look like this:

```
<%@ Control Language="c#" %>
<%@ Register TagPrefix="CS" Namespace="CommunityServer.Controls"
Assembly="CommunityServer.Controls" %>
<%@ Import Namespace="System.Data" %>
<%@ Import Namespace="System.Data.SqlClient" %>
<%@ Import Namespace="CommunityServer.Components" %>
<%@ Import Namespace="CommunityServer.Blogs.Components" %>

<script language="C#" runat="server">
    private void Page_Load(object sender, System.EventArgs e)
```

```
{
    CSContext context = CSContext.Current;

    DataSet ds = new DataSet();
    ds = getFeedbacks(context.SectionID, 10, true, true, true);

    RecentFeedbacksList.DataSource = ds;
    RecentFeedbacksList.DataBind();
}

private DataSet getFeedbacks(int sectionID, int count, bool hasComment,
    bool hasTrackBack, bool excerpt)
{
    BlogThreadQuery query = new BlogThreadQuery();

    ThreadSet feedbacks = new ThreadSet();

    if ((hasComment == false) && (hasTrackBack == false))
        return null;
    if (hasComment == true)
        query.BlogPostType = BlogPostType.Comment;
    if (hasTrackBack == true)
        query.BlogPostType = BlogPostType.Trackback;
    if ((hasComment == true) && (hasTrackBack == true))
        query.BlogPostType = (BlogPostType.Comment | BlogPostType.Trackback);
    query.SortBy = BlogThreadSortBy.MostRecent;
    query.SortOrder = SortOrder.Descending;
    query.PublishedFilter = BlogPostPublishedFilter.Published;
    query.PageSize = count;
    query.SectionID = sectionID;


    feedbacks = WeblogPosts.GetBlogThreads(query, false);

    DataSet ds = new DataSet();
    DataTable dt = new DataTable();


    dt.Columns.Add("ID");
    dt.Columns.Add("Date");
    dt.Columns.Add("UserName");
    dt.Columns.Add("Url");
    dt.Columns.Add("Subject");
    dt.Columns.Add("PostUrl");
    dt.Columns.Add("FeedbackType");
    dt.Columns.Add("BlogName");
    dt.Columns.Add("BlogUrl");

    ds.Tables.Add(dt);

    foreach (Post feedback in feedbacks.Threads)
    {
        WeblogPost post = WeblogPosts.GetPost(feedback.PostID, false, true,
            false);
        WeblogPost parentPost = WeblogPosts.GetPost(feedback.ParentID, false,
```

```
                        true, false);

            DataRow Row = ds.Tables[0].NewRow();

            Row["ID"] = feedback.PostID;

            if ((feedback.GetExtendedAttribute("SubmittedUserName") != null) &&
                (feedback.GetExtendedAttribute("SubmittedUserName") !=
                    string.Empty))
            {
                Row["UserName"] =
                    feedback.GetExtendedAttribute("SubmittedUserName");
                Row["FeedbackType"] = "Comment";
            }
            else
            {
                Row["Username"] = feedback.Username;
                Row["FeedbackType"] = "Comment";
            }

            if (feedback.GetExtendedAttribute("trackbackName") != null &&
                feedback.GetExtendedAttribute("trackbackName") != string.Empty)
            {
                Row["UserName"] = feedback.GetExtendedAttribute("trackbackName");
                Row["FeedbackType"] = "TrackBack";
            }
            Row["Url"] =
                SiteUrls.Instance().Redirect(post.GetExtendedAttribute("TitleUrl"));
            Row["Date"] = post.PostDate;
            Row["Subject"] = post.Subject;
            Row["BlogName"] = post.Section.Name;
            Row["BlogUrl"] = post.Section.Url;
            Row["PostUrl"] = BlogUrls.Instance().Post(parentPost);

            ds.Tables[0].Rows.Add(Row);
        }

        return ds;
    }
</script>

<div class="CommonSidebarArea">
    <h4 class="CommonSidebarHeader">
        Recent Feedbacks</h4>
    <div class="CommonSidebarContent">
        <ul class="CommonSidebarList">
            <asp:Repeater ID="RecentFeedbacksList" runat="server">
                <ItemTemplate>
                    <li>
                        <asp:HyperLink runat="server" ID="Author" title='<%#
DataBinder.Eval(Container.DataItem,"FeedbackType") %>'
                            NavigateUrl='<%# "http://" + CSContext.Current.SiteUrl
+ DataBinder.Eval(Container.DataItem, "Url") %>'
                            Target="_blank">
```

```
                        <%# DataBinder.Eval(Container.DataItem,"UserName") %>
                            </asp:HyperLink>
                            on
                            <asp:HyperLink runat="server" ID="Post" title='<%#
DataBinder.Eval(Container.DataItem,"Subject") %>'
                                NavigateUrl='<%#
DataBinder.Eval(Container.DataItem,"PostUrl") %>'>
                    <%# DataBinder.Eval(Container.DataItem,"Subject") %>
                            </asp:HyperLink>
                             at
                            <asp:Literal runat="server" ID="Literal" Text='<%#
Convert.ToDateTime(DataBinder.Eval(Container.DataItem, "Date")).ToString("d MMM
yyyy") %>' />
                        </li>
                    </ItemTemplate>
                </asp:Repeater>
            </ul>
        </div>
</div>
```

Now, add this control to the default blog theme sidebar. To do this, add a reference to this user control in the `Blog-Sidebar.ascx` control and put it somewhere in sidebar, as the following code shows:

```
<%@ Control Language="C#" %>
<%@ Register TagPrefix="CS" Namespace="CommunityServer.Controls"
Assembly="CommunityServer.Controls" %>
<%@ Register TagPrefix="Blog" Namespace="CommunityServer.Blogs.Controls"
Assembly="CommunityServer.Blogs" %>
<%@ Register TagPrefix="Keyvan" TagName="RecentFeedbacks"
Src="~/Themes/Blogs/default/Skins/RecentFeedbacks.ascx" %>
<%@ Import Namespace="CommunityServer.Components" %>
<Blog:WeblogLinks runat="Server" ID="wl" />
<Blog:WeblogQuickLinks runat="Server" ID="wql" />
<Blog:Subscriptions runat="Server" ID="s" />
<Blog:RecentPosts runat="server" ID="rp" />
<div class="CommonSidebarArea">
    <h4 class="CommonSidebarHeader">
        <CS:ResourceControl runat="Server" ResourceName="Tags" />
    </h4>
    <div class="CommonSidebarContent">
        <Blog:TagCloud
TagCloudCSSClasses="CommonTag6,CommonTag5,CommonTag4,CommonTag3,CommonTag2,CommonTa
g1"
            runat="server" IgnoreFilterTags="true" CssClass="CommonSidebarTagCloud"
ID="TagCloud" />
    </div>
</div>
<Blog:BlogNews runat="Server" ID="n" />
<Blog:ArchiveList runat="Server" ID="al" />
<!-- Recent Feedbacks Control -->
<Keyvan:RecentFeedbacks id="RecentFeedbacks1" runat="server">
</Keyvan:RecentFeedbacks>
```

Now, it's time to see your output. Figure 13-1 shows the output of this example.

Figure 13-1: Recent Feedback

Attachments

You've probably used an attachment in forum posts or blog posts. They allow you to include additional files that can be downloaded by visitors who view your post. `CommunityServer.Components` `.PostAttachment` is a commonly used class in the Community Server APIs that represents the attachments that you use.

As seen in previous examples, the `post` base class has an attachment property, so all of its children inherit attachments. Thankfully, the process of working with attachments is similar for all applications and post types. You should know that with current Community Server APIs, each `Post` object can only have one attachment.

The `CommunityServer.Components.PostAttachment` class and the `CommunityServer.` `Components.PostAttachments` namespace serve the main roles in this scenario. The static methods in the `PostAttachments` namespace help you get, add, delete, and update `PostAttachments` (compare this with doing the same operations for `WeblogPost`, `ForumPost`, and `GalleryPost` in the Query/Set model discussed earlier).

It's important to note that there are two types of attachments in Community Server, and both of them are represented by the `PostAttachment` object:

❏　　`Local` — Content for this type of attachment is stored on local storage systems for applications such as databases and file systems.

❏　　`Remote` — Content for this type of attachment is stored on a third-party server, and the application only refers to it with a link and doesn't save the content locally. There is no guarantee for the content of remote attachments.

Table 13-5 provides a list of the important properties of the `PostAttachment` class with a short description about each one.

Table 13-5 PostAttachment Properties

Property	Description
Content	System.IO.Stream object of attachment content.
ContentType	String value of attachment's MIME type.
DateCreated	DateTime value of when attachment has been created.
FileName	String value of attachment's file name.
FriendlyFileName	String value of attachment's friendly file name.
HasDateCreated	Boolean value to check if PostAttachment has a DateCreated property available.
Height	If attachment is an image, this integer value specifies its height.
IsImage	Boolean value to check if attachment is an image.
IsRemote	Boolean value to check if attachment is remote.
Length	Long value of attachment's file length.
PostID	Integer value of the post ID that is using attachment.
SectionID	Integer value of section ID where attachment is being used.
UserID	Integer value of user ID who has created the attachment.
Width	If attachment is an image, this integer value specifies its width.

The next code listing is an example for the PostAttachment class. In this code, you first read the content of an image from a local file system as a MemoryStream and then create a new instance of a PostAttachment. Finally, we add this attachment to a post that is currently being viewed:

```
void AddAttachment()
{
    CSContext context = CSContext.Current;
    String path = context.MapPath("~/Downloads/MyFile.zip");

    FileStream content = new FileStream(path, FileMode.Open);

    PostAttachment attachment = new PostAttachment();
    attachment.Content = content;
    attachment.Length = content.Length;
    attachment.ContentType = "application/zip";
    attachment.DateCreated = DateTime.Now;
    attachment.FileName = Path.GetFileName(path);
    attachment.IsRemote = false;

    PostAttachments.Add(context.Post, attachment);
}
```

Users

Dealing with users and their roles is a common task in Community Server development (and in most web applications, for that matter). The following sections discuss users and roles.

The foundation of this topic is the User object, which is the code representation of a user. Table 13-6 lists important properties for a User object with a short description about each one.

Table 13-6 User Properties

Property	Description
AccountStatus	UserAccountStatus enumeration value that specifies the status of user's account. Possible values are All, ApprovedPending, Approved, Banned, and Disapproved.
AvatarUrl	String value of avatar URL.
BannedUntil	DateTime value to ban user's account until then.
BannedReason	UserBanReason enumeration value to specify the reason to ban user's account. Possible values are Advertising, Aggressive, BadSignature, BadUsername, Baddodging, Other, Profanity, Spam.
CommonNameOrUserName	If a DisplayName is available this will be set to it; otherwise, Username will be used.
ControlPanelManageView	ControlPanelManageView enumeration value to specify the default view type for users in the Control Panel. Possible values are Grid and Tree.
DateCreated	DateTime value of when user account is created.
DisplayName	String value of user's DisplayName.
Editor	SelectableEditor object of default editor.
EditorType	String value of default editor's name.
Email	String value of user's email.
EnableAvatar	Boolean value to check if avatar must be enabled.
EnableCollapsingPanels	Boolean value to check if collapsing panels are enabled.
EnableDisplayInMemberList	Boolean value to check if user must be displayed in members list.
EnableDisplayName	Boolean value to check if DisplayName must be enabled.
EnableEmail	Boolean value to check if email must be enabled.
EnableHtmlEmail	Boolean value to check if HTML emails must be enabled.

Table continued on following page

Property	Description
EnableInk	Boolean value to check if ink must be enabled.
EnableOnlineStatus	Boolean value to check if the user's online status must be displayed.
EnablePrivateMessages	Boolean value to check if private messages must be enabled for the user.
EnableThreadTracking	Boolean value to check if thread tracking must be enabled for the user.
EnableUserAvatar	Boolean value to check if the user's avatar must be enabled.
EnableUserSignatures	Boolean value to check if the user's signature must be enabled.
ExtendedAttributesCount	Integer value of extended attributes count for User object.
FavoritesShared	FavoriteType enumeration value to check which user's favorites are shared. Possible values are None, Post, Section, and User.
HasAvatar	Boolean value to check if the user has an avatar available.
HasProfile	Boolean value to check if the user has a profile.
IsAdministrator	Boolean value to check if the user is in Administrator role.
IsAnonymous	Boolean value to check if the user is anonymous.
IsAvatarApproved	Boolean value to check if the user's avatar is approved by site administrators.
IsBanned	Boolean value to check if the user is banned.
IsEditor	Boolean value to check if the user is in the Editor role.
IsIgnored	Boolean value to check if the user is ignored.
IsModerator	Boolean value to check if the user is in the Moderator role.
IsRegistered	Boolean value to check if user is in the Registered role.
LastAction	String value of user's last action on the site.
LastActivity	DateTime value indicating when the user performed his or her last activity on the site.
LastLogin	DateTime value indicating when the user logged in to site.
ModerationLevel	ModerationLevel enumeration value to specify the user's moderation level. Possible values are Moderated and Unmoderated.
Password	String value of the user's password.
PasswordAnswer	String value of the user's answer to a security question to retrieve a forgotten password.

PasswordQuestion	String value of the user's question to retrieve a forgotten password.
Points	Integer value of the user's points.
PostRank	Array of bytes for the user's post rank.
PostsModerated	Integer value of the number of the user's posts that are moderated.
PostViewType	PostViewType enumeration value specifying the user's default post view type. Possible values are Flat and Threaded.
Profile	An instance of the Profile object for the user's profile.
SettingsID	Integer value of the SettingsID for the site where this user is registered.
Theme	String value of the user's default theme name.
TotalPosts	Integer value of the user's total posts.
UserID	Integer value of the user ID.
UserName	String value of Username.

Table 13-7 lists important methods for the User class.

Table 13-7 User Methods

Method	Description
ChangePassword	Gets string value of current and new passwords and changes user's password to the new one.
ChangePasswordAnswer	Gets string values of current password answer, a new question, and a new answer, and changes the user's password answer to the new value.
GetExtendedAttribute	Returns the string value of an extended property by getting its key value.
GetTimeZone	Returns a DateTime value of current time on basis of user's time zone.
GetUserCookie	Returns a UserCookie object.
IsInRoles	Gets an array of strings for role names and returns a Boolean value to check whether user is in all of those roles or not.
ResetPassword	Resets user's password and returns a Boolean value to check whether operation was successful or not.
SetExtendedAttributes	Gets string values for extended attribute name and value and adds it to extended attributes.

Getting a collection of User objects follows the same process as in the Query/Set model: defining a CommunityServer.UserQuery and getting a list of users via a CommunityServer.Components.

UserSet object. Here is an example of this usage. It uses a UserQuery to get the top five most active users; then returns the Username of the member who has joined site most recently.

```
String OldestActiveUser()
{
    UserQuery query = new UserQuery();
    query.Status = UserAccountStatus.Approved;
    query.SortBy = SortUsersBy.Posts;
    query.Order = SortOrder.Descending;
    query.PageSize = 5;

    UserSet users = Users.GetUsers(query, false);

    String username = String.Empty;
    DateTime joinDate = DateTime.Now;

    foreach (User user in users.Users)
    {
        if (user.DateCreated < joinDate)
        {
            username = user.Username;
            joinDate = user.DateCreated;
        }
    }

    return username;
}
```

The model for user manipulation is similar across many applications. The CommunityServer.Users namespace provides several static methods that help you get, add, delete, and update User objects.

The next code example gets the User object for the current user who is viewing the site and then removes this user and reassigns his or her posts to the anonymous user:

```
void RemoveCurrentUser()
{
    CSContext context = CSContext.Current;

    User user = context.User;

    Users.DeleteUser(user, "Anonymous");
}
```

Roles

Community Server comes with some predefined roles as well as user-defined roles. Each role is represented by the CommunityServer.Components.Role class in code. The CommunityServer.Components .Roles namespace is where you can use some static methods to get, add, delete, or update instances of the Role class.

Community Server identifies each role with a GUID. This identifier can be found in the application's Control Panel as well. On the other hand, Community Server has some predefined roles that it uses in its APIs so there are separate properties and methods to support them in some classes.

Table 13-8 lists the `Role` class's properties with a description about them.

Table 13-8 Role Properties

Property	Description
Description	String value of a description about `Role`.
IsRoleIDAssigned	Boolean value to check if the `Role` object has an ID assigned to it.
Name	String value of `Role`'s name.
RoleID	GUID value of `Role`'s identifier.

Let's finish our discussion about roles by giving an example of the `Roles` class's static methods. This example consists of three simple steps: creating a new role (named `NewRole`), getting this new role and updating its `Name` and `Description`, and adding a current user who is viewing the site to this newly added role.

```
void CreateNewRole()
{
    // Create new role
    Roles.AddRole("NewRole");

    // Get this new role.
    Role role = Roles.GetRole("NewRole");

    // Update role
    role.RoleID = Guid.NewGuid();
    role.Name = "MyRole";
    role.Description = "A sample role";

    Roles.UpdateRole(role);

    // Add current user to this role
    CSContext context = CSContext.Current;

    Roles.AddUserToRole(context.User.Username, role.Name);
}
```

Site URLs

Community Server has a great `SiteUrls` provider, which lets you change the address of your applications easily. There are two types of `SiteUrl` APIs available for developers:

❑   **Global** — URLs that are used in all parts of a Community Server application such as the URL of a weblog application, forums application, redirector page, and FAQ page.

❑   **Application specific** — URLs that are used for a specific application are useful only for that application. For example, URLs for blog posts or individual blogs are application-specific URLs.

On the basis of these two types of URLs, there are two different groups of APIs available. APIs for global URLs are available in the CommunityServer.Components namespace, and APIs for each application are available in each respective application's namespace.

Global URL APIs are available in the CommunityServer.Components.SiteUrls namespace. In addition to some static methods that help you to do some global tasks, the Instance() function returns an instance of the SiteUrls object, which is the main object that plays the role in global URL APIs.

The SiteUrls class provides various string properties and static string functions. All of these properties and functions return a URL. Properties are used for those URLs that are constant and don't need dynamic parameters (i.e., Control Panel home page) and functions are used for those URLs that need some parameters (i.e., the Private Message page for each user on basis of the UserID).

This is an example of properties for global URLs. It simply returns the URL of the weblog's homepage:

```
String GetWeblogsHomePageUrl()
{
    SiteUrls urls = SiteUrls.Instance();

    return urls.WeblogsHome;
}
```

The following is an example of string functions for global URLs. It uses the Message() function and gets a CSExceptionType enumeration value to return the URL of the Access Denied message.

```
String GetAccessDeniedMessageUrl()
{
    SiteUrls urls = SiteUrls.Instance();

    return urls.Message(CSExceptionType.AccessDenied);
}
```

The other type of URL API is for application-specific URLs. These APIs are similar to global URLs, but will be used within an application. This is a sample code that returns the URL for current blog post that is being viewed.

```
String GetCurrentBlogPostUrl()
{
    BlogUrls urls = BlogUrls.Instance();

    CSContext context = CSContext.Current;

    WeblogPost currentPost = WeblogPosts.GetPost(context.PostID, false, true,
false);

    return urls.Post(currentPost);
}
```

Event Logs

Nowadays, event-logging systems are a common part of every application. They are a useful tool for site administrators and developers to monitor events and errors and track other information about their site. This feature was common enough to encourage the Microsoft ASP.NET team to add a built-in Health-Monitoring feature to ASP.NET 2.0.

Community Server has its own event-logging system. This system logs events into the Community Server database in the `cs_EventLog` table. A full report for event log entries with useful details is available in a site's Control Panel for administrators as well. This logging system logs some events in a Community Server application, such as an application's start and stop time, spam blocker events, and incoming and outgoing trackback reports, as well as other events.

Obviously, any good custom module will use this mechanism to log events. Thankfully, it's easy to use the Event Log APIs in order to log events in Community Server. For background, you should know that there are four types of events in Community Server, which are represented as an `EventType` enumerator:

- ❑ `Debug` — An event that is used to log something in order to help a developer debug code.

- ❑ `Error` — An event that is used to report an occurrence of an error in an application to the site administrator.

- ❑ `Information` — An event that is used to inform the site administrator about something such as the application's starting or stopping.

- ❑ `Warning` — An event that should be attended to by a site administrator or developer such as the automoderation of blog posts by spam add-on rules.

The `CommunityServer.Components.EventLogEntry` class plays the main role in the event logs subsystem. It represents an event log entry in code. Table 13-9 lists all properties for this class, with a short description about each one.

Table 13-9 EventLogEntry Properties

Property	Description
Category	String value of the event's category.
EntryID	Integer value of entry ID.
EventDate	`DateTime` value indicating when an event has occurred.
EventID	Integer value of an event ID. Each event has an identifier. All events are listed in the `cs_EventDescription` table in database. It's worth to add a new row with description for your new event types.
EventType	`EventType` enumeration value of event's type.
MachineName	String value of machine's name where an event has occurred.
Message	String value of an event's message.
SettingsID	Integer value of the settings ID.

Static methods in the `CommunityServer.Components.EventLogs` namespace allows you to add a new `EventLogEntry` to the system or to clear all items that were added before a specific date. There are also some overloads and static methods that work as a shortcut to help you add a new entry by providing default values to methods parameters and avoid creating a new instance of `EventLogEntry`. Table 13-10 lists them with descriptions.

Table 13-10 EventLogs Static Methods

Method	Description
Clear	Gets a `DateTime` value and clears all event logs entry older than specified date.
Debug	Adds a new `Debug` event type entry to event log. It saves you from having to create a new instance of the `EventLogEntry` object by getting all required properties from its parameters.
Info	Adds a new Information event type entry to the event log. It saves you from having to create a new instance of the `EventLogEntry` object by getting all required properties from its parameters.
Warn	Adds a new `Warning` event type entry to the event log. It saves you from having to create a new instance of the `EventLogEntry` object by getting all required properties from its parameters.
Write	Adds a new `EventLogEntry` to the event log by getting an instance of `EventLogEntry` or all required properties.

The next example creates an `EventLogEntry` to warn site administrators about there being an unexpected number of online anonymous users (suppose that more than 500 online anonymous users are unexpected):

```
void UnexpectedAnonymousUsers()
{
    CSContext context = CSContext.Current;

    if (context.Statistics.CurrentAnonymousUsers > 500)
    {
        EventLogEntry entry = new EventLogEntry();
        entry.Category = "Unexpected Anonymous Users";
        entry.EventDate = DateTime.Now;
        entry.EventID = 1002;
        entry.EventType = EventType.Warning;
        entry.MachineName = context.Context.Server.MachineName;
        entry.Message = String.Format("There are {0} online anonymous users.",
            context.Statistics.CurrentAnonymousUsers);
        entry.SettingsID = context.SettingsID;

        EventLogs.Write(entry);
    }
}
```

CSException

Like the event log, Community Server comes with its own exception types for what it wants to do. Community Server uses `CommunityServer.Components.CSException` as the class for its exceptions. This class is derived from the `ApplicationException` class in .NET, but it has several extra properties and methods that are suitable for a Community Server application.

There are two different constructors for the `CSException` class that are used to log exceptions that occur during user creation and then to log exceptions that occur at other times (see `CreateUserStatus` in Table 13-11).

The `CSException` class has some properties, which are listed in Table 13-11.

Table 13-11 CSException Properties

Property	Description
Category	Integer value of the exception's category.
CreateUserStatus	The `CreateUserStatus` enumerator value that specifies the type of exception on user creation.
DateCreated	`DateTime` value of when exception has occurred.
DateLastOccurred	`DateTime` value of when the exception has occurred for the last time.
ExceptionID	Integer value of the exception ID.
ExceptionType	The `CSExceptionType` enumerator that specifies the type of exception.
Frequency	Integer value of the number of same exception instances that have occurred so far.
HttpPathAndQuery	String value of the `HttpPathAndQuery` where the exception has occurred.
HttpReferrer	String value of the `HttpReferrer` for the exception.
HttpVerb	String value of the HTTP method for the exception.
IPAddress	String value of the IP address of the user who has thrown this exception.
LoggedStackTrace	String value of logged stack trace for the exception.
Message	String value of the exception message. It's read-only.
UserAgent	String value of the user agent for the user who has thrown this exception.

After handling an exception with the appropriate `CSException` object, you can log it by calling the `Log()` method. This method will add information about this exception to the `cs_Exceptions` table in the Community Server database and will let you view the exception in the Control Panel.

This code shows an example of `CSException` usage to handle an exception.

```
void CreateUserWithAge(String Username, String Password, String Email, int Age)
{
    if (!DisallowedNames.NameIsDisallowed(Username))
    {
        throw new CSException(CreateUserStatus.DisallowedUsername, "Username is
            disallowed");
    }
    else
    {
        User user = new User();
        user.Username = Username;
        user.Password = Password;
        user.Email = Email;
        user.SetExtendedAttribute("age", Age.ToString());

        Users.Create(user, true);
    }
}
```

Sending Emails

Community Server uses email for system notifications of various types and to allow members to interact with each other; it also includes a mass emailing feature. Therefore, emails are another frequently used tool in Community Server. All emails are stored in the `cs_EmailQueue` table in the Community Server database. A `CSJob` will run on regular basis in order to send emails from the `cs_EmailQueue` to recipients.

Community Server email functionality is built atop ASP.NET email features. Several types of predefined email templates in Community Server help you send emails for a variety of common scenarios. Templates will be discussed in Chapter 15, but here we will use them in API calls.

`CommunityServer.Components.Emails` contains various static methods that send emails by using the predefined templates. In addition to these methods, there are two static methods available that let you to get an `ArrayList` of queued emails or to process the queue. `Emails.EmailsInQueue` takes a settings ID and returns an `ArrayList` of queued emails. `Emails.SendQueuedEmails` sends all queued emails to recipients.

As an example, the following code implements the `Emails.UserCreate` method to notify a new user about his new account creation:

```
void NewUserNotification()
{
    CSContext context = CSContext.Current;
    Emails.UserCreate(context.User, context.User.Password);
}
```

These methods work as a shortcut and save you from doing a longer manual process. However, you sometimes need to send an email for which a template isn't provided. In this case, you need to create an email, set its properties, and add it to the email queue manually.

CommunityServer.Components.EmailQueueProvider comes in handy in this instance. It lets you add a System.Web.Mail.MailMessage to the email queue. It also enables some ways to delete a queued email, dequeue an email, and send queued emails.

The EmailQueueProvider.QueueEmail() method gets a MailMessage object and adds it to the email queue. This email will be processed by the next email job iteration, and the email will be delivered to recipients.

This code listing is an example where the system sends an email to the site owner to let him know about an unexpected number of anonymous users on his site. This method can be added to a CSJob to run on regular basis. You'll learn more about CSJobs later in this chapter.

```
void NotifyUnexpectedAnonymousUsers()
{
    CSContext context = CSContext.Current;

    if (context.Statistics.CurrentAnonymousUsers > 500)
    {
        MailMessage mail = new MailMessage();
        mail.From = "sender@server.com";
        mail.To = context.SiteSettings.AdminEmailAddress;
        mail.Priority = MailPriority.Normal;
        mail.BodyFormat = MailFormat.Text;
        mail.Body = String.Format("There are {0} online anonymous users on {1}",
            context.Statistics.CurrentAnonymousUsers,
                context.SiteSettings.SiteName);
        mail.Subject = String.Format("[{0}] Unexpected Anonymous Users",
            context.SiteSettings.SiteName);

        EmailQueueProvider.Instance().QueueEmail(mail);
    }
}
```

Here is a short description about other available methods in the EmailQueueProvider:

❑   DeleteQueuedEmail — Takes the GUID of an email's identifier and removes it from the email queue.

❑   DequeueEmail — Takes a settings ID for a site and returns an ArrayList of dequeued emails.

❑   QueueSendingFailure — Takes an ArrayList of emails, an integer value for the failure interval, and an integer value to specify the maximum number of tries if failure occurred, and sends emails from ArrayList to their recipients.

> At the time of writing, Community Server 2.1 and older versions are using the previous APIs, but the team is working on new APIs for emailing in Community Server 3.0, which can change these items and is compatible with .NET 2.0.

Configuration

You learned about configurations in Chapter 10, but this section walks you through the APIs available to work with configurations in the `communityserver.config` file to help you retrieve configuration information for your site.

You can work with APIs through code using the `CommunityServer.Configuration` namespace. There are appropriate classes for you to deal with configurations, but the most common one is `CSConfiguration`. Instances of this class can provide a site's configurations through their properties and methods. The following code shows a function that returns the cache factor for a site:

```
int CacheFactor()
{
    CSConfiguration configuration = CSConfiguration.GetConfig();

    return configuration.CacheFactor;
}
```

The purpose of the `CSConfiguration` properties is obvious from their names and what you saw in Chapter 10, but there is an important method for this class that you should learn about.

The `GetConfigSection()` method helps you to retrieve any configuration settings from the `communityserver.config` file. While most default configuration settings can be accessed through the `CSConfiguration` properties discussed previously, this method can be used to select XML nodes for any configuration element, including those from custom configuration settings. The function takes an XPath expression as an argument and returns a corresponding `XmlNode`. You apply XML manipulations on this `XmlNode` to get any configuration information you want.

> XPath is one of the XML-related technologies that lets you select specified information from an XML document. You can read the *XPath 2.0 Programmer's Reference* (Wrox Press, 0-7645-6910-4) or *Beginning XML*, 3rd Edition (Wrox Press, 0-7645-7077-3) for more information.

In the following code listing, you can see a function that uses the `GetConfigSection` method to return the cache factor. It uses an XPath expression and some XML manipulations to retrieve appropriate data:

```
int CacheFactor()
{
    CSConfiguration configuration = CSConfiguration.GetConfig();

    XmlNode node = configuration.GetConfigSection("/CommunityServer/Core");

    if (node != null)
    {
        return int.Parse(node.Attributes["cacheFactor"].InnerText);
    }
    return 0;
}
```

CSModule

CSModules were introduced in Chapter 11. CSModules are a great feature in Community Server development. They can solve many extending problems quickly and easily. They are easy to develop and deploy — and they have a straightforward definition, which makes them even sweeter. This section shows you some advanced concepts about CSModules and how to write a simple CSModule, using what you've seen in this chapter to understand the relationship between APIs in action.

After reading Chapter 11, you probably asked yourself, "How can I apply my configurations and send my parameters to a CSModule?" The answer is simple. When you implement the ICSModule interface, the Init() method takes two parameters: the first one is a CSApplication, and the second one is an XmlNode. This XmlNode object helps you to pass your configuration information and parameters to CSModules. Actually, this XmlNode is a node in the communityserver.config file under the <CSModules> element, which contains the definition for your CSModule. There you can add XML elements or attributes and pass them to your CSModule. Finally, you can use XML manipulations to retrieve this information and use it in your CSModule.

The event that your module subscribes to will determine the first parameter that your event handler accepts; however, the second one is always a CSEventArgs object. Both of these parameters provide information to your event subscriber.

To get information from the first parameter in your event subscriber method, you need to have a good background in Community Server APIs. From reading this chapter, you will have most of this knowledge. There are some techniques, such as casting a Community Server object to another object type, which can help you in some scenarios as well. For example, if you use the PreRenderPost event handler to write your CSModule and want to implement something for your blog posts, you may need a WeblogPost. The problem is that a Post object is provided by this event handler. As discussed before, a Post object can be converted to one of its children (WeblogPost, ForumPost, or GalleryPost), so you can use this as your solution.

The second parameter in your event handler is a CSEventArgs object. This object comes in handy when you want to find some information about the application where your object is going to be used. For example, in a PreRenderPost event, you can use this CSEventArgs object to apply your CSModule only to weblog application feeds.

The following is a simple example that applies these techniques in a real-world scenario. In this example, you will write a CSModule that takes the address of a text file and adds the content of this file to the end of all feed entries in all individual blogs. This CSModule can be used to add advertisement or copyright notices to feeds.

The address of that text file will be passed as a relative address for the filePath attribute in the communityserver.config file under the appropriate node. The PreRenderPost event handler is used in conjunction with some casings to target my changes to weblog feeds.

The following code is the simple source code for this CSModule:

```
using System;
using System.Xml;
using System.IO;
```

```
using CommunityServer;
using CommunityServer.Components;


namespace WroxProCS.Chapter13
{
    public class FeedCopyright : ICSModule
    {
        private string filePath;

        public void Init(CSApplication csa, XmlNode node)
        {
            CSContext context = CSContext.Current;

            csa.PreRenderPost += new CSPostEventHandler(csa_PreRenderPost);

            XmlAttribute filePathNode = node.Attributes["filePath"];
            try
            {
                this.filePath = context.MapPath(filePathNode.Value);
            }
            catch
            {
                throw new CSException(CSExceptionType.UnknownError,
                    "Enter a valid relative address for your text file.");
            }
        }

        private void csa_PreRenderPost(IContent Content, CSPostEventArgs e)
        {
            if ((e.ApplicationType == ApplicationType.Weblog) &&
                (e.Target == PostTarget.Syndication))
            {
                Content.FormattedBody += getCopyright();
            }
        }

        private string getCopyright()
        {
            StreamReader Reader = new StreamReader(File.Open(this.filePath,
                FileMode.Open,
                FileAccess.Read, FileShare.ReadWrite));
            string copyright = Reader.ReadToEnd();

            Reader.Close();

            return copyright;
        }
    }
}
```

In the `Init()` method of this CSModule, first you get the relative address of the text file from an XML node and then use the `CSContext.MapPath()` method to convert the relative address to a physical path. Finally, you'll call the `PreRenderPost` event handler.

In the `PreRenderPost` handler, use the `CSEventArgs` object to target changes to feeds of the weblog application and add the content of the text file to the end of each post.

Now, compile this code and deploy it to the application by copying the assemblies to the `bin` folder and then add the following line to the `communityserver.config` file under the `<CSModules>` element:

```xml
<?xml version="1.0" encoding="utf-8" ?>
<CommunityServer>
    <!-- Other elements are removed to save space -->        <CSModules>
        <add name = "FeedCopyright" type = "WroxProCS.Chapter13.FeedCopyright,
WroxProCS.Chapter13" filePath = "~/utility/copyright.txt" />
    <!-- Other elements are removed to save space -->        </CSModules>
<!-- Other elements are removed to save space -->
</CommunityServer>
```

You should note that `WroxProCS.Chapter13` is the name of the project that you should create in this example. Also, you should ensure that your class is named `FeedCopyright` so that the previous entry in the `CSModules` section corresponds to the appropriate namespace and assembly. For more information about the `CSModules` section in the `communityserver.config` file, please refer to Chapter 11. Now, if you put a copyright notice in the `copyright.txt` file, create a new post, and check the RSS feed in a feed reader, the result should look like Figure 13-2.

Hello World!

This is a test post.

© 2006-2007 Keyvan Nayyeri.

Figure 13-2: Copyright Module Working

`CSModules` are a sweet concept in Community Server. I recommend you write some `CSModules` to practice using Community Server APIs and to extend Community Server to fit your needs.

CSJob

A second way to extend Community Server for special requirements is through the use of a `CSJob`. A `CSJob` is a module that runs on a schedule that can be configured in the `communityserver.config` file. Refer to configuring jobs in Chapter 10.

Writing a `CSJob` is very similar to writing a `CSModule`. There is only one difference, and that is you must implement the `IJob` interface instead of `ICSModule`. This interface needs one method to be implemented: `Execute()`. This method will be called on each job's iteration and takes an `XmlNode` object as its parameter. Like `CSModules`, this `XmlNode` object can be used to pass custom configurations into your `CSJob`.

The next code snippet is an example of a `CSJob` that takes an integer via configurations and runs on regular intervals to notify about an unexpected number of online anonymous users. This job will send an email to site administrators when the threshold is exceeded.

```
using System;
using System.Xml;
using System.Web.Mail;
using CommunityServer.Configuration;
using CommunityServer.Components;

namespace WroxProCS.Chapter13
{
    public class AnonymousUserNotify : IJob
    {
        private int number = 1000;

        public void Execute(XmlNode node)
        {
            XmlAttribute numberAtribute = node.Attributes["number"];
            if (numberAtribute != null)
                this.number = Convert.ToInt32(numberAtribute.Value);


            CSContext context = CSContext.Current;

            if (context.Statistics.CurrentAnonymousUsers > this.number)
            {
                MailMessage mail = new MailMessage();
                mail.From = "noreply@" + context.SiteUrl;
                mail.To = context.SiteSettings.AdminEmailAddress;
                mail.Priority = MailPriority.Normal;
                mail.BodyFormat = MailFormat.Text;
                mail.Subject = String.Format("[{0}] Unexpected Anonymous Users",
                    context.SiteSettings.SiteName);
                mail.Body = String.Format("There are {0} online anonymous users on
                    {1}",
                    context.Statistics.CurrentAnonymousUsers,
                    context.SiteSettings.SiteName);

                EmailQueueProvider.Instance().QueueEmail(mail);
            }
        }
    }
}
```

After compiling this code into an assembly, deploy it to your site by adding the following line to your communityserver.config file:

```
<?xml version="1.0" encoding="utf-8" ?>
<CommunityServer>
    <!-- Other elements are removed to save space -->
  <Jobs minutes = "15" singleThread = "true">
    <job singleThread = "false" minutes="10" name = "AnonymousUserNotify" type =
"WroxProCS.Chapter13.AnonymousUserNotify, WroxProCS.Chapter13" enabled="true"
enableShutDown = "false" number="500" />
        <!-- Other elements are removed to save space -->
    </Jobs>
  <!-- Other elements are removed to save space -->
</CommunityServer>
```

Now, if you navigate to the Jobs Report page in the Control Panel, you should see a new entry for your CSJob there (see Figure 13-3). If you don't see the job right away, you may want to try restarting Community Server by touching the web.config file.

Figure 13-3: Jobs Report

Spam Rule

Spam Rules aren't a way to extend Community Server and customize its behavior but are a great way to fight spammers and prevent them from disrupting a community. Nowadays, the Web is full of spammers and spam messages advertising something or trying to improve the rank of a page. Spammers send many spam messages every day and change their strategies to meet their goals (I get more than 300 spam messages every day). The Community Server team decided to add the Spam Blocker add-on to Community Server 2.0 as one of the free features. They improved it for Community Server 2.1. It's helpful to know that the Spam Blocker is a CSModule itself. As an aside, the rules the CS team developed and integrated into the application work very well, and now I don't see any published spam in my blog.

The Spam Blocker uses a set of Spam Rules. Each incoming comment is checked against the Spam Rules and is assigned a spam score. The Spam Blocker compares the spam score of the comment against user-configured thresholds to determine if the comment is Not Spam, Possible Spam, or Spam. Users may configure the spam system to handle each of these categories by deleting spam immediately or simply keeping the comment unpublished for a moderator to review. The system is highly configurable.

There are some default rules written by the Community Server team as well as several great rules written by the community to fight spam. Here, we'll walk through the steps to write a new Spam Rule, and you can write your own rules to protect your site against spammers.

In a nutshell, writing a Spam Rule consists of these steps:

1. Create a Class Library project.
2. Implement the CommunityServer.Spam.SpamRule abstract class or one of its children such as BlogSpamRule, ForumSpamRule, GallerySpamRule, or FileSpamRule.
3. Compile your class into a DLL file.
4. Deploy this DLL file to your bin folder.
5. Go to Manage Spam Blocker page in Control Panel and configure your Spam Rule.

Community Server identifies each role via a GUID as its identifier. This ID is named `RuleID` and is a part of the abstract base class that you must override for your Spam Rule. Rules also have two other properties that must be overridden: `Name` and `Description`.

The `GetAvailableSettings()` method is the only method that must be implemented, but the `CalculateSpamScore()` method should generally be implemented as well. Here are two methods with a description about each one:

❑ `GetAvailableSettings` — Must return an `ArrayList` of `CommunityServer.Spam`
`.RuleSetting` objects. These objects will provide the user interface in Control Panel when users are configuring your rule.

❑ `CalculateSpamScore` — Takes a `WeblogPost`, `ForumPost`, `GalleryPost` or file gallery `Entry` (which are actually comments), and a `CSPostEventArgs` object as a parameters, and calculates and returns a post score. Here is where most of the process happens.

`RuleSetting` is an object that will be used by the `GetAvailableSettings()` method to make the rule configuration user interface. Each `RuleSetting` makes a row in a pop-up window where you can configure your rule.

By using `RuleSetting` objects that will be returned by the `GetAvailableSettings()` method, you can get parameters for your rule. By calling the `GetSettingValue()` function and passing a `RuleSetting` name from the `CommunityServer.Spam.SpamRule` base class, you can retrieve the value that is entered by user.

Let's apply these theories to a custom Spam Rule. The next example is source code of a Spam Rule that checks the length of a blog comment and assigns some spam points to the comment if its length is shorter than the configured value. It takes two parameters in Control Panel to configure this rule: the minimum allowed length of the comment and the number of points that must be assigned to the comment if its length was shorter than the specified value.

> In a Community Server development, you should always use resources to show text values in the user interface. This step is not included in the Spam Rule example to keep things simple, as you're learning. You will learn about resources in Chapter 15.

```
using System;
using System.Collections;
using CommunityServer.Blogs.Components;
using CommunityServer.Components;
using CommunityServer.Spam;

namespace WroxProCS.Chapter13
{
    public class LengthRule : BlogSpamRule
    {
```

```csharp
        private static Guid ruleGuid = new Guid("37707773-F146-4d68-A1A7-
            F989C0086B4F");

        public override string Description
        {
            get { return "Checks comments for being spam on basis of their
                length."; }
        }

        public override ArrayList GetAvailableSettings()
        {
            ArrayList settingsList = new ArrayList();

            settingsList.Add(new RuleSetting(ruleGuid, "minlength",
                "Enter the minimum expected length of comments:", "10"));
            settingsList.Add(new RuleSetting(ruleGuid, "points",
                "Number of points to assign to post if its length was shorter than
                specified value:", "0"));

            return settingsList;
        }

        public override string Name
        {
            get { return "Comment Length Rule"; }
        }

        public override Guid RuleID
        {
            get { return ruleGuid; }
        }

        public override int CalculateSpamScore(WeblogPost blogPost, CSPostEventArgs
            e)
        {
            base.CalculateSpamScore(blogPost, e);

            if (blogPost.BlogPostType == (BlogPostType.Comment |
                BlogPostType.Trackback))
            {
                if (blogPost.Body.Length <
                    Convert.ToInt32(base.GetSettingValue("minlength")))
                    return Convert.ToInt32(base.GetSettingValue("points"));
            }

            return 0;
        }
    }
}
```

Now, if you compile this code into an assembly and copy it to the `bin` folder and then navigate to the Manage Spam Blocker page in the Control Panel, should see a new rule added there (see Figure 13-4). Note that there is nothing to configure to add your rule to your site. If you click the Configure button, you can configure your custom Spam Rule (see Figure 13-5).

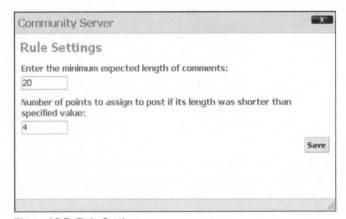

Enabled	Rule Name	Settings
☐	**Forbidden Word** Rates spam factor based on the existence of configured forbidden words	Configure
☐	**Bad Word Count** Rates spam factor based on number of occurences of configured bad words	Configure
☐	**Link Count** Rates spam factor based on number of links (href's) in the post	Configure
☐	**IP Count** Rates spam factor based on the number of recent posts from the same ip address	Configure
☐	**Comment Length Rule** Checks comments for being spam on basis of their length.	Configure

Figure 13-4: Spam Rule List

Community Server [X]

Rule Settings

Enter the minimum expected length of comments:

`20`

Number of points to assign to post if its length was shorter than specified value:

`4`

Save

Figure 13-5: Rule Settings

Add a New Page or User Control to Control Panel

As mentioned previously, you can retrieve a `SectionID` from the `CSContext` class for private Control Panel pages. There is another technique you can use to accomplish this.

Community Server has its own base page class for Control Panel pages or user controls. There are different base classes for each application type and common controls available in the `CommunityServer.ControlPanel.UI` namespace. For example, you can use `BaseBlogPage` for a blog Control Panel page, `BaseBlogControl` for a blog Control Panel user control, or `BaseBlogGridControl` for a control that is derived from the blog Control Panel grid.

This listing shows how to inherit a new user control from the `BaseBlogControl` class:

```csharp
using System;
using CommunityServer.ControlPanel.UI;

namespace WroxProCS.Chapter13
{
    public class MyControl : BaseBlogControl
    {
        // Code
    }
}
```

This code shows equivalent code for a user control markup:

```aspx
<%@ Control Language="c#"
Inherits="CommunityServer.ControlPanel.UI.BaseBlogControl"%>
```

Once you do this, you have access to the `SectionID` for the current blog in the Control Panel by using the `CurrentWeblog.SectionID` property from the base class:

```csharp
int sectionID = base.CurrentWeblog.SectionID;
```

Summary

This chapter showed you the power of Community Server APIs, which let you extend it and write your own modules. After talking about important topics in APIs such as `CSContext`, `Post`, the Query/Set model, `Attachments`, `Users` and `Roles`, `SiteUrls`, event logs, `CSException`, and emails and configuration as well as some other related topics, we jumped into three concepts in Community Server that are easy to develop using these APIs: `CSModule`, `CSJob`, and Spam Rules. You examined real-world examples for these concepts. Finally, we discovered how to add a new page or control to Control Panel by inheriting from the Community Server base classes in order to be able to retrieve information about the current section and application.

In the next chapter, you will learn more about the Community Server database, including how to extend the database. You will also learn how to extend parts of Community Server by using providers.

14

Extending the Database

Community Server has a great data layer and database. Community Server uses SQL Server as its default data store to save data. There are several different providers available to interact with the default database that allows you to select, add, delete, and update data. In addition, you can create your own provider to interact with different types of data stores such as Oracle or MySQL.

In many instances, when you want to extend Community Server or write a custom module for it, you shouldn't need to change the database because APIs help you to work with data. Server development using APIs is explained in Chapter 13. Chapter 13 also introduced the concept of extended properties in Community Server. These are a great way to help you to store custom data in and retrieve it from the database without writing data layer code.

It is important to understand that a default Community Server installation does not require a developer to alter or work directly with database objects. A majority of the time, a developer will not need to alter any portion of the database except for the creation of custom solutions, which can include, but are not limited to, custom stored procedures or data providers. Even though there are few instances where developers need to alter the Community Server database, it is helpful to know how altering the database can be accomplished if the need arises.

The main goal of this chapter is to assist you in becoming more familiar with the Community Server database schema and give you some basic information about providers and how to write your own.

Overview of Database

It's important to choose a data store that is capable of handling the expected number of requests your site will make. For example, an Access database will be down on the first hit to your Community Server site because there are many subsequent database requests from a Community Server application. SQL Server is the best choice for Community Server, since it's completely compatible with ASP.NET, and Microsoft development technologies are capable of handling many requests.

One interesting feature of the Community Server data model is that it allows you to choose different data stores for different applications. For example, you can use an Oracle database for photo galleries while you are simultaneously using SQL Server for blogs or forums. This is one of the ways that the provider pattern and the providers inside of Community Server make it easy to extend the default database.

Understanding the structure of the Community Server database, including tables, views, and stored procedures, is very beneficial when working with the database. A full discussion of each table is beyond the scope of this chapter, but refer to Table 14-1 for a brief description of each table and its role in Community Server.

The great data layer for Community Server 2.1 for ASP.NET 2.0 is made up of 105 tables, 14 views, and 374 stored procedures.

The purpose and use of the various Community Server database tables is a common question on Community Server forums. Table 14-1 represents this list.

Table 14-1 Community Server Database Tables

Table	Description
aspnet_Applications	One of ASP.NET 2.0 tables. It keeps all data about applications that have access to information of this database. It lets you host multiple applications in one database while they have their own membership, personalization and data.
aspnet_Membership	One of ASP.NET 2.0 tables. It keeps data for membership provider.
aspnet_Paths	One of ASP.NET 2.0 tables. It keeps data for paths.
aspnet_PersonalizationAllUsers	One of ASP.NET 2.0 tables. It keeps data for general personalization for all users in personalization provider.
aspnet_PersonalizationPerUser	One of ASP.NET 2.0 tables. It keeps data for personalization for individual users in personalization provider.
aspnet_Profile	One of ASP.NET 2.0 tables. It keeps data for user profiles in ASP.NET 2.0.
aspnet_Roles	One of ASP.NET 2.0 tables. It keeps data for role provider.
aspnet_SchemaVersions	One of ASP.NET 2.0 tables. It keeps data for ASP.NET 2.0 database schema versions.
aspnet_Users	One of ASP.NET 2.0 tables. It keeps data for users.
aspnet_UsersInRoles	One of ASP.NET 2.0 tables. It's an intermediate table between aspnet_Users and aspnet_Roles that keeps relationship data for users and their roles.

Table	Description
aspnet_WebEvent_Events	One of ASP.NET 2.0 tables. It keeps data for ASP.NET 2.0 Health Monitoring feature. This table is useless in Community Server because it has its own event-logging system.
cs_AnonymousUsers	Keeps information about site anonymous users and their activities.
cs_ApplicationConfigurationSettings	Keeps information about different application configurations.
cs_ApplicationType	You saw different ApplicationType enumeration values in Chapter 13 when you were learning APIs. Here, ApplicationTypes are stored in a table.
cs_BannedAddresses	List of banned addresses is stored here.
cs_BannedNetworks	List of banned networks is stored here (the Commercial IP Banning add-on uses this table).
cs_BlogActivityReport	Keeps data for blog activity reports. Later, you can check this information to analyze blogs activity in Control Panel.
cs_CensorShip	Keeps data for censorships. You can manage censorships in Control Panel to replace censored words with new characters.
cs_Content	Data for content management are stored in this table. For example, all the text data you enter in Feature Item in your home page will be stored in a row in this table.
cs_DisallowedNames	List of disallowed names is stored here.
cs_EmailsQueue	All queued emails will be stored here until Emails Jobs sends them to recipients. You learned about email APIs in Chapter 13.
cs_es_Search_RemoveQueue	Keeps a list of posts that should be removed from queue in Enterprise Search add-on. This table is useful for Enterprise Search commercial add-on.
cs_EventDescriptions	Keeps a list of various event types with their description for the event-logging system. There is a relationship between this table and cs_EventLog, which lets you see a description of every event that has occurred.
cs_EventLog	Keeps the list of Event Log entries. You learned about event logging feature in Chapter 13.
cs_Exceptions	Keeps the list of all exceptions that have occurred. You learned about CSExceptions in Chapter 13.

Table continued on following page

Table	Description
cs_FavoritePosts	Keeps the list of favorite posts with some information about them.
cs_FavoriteSections	Keeps the list of favorite sections with some information about them.
cs_FavoriteUsers	Keeps the list of favorite users with some information about them.
cs_Feed	Keeps the list of all subscribed feeds in Reader application with information about them.
cs_FeedPost	Keeps the list of all fetched posts from subscribed feeds in Reader application.
cs_FeedState	Keeps a list of names and descriptions about possible states for a feed in Reader application.
cs_Folder	Keeps a list of folders and information about them in Reader application.
cs_FolderFeed	Keeps a list of feeds in folders in Reader application.
cs_ForumPingback	Keeps a list of pingbacks to forum posts.
cs_Groups	Data for different groups in applications will be stored here. For example list of weblog groups will be stored in this table.
cs_InkData	Data for inks will be stored in this table.
cs_Licenses	Keeps data for application licenses.
cs_LinkCategories	Keeps data for links category.
cs_Links	Keeps data for links.
cs_Messages	Actually, this table is useless since Community Server stores its messages as XML files on local file system storage. You'll learn about messages in Chapter 15.
cs_ModerationAction	Keeps the list of various moderation actions that a moderator can do.
cs_ModerationAudit	Keeps the list of all moderations that are occurred in an application with information about each one.
cs_Moderators	By using a relationship to cs_Users it lists all users who have moderation access to application.
cs_nntp_NewsGroups	Keeps the list of newsgroups for NNTP add-on in an application. NNTP is a commercial add-on.
cs_nntp_Posts	Keeps the list of posts for NNTP add-on in an application. NNTP is a commercial add-on.
cs_PageViews	Keeps all statistic data for page views in an application.

Table	Description
cs_Post_Categories	Keeps the list of post categories in blog applications.
cs_Post_Categories_Parents	Keeps the list of parent categories for categories that are available in cs_Post_Categories table.
cs_PostAttachments	Content and information about post attachments, file gallery items, and photos will be stored here. You can disable database storage by configuring your application to have smaller database.
cs_PostAttachments_Temp	This table is a temporary table for cs_PostAttachments to keep attachment data before moderators approve them.
cs_PostEditNotes	Keeps edit notes for edited posts.
cs_PostMetaData	Keeps some meta data information for posts.
cs_PostRating	Keeps the list of post ranks.
cs_Posts	Keeps all posts for all application that are hosted in this database.
cs_posts_deleted_archive	Keeps a history of all deleted posts in applications. When you delete a post in your applications, an entry will be added to this database.
cs_PostsInCategories	This intermediate table makes a many-to-many relationship between cs_Posts and cs_Post_Categories tables.
cs_PostsArchive	Keeps a list of all archived posts.
cs_PrivateMessages	Keeps a list of private messages by making a relation to original private messages in cs_Posts table.
cs_ProductPermissions	Keeps all default permissions for applications.
cs_Ranks	Keeps a list of all ranks, their icons, and some other related information.
cs_Referrals	Keeps a list of referrals to blog posts and photo gallery photos.
cs_Reports	Keeps a list of application reports. This table can be used to add a new report to system.
cs_RoleQuotas	Keeps data for each role quotas to configure the maximum amount of resource that a role can use.
cs_RollerBlogFeeds	Keeps a list of all feeds that are added to Roller application and their settings.
cs_RollerBlogUrls	Keeps a list of URLs for Roller feeds.

Table continued on following page

Table	Description
cs_RollerBlogPost	Keeps a list of all fetched posts in the Roller application.
cs_SchemaVersion	Keeps the schema version numbers for upgrade patches.
cs_SearchBarrel	Keeps data for the default Community Server search engine. You site content will be indexed here.
cs_SearchIgnoreWords	Keeps a list of ignored words from search engine to improve search results.
cs_SectionPermissions	Keeps a list of permissions for each section.
cs_Sections	Keeps a list of sections in an application with information about them.
cs_SectionsRead	Keeps a list of read sections for users.
cs_SectionTokens	Keeps a list of token sections. Users will be prevented from creating same sections.
cs_SiteMappings	This table maps SiteIDs for all hosted sites in the current database to a corresponding SettingsID.
cs_Sites	Keeps a list of all hosted sites in current database with their URL.
cs_SiteSettings	Keeps settings for all hosted sites in current database.
cs_Smilies	Keeps a list of available smilies and their URLs.
cs_statistic_Site	Keeps a list of general statistic information for all sites.
cs_statistic_user	Keeps a list of general statistic information for users.
cs_Styles	Keeps data for custom styles that are defined by users. For example, you can add your own CSS styles to your blogs from Control Panel.
cs_ThreadRating	Keeps rating data for threads.
cs_Threads	Keeps all threads.
cs_ThreadsRead	Keeps a list of read threads.
cs_TrackedSections	Keeps a list of user subscriptions in an application. For example, a user can subscribe to all new topics in a forum.
cs_TrackedThreads	Keeps a list of user subscriptions to threads.
cs_UrlRedirects	All URLs for redirector will be stored here. This feature lets you to create short links and have statistic information about number of clicks on each one.

Table	Description
cs_Urls	This table is in use by a relationship between it and the cs_Referrals table and stores all incoming URLs.
cs_UserAvatar	Keeps a list of user avatars and their content.
cs_UserInvitation	Keeps a list of user initiations. Invitation is one of new user registration options.
cs_UserProfile	Keeps data for users profiles.
cs_UserReadPost	Keeps a list of read posts for users.
cs_Users	Keeps data for all users. Community Server uses a relationship between this table and ASP.NET 2.0 membership tables in order to add its own requirements to membership.
cs_Version	Keeps version information for sites.
cs_Visits	Keeps a list of visits on the basis of the client's IP address. Some configuration is needed to enable this feature.
cs_VisitsDaily	Keeps list of visits on the basis of the client's IP address per day. Some configuration is needed to enable this feature.
cs_Votes	Keeps a list user's votes data with their PostID.
cs_VotesSummary	Keeps a summary of user's votes.
cs_weblog_Weblogs	Some statistic information about individual weblogs will be stored in this table.
csm_EmailIds	Keeps a list of email IDs and their corresponding user IDs.
csm_MailingLists	Keeps a list of mailing lists for each section.
Files_Downloads	Keeps a report of downloads for file gallery items.

Tables whose names start with an aspnet prefix, are installed by ASP.NET 2.0 database scripts. Some of these tables are not used by Community Server; instead, Community Server has its own mechanisms for the functions they are used for. For example, the Health Monitoring feature in ASP.NET 2.0 is replaced by Event Logs in Community Server (Event Logs are covered in Chapter 13).

A common issue that seems to occur when some users upgrade their databases from an older version of Community Server to a newer version is corrupting their database schema. Once the schema is changed, it's difficult to find the issue and correct it. Community Server has a built-in mechanism to help track schema versions. Upgrade scripts are made of several patches. When you install a patch on your database, the script will add a new row to the cs_SchemaVersion table and provide Major, Minor, and Patch version numbers. Later, other upgrade scripts or database administrators can check these version numbers to make sure that older patches were installed successfully.

Two tables play a key role in the Community Server database: cs_Threads and cs_Posts. Most of Community Server content is stored in the cs_Posts table. In Chapter 13, you learned about the cs_Posts table from the development point of view, but here you will learn more about how the tables work together.

Every blog post, comment, trackback, pingback, forum post, photo gallery item, and private message will be stored as a new row in the cs_Posts table with different SectionID values to distinguish them. Each post has a thread as its unique container. For example, a thread for a forum post is the post that starts its discussion, a thread for a blog comment or trackback is its parent post, and a thread for a photo gallery comment is its parent item. So, each row in cs_Posts table has a unique corresponding row in the cs_Threads table, which helps you to select items based on post threads.

On the other hand, each row in the cs_Posts table has a parent row. A row's parent can be itself, as is the case for the first post in a thread in forums or a blog post. The PostID of the parent is stored in a row's ParentID field. You can use the ParentID and PostID fields to select items based on the post's parents. Generally, the cs_Posts table is the heart of data for a Community Server application.

Adding Stored Procedures

Like other SQL databases, the Community Server database is extensible, making it not only convenient for adding new stored procedures but also straightforward for changing the existing schema. However, you should attempt to use the resources already available in the database before you create any new ones.

It is usually a good idea to create brand-new stored procedures instead of altering existing ones. The reason that you want to avoid changing an existing stored procedure is that whenever you upgrade your site you will not have to worry about rolling back any changes that you have made. By doing this, you can perform an upgrade on Community Server, which may include database changes, without worrying about if you will need to reapply changes that you have made.

One of the instances that may require the use of creating a custom stored procedure is when you plan to create a new report. Perhaps you would like to look at the data of your site in a different way, one that is not offered currently and that is not easily possible with the existing resources. Therefore, you decide to create a new stored procedure that you can then query to report on different data trends.

For the purposes of this example, assume that you need to keep track of the trends related to post ratings. This can be a good gauge for determining the activity of a site, because of the simple fact that a user is required to be registered in order to rate a post and also because rating posts usually indicates that a person has read the content. Most people do not go around rating content that they have not read, because that would be dishonest. Therefore, the data gathered regarding post rating activities can be useful in determining how involved your community members are. One of the ways that you can report this information is with a simple stored procedure that returns the number of ratings that have occurred in a specific time frame. Therefore, the input for gathering the data will be a start date and an end date that you can calculate the number of ratings for. This statistic can be gathered by writing the following stored procedure and adding it to the Community Server database:

```
CREATE PROCEDURE GetRatingActivity
  @StartDate DateTime,
  @EndDate DateTime
AS
BEGIN
  SET NOCOUNT ON;

  SELECT count(Rating) FROM cs_PostRating
  WHERE
    DateCreated >= @StartDate AND
    DateCreated <= @EndDate
END
GO
```

To add the preceding stored procedure to your Community Server database, you need to first be logged in to the database, using a tool such as Microsoft SQL Server Management Studio. The next things you can do are to right-click on the Stored Procedures folder and select New Stored Procedure. Now, you will only need to type in the stored procedure given previously and execute the SQL. As a result, a new stored procedure named GetRatingActivity will be added to the Community Server database. Whenever you run this stored procedure you will need to provide a date range. The results of a query that you make to this stored procedure will simply be an integer that represents the number of ratings that occurred during that date and time range.

Modifying Tables

Aside from creating and updating stored procedures, there can also be a situation in which you need to extend a Community Server table. Perhaps there is data that you need to store that is not currently being stored. Another situation might be that you want to create an entirely new table for storing information about a part of the site that is not currently being stored. Whatever the reason may be, it is a good idea that you understand some of the basics for how to modify and extend a table in Community Server.

The nice fact about the Community Server database is that you will find it to be similar to other application databases. As a result, it should be just as simple to extend the database as it would be to extend a custom database. You can modify the tables just as you would any other SQL Server table, only be sure not to remove any of the existing columns.

An example where you may want to modify a table is with the cs_Messages table, which you can add a column for storing when a message was last updated. While this table is not particularly useful at this point in the Community Server application, it can serve as a basic example for extending a table. Here are the steps that you can take to add a new column to this table and update the stored procedure to populate this new column:

1. Log in to your database using a tool similar to Microsoft SQL Server Management Studio.

2. Navigate to your Community Server database and expand the Tables folder.

3. Right-click on the cs_Messages table and select Modify.

4. Add a new column called `LastModifiedDate` and make its Data Type `datetime`, as pictured in Figure 14-1.

5. Save the changes to `cs_Messages` by pressing Ctrl+S.

6. Expand the Programmability and Stored Procedures folders.

7. Right-click on the `cs_Message_CreateUpdateDelete` stored procedure and select Modify.

8. Change the Update action in the stored procedure to look like the following code:

```
-- UPDATE
ELSE IF @Action = 1
BEGIN
    UPDATE
        cs_Messages
    SET
        Title = @Title,
        Body = @Body,
        LastModifiedDate = getdate()
    WHERE
        MessageID = @MessageID and SettingsID = @SettingsID
END
```

9. Press F5 or press the Execute button to save the changes to the stored procedure.

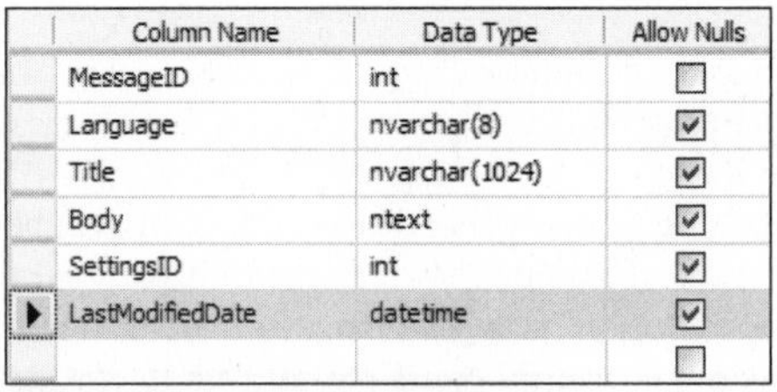

Column Name	Data Type	Allow Nulls
MessageID	int	☐
Language	nvarchar(8)	☑
Title	nvarchar(1024)	☑
Body	ntext	☑
SettingsID	int	☑
▶ LastModifiedDate	datetime	☑
		☐

Figure 14-1: cs_Messages Table

After you make the previous changes, the new information will be stored whenever a message is updated. From this example it should be clear that you can modify the Community Server tables and stored procedures just as you would in other SQL databases.

Providers

To demonstrate how to create a custom SQL data provider, a new email template provider will be created. By default, the email template provider that ships with Community Server is an XML provider and reads the data for the various email templates from an XML file called `emails.xml`. In this example, that file will be converted into a table in the database.

To begin with, you will need to create this new table, which will be called `cs_EmailTemplates`. The `cs_EmailTemplates` table structure should contain the following columns with the appropriate data types:

```
EmailType nvarchar(256)

Subject nvarchar(256)

MsgFrom nvarchar(256)

Body nvarchar(MAX)
```

Once you have created the previous table in the Community Server database, you will want to also create a new stored procedure to select the appropriate email type. Therefore, create a new stored procedure in your Community Server database called cs_GetEmailTemplate. The stored procedure is relatively simple and should contain the following SQL code to select the email template:

```
CREATE PROCEDURE cs_GetEmailTemplate
  @EmailType nvarchar(256)
AS
BEGIN
  SET NOCOUNT ON;

  SELECT Subject, [From], Body FROM [cs_EmailTemplates]
  WHERE
    EmailType = @EmailType
END
GO
```

When you have the preceding stored procedure in place for retrieving the appropriate email template, you should execute the code so that the new stored procedure is created in the database. At this point, you have the basic structure of the database in place, and now it is time to proceed to creating the customer email template provider.

To create the new email template data provider, you should have a separate project to house the provider. If you do not already have projects created for this purpose, create a new class library in Visual Studio called CustomProviders. You will want to add references to all of the Community Server assemblies that exist in the web projects bin folder. This will allow you to implement a new EmailTemplateProvider and access portions of the Community Server API. Once you have added the references to these assemblies, you should create a new class in your project called SqlEmailTemplateProvider and make the new class file look like this:

```
using System.Data;
using System.Web.Mail;
using System.Data.SqlClient;
using CommunityServer.Components;

namespace CustomProviders
{
    class SqlEmailTemplateProvider : EmailTemplateProvider
    {
        protected string databaseOwner = "dbo";
        string connectionString = null;
        ProviderHelper sqlHelper = null;

        public SqlEmailTemplateProvider(string databaseOwner,
            string connectionString)
```

```
        {
            this.connectionString = connectionString;
            this.databaseOwner = databaseOwner;
            sqlHelper = ProviderHelper.Instance();
        }

        protected SqlConnection GetSqlConnection()
        {
            try
            {
                return new SqlConnection(connectionString);
            }
            catch
            {
                throw new CSException(CSExceptionType.DataProvider,
                    "SQL Connection String is invalid.");
            }
        }

        public override System.Web.Mail.MailMessage GetTemplate(string emailType,
            User userEmailTo)
        {
            MailMessage email = new MailMessage();
            using (SqlConnection myConnection = GetSqlConnection())
            {
                SqlCommand myCommand = new SqlCommand(databaseOwner +
                        ".cs_GetEmailTemplate", myConnection);
                SqlDataReader reader;

                myCommand.CommandType = CommandType.StoredProcedure;

                myCommand.Parameters.Add("@EmailType", SqlDbType.NVarChar,
                    256).Value = emailType;

                myConnection.Open();

                using (reader =
                    myCommand.ExecuteReader(CommandBehavior.CloseConnection))
                {
                    while (reader.Read())
                    {
                        email.Subject = (string)reader["Subject"];
                        email.From = (string)reader["From"];
                        email.Body = (string)reader["Body"];
                    }
                    reader.Close();
                    myConnection.Close();
                }
            }
            return email;
        }

    }
}
```

The only required method of the `EmailTemplateProvider` is the `GetTemplate` method, which will return an email message. The other method and fields are used for creating the connection to the database in order to retrieve the email message. Also, you should notice that the constructor takes a couple of parameters that will be used to help create the database connection.

The bulk of the code for the new provider is in the `GetTemplate` method. However, the code itself is not as massive as it could be as a result of using a stored procedure in the database. Very simply, the `GetTemplate` method connects to the database, executes the stored procedure that was created previously in this section, and then reads the results if there are any. The part of this class that makes it a template provider is the fact that it implements the `EmailTemplateProvider` abstract class.

After you have all of the code in place, it is time to compile the `CustomProviders` project and test the results with a Community Server installation. To do this, you will simply need to compile the project and copy the output assembly into a Community Server sites `bin` directory. Once you have copied the assembly, you will need to edit the `communityserver.config` file to point to the new provider. To do this, simply open `communityserver.config` and replace the existing `EmailTemplateProvider` entry in the providers section with a new entry that looks like this:

```
<add name = "EmailTemplateProvider"
     type = "CustomProviders.SqlEmailTemplateProvider, CustomProviders,
             Version=1.0.0.0, Culture=neutral, PublicKeyToken=null"
/>
```

Now that you have done this, you can save the changes and run your site. When you try to send an email, you should not see it being sent because it does not yet exist in the database. To get the provider functioning completely, you will want to populate the `cs_EmailTemplates` table with the entries from the `emails.xml` file that is located in the Languages folder of your Community Server site. Once you have updated the table with these new entries, you will have a fully functioning `SqlEmailTemplateProvider`.

Summary

The Community Server database is extensible, allowing new tables and functionality to be added to it. Also, Community Server is easily extensible using the Provider Pattern. As a result, you are open to extend your site in many exciting ways.

In the next chapter, you will learn how to localize Community Server. The chapter will also extend your knowledge about the database with some of the methods used to localize Community Server.

15

Localizing Community Server

Nowadays, companies try to release their software with features to make it localizable for various languages in order to attract more clients.

People around the world need applications written in their native language. The default language for Community Server is English, but the team has created great features that make it easy to localize your Community Server application.

There are two major groups of languages in our world based on the direction they're written: from left to right (abbreviated as LTR) and from right to left (abbreviated as RTL). Most languages such as English, Spanish, German, and French are written from left to right, but some Eastern languages such as Persian and Arabic are written from right to left. There are also different calendars for each culture. We often see Georgian calendar for most cultures, but some cultures use other types such as the Islamic calendar and the Hebrew calendar.

Thankfully, Community Server stores your data in the database in a way that allows for your data to be encoded in a way that will work for your language. Community Server uses UTF-8 encoding, which guarantees that your site works for every culture properly.

In this chapter, we walk through the localization features in Community Server and provide a short introduction to localization for right to left languages. Our main focus is on common localization steps that you can use to localize your site for your language.

Before you start working on localizing your site for a particular culture, you should first check the international forums on Community Server's official web site at `http://communityserver.org`. There are many active forums for almost all spoken languages around the world. There you can find good information about the localization process as well as any available language packs for your native language. You may find that someone has already published a language pack for your culture!

Translation

Translation is the most important part of localization. It consists of changing static text values or text patterns from the default language (English) to a local language. This translation is shown to end users. A good translation produces a good localization, so it is important to pay attention to it. Thanks to great localization features in Community Server, the translation step is as easy as translating string values in XML files. The architects behind Community Server chose to use XML files to save and retrieve all text elements for the user interfaces.

To have a good translation, you have to pay attention to some guidelines:

1. Assign the role of translation to someone who knows English as well as the local language very well and has worked with Community Server. This helps them to choose better equivalents for original words.

2. Be consistent. When you choose a word in the local language for an element in the site, try to use that word consistently throughout the system.

3. Many of the words and phrases in the localization XML files have a variety of good translations in other languages, but you should consider where the translated string will be used within your site when you pick the phrase to use. Try to locate where each string is displayed on your site; you may find that spacing is limited or that you don't like the English phrase and want to provide a description that actually says something that's not very close to the original English version.

Later in this chapter, we will cover translation process in detail.

Languages Folder

Almost all localization data for a Community Server application is stored in the Languages folder. This folder has an XML file, named languages.xml, which plays the role of an index for available languages in the application and represents the key information for each language. This file has a structure similar to the following code example of Languages.xml.

```
<?xml version="1.0" encoding="UTF-8" ?>
<root>
<!--
Specify enabled languages here
-->
  <language name="U.S. English" key="en-US" emailCharset="iso-8859-1" />

<!-- Disabled since they are not fully complete

 note: the folders and files must exist on your server before enabling these
 If a user / site has a disabled theme selected, it will default to en-US

  <language name="Chinese Simplified" key="zh-CN" />
  <language name="Chinese Traditional" key="zh-TW" />
  <language name="Danish" key="da-DK" emailCharset="iso-8859-1" />
```

```
      <language name="Hellenic" key="el-GR" />
      <language name="Italian" key="it-it" emailCharset="iso-8859-1" />
      <language name="Netherlands" key="nl-NL" emailCharset="iso-8859-1" />
      <language name="Portuguese" key="pt-PT" emailCharset="iso-8859-1" />
      <language name="Russian" key="ru" emailCharset="iso-8859-5" />
      <language name="Swedish" key="sv" emailCharset="iso-8859-1" />
      <language name="Japanese" key="ja-jp" emailCharset="iso-2022-jp" />
      <language name="Catalan" key="ca-ca" emailCharset="iso-8859-1" />
      <language name="Czech" key="cs-CZ" emailCharset="iso-8859-2" />
      <language name="German" key="de-de" emailCharset="iso-8859-1" />
      <language name="French" key="fr-fr" emailCharset="iso-8859-1" />
      <language name="Slovak" key="sk-SK" emailCharset="iso-8859-2" />
  -->

</root>
```

This file has a `root` element and one or more `language` elements. By default, only English is listed in the file and all other languages are commented out (as shown in the preceding listing). When you create your custom translation, you will add your own language to the listing as well.

Each `language` element has three attributes:

❑   `name` — Represents the name of the language you want to declare. This will be shown to end users in the user interface.

❑   `key` — This attribute is an identifier for your language. Community Server looks for a subfolder with the same name in the `Languages` folder that you must copy your resource files there.

❑   `emailCharset` — The `Charset` that will be used in any email your site sends to its users.

For each element in this file, you should have a subfolder with the same name as the key attribute. The default language pack, English, found in the `/languages/en-US` folder uses a folder structure that you should mimic with your translations:

```
docs
    faq.ascx
    faq.aspx
emails
    emails.xml
errors
    BlockedIpAddress.htm
    BlogRollerDisabled.htm
    BlogsDisabled.htm
    DataProvider.htm
    DataStoreUnavailable.htm
    FeedReaderDisabled.htm
    FileGalleriesDisabled.htm
    ForumsDisabled.htm
    GalleriesDisabled.htm
    SiteIDUnavailable.htm
    SiteUrlData.htm
    UrlReWriteProvider.htm
```

```
metadata
    ExifMetadata.xml
    LinkRelations.xml
ControlPanelResources.xml
FeedReader.xml
FileGallery.xml
Messages.xml
Resources.xml
Templates.xml
```

Here is a brief description about each of the subfolders within the en-US folder:

- ❏ docs — Keeps an ASP.NET user control and a page. The user control contains all of the HTML content for the FAQ page. You need to translate the content of the user control by changing its source HTML.

- ❏ emails — Contains an XML file, emails.xml, which keeps all available email templates for your application. You can add your own templates or translate default templates.

- ❏ errors — It has a collection of HTML files that represent an error for application and will be shown to the end user on any error.

- ❏ metadata — It contains two XML files, ExifMetadata.xml and LinkRelations.xml, which keep the resource files for photo EXIF data.

Later in this chapter you will see the resource files in these folders in some details.

Resources

Resources are the main part of translation. The data for all text values or text patterns that will be shown to end users via web browser, emails, and feeds are stored in four files: Resources.xml, ControlPanelResources.xml, FileGallery.xml, and FeedReader.xml. These XML files have the same structure as the following code, Resources.xml, keeps data for public pages, while ControlPanelResources.xml keeps data for the Control Panel pages. The content stored in the FileGallery.xml and FeedReader.xml files is used by the File Gallery and Feed Reader applications, respectively.

```xml
<?xml version="1.0" encoding="utf-8" ?>
<root>
  <resource name="ResourceName">ResourceValue</resource>
</root>
```

Each resource file consists of a root element as well as a collection of resource elements. Resource elements have a name attribute and a string value. The name attribute is an identifier that you will use to refer to a resource element, and the string value is what the end user sees. In order to translate a resource element, you need to translate its corresponding string value. These texts may contain some string placeholders that are presented as {0}, {1}, or other indexes. These placeholders are used in conjunction with dynamic values.

In the resource files, you will find several XML comments that group resources based on where they will be applied. The following code example is a sample translation of the Main Navigation section in Persian. You can see the result in Figure 15-1.

```
<!-- Other elements are removed to save space -->

<resource name="files">____ __</resource>
<!-- Main Navigation -->
<resource name="home">____</resource>
<resource name="weblogs">____ __</resource>
<resource name="forums">_____ __</resource>
<resource name="discussions">___ __</resource>
<resource name="photos">_____</resource>
<resource name="admin">_____</resource>
<resource name="controlpanel">____ _____</resource>
<resource name="register">_____</resource>
<resource name="invite">____</resource>
<resource name="mainnavigation">_____</resource>
<resource name="user_myprofile">_____</resource>
<!-- End MainNavigation -->

<!-- Other elements are removed to save space -->
```

Figure 15-1: Localized Navigation Code

But you might ask: *How easy is this when you want to translate tons of elements via a common editor?* I agree it's not easy, and others agree too, because there are now some free tools that help you translate your application using a Windows application. One of the best applications for this purpose is CS Localization Ultra, which is available at www.ruri.com.tw/product/CSLU.

Not only can you use default resources, but it's also possible to declare your own resources and add them to the default resource files or your own files.

What if you want to use default or user-defined resources in your skins? It's pretty simple. There are two Community Server controls that come in handy in this case. The first one is the template you frequently see in default skins, and it lets you retrieve a resource value from default resource files. The second template takes a resource file name as a parameter, and you can use it to retrieve values from your custom resource files. The following code listing represents the structure of both templates. In the first template, you pass only the name of a resource through the `ResourceName` attribute, and in the second template you can pass an extra `resourcefile` attribute for your resource file name.

```
<CS:ResourceControl ResourceName="ResourceName" runat="server" />

<CS:ResourceControl ResourceName="ResourceName" resourcefile="my_resource_file.xml"
runat="server" />
```

Let's take a look at an example. The following code uses resource file entries for the content of a contact form for the default blog theme:

```
<!-- Other elements are removed to save space -->
<asp:PlaceHolder runat="Server" ID="CommentFormWrapper">
    <div id="CommonCommentForm">
        <h3>
            <CS:ResourceControl runat="server"
                ResourceName="Weblog_CommentForm_WhatDoYouThink"
                ID="rc_think" />
        </h3>
        <dl>

            <h4>
                <CS:ResourceControl runat="server"
                    ResourceName="Weblog_CommentForm_Policy" />
            </h4>

            <dt id="NameTitle" runat="server">
                <label for="<%=tbName.ClientID %>">
                    <CS:ResourceControl runat="server"
                        ResourceName="Weblog_CommentForm_Name" />
                </label>
                <em>(<CS:ResourceControl runat="server" ResourceName="Required" />
                    )</em>
                <asp:RequiredFieldValidator runat="server" ErrorMessage="*"
                    ControlToValidate="tbName"
                    ID="Requiredfieldvalidator2" />
            </dt>
            <dd id="NameDesc" runat="server">
                <asp:TextBox ID="tbName" runat="server" CssClass="smallbox" />
            </dd>
            <dt>
                <label for="<%=tbUrl.ClientID %>">
                    <CS:ResourceControl runat="server"
                        ResourceName="Weblog_CommentForm_YourUrl" />
                </label>
                <em>(<CS:ResourceControl runat="server" ResourceName="Optional" />
                </em>) </dt>
            <dd>
                <asp:TextBox ID="tbUrl" runat="server" CssClass="smallbox" />
            </dd>
            <dt>
                <label for="<%=tbComment.ClientID %>">
                    <CS:ResourceControl runat="server"
                        ResourceName="Weblog_CommentForm_Comments" />
                </label>
                <em>(<CS:ResourceControl runat="server" ResourceName="Required" />
                    )</em>
                <asp:RequiredFieldValidator runat="server" ErrorMessage="*"
```

```
                ControlToValidate="tbComment"
                ID="Requiredfieldvalidator3" />
        </dt>
        <dd>
            <asp:TextBox ID="tbComment" runat="server" Rows="5" Columns="25"
                TextMode="MultiLine" />
        </dd>
        <dt>
            <asp:CheckBox ID="chkRemember" runat="server" Text="Remember
                Me?"></asp:CheckBox>
        </dt>
        <dt>
            <asp:LinkButton CssClass="CommonTextButton" ID="btnSubmit"
                runat="server" Text="Submit"></asp:LinkButton>
        </dt>
    </dl>
  </div>
</asp:PlaceHolder>
<!-- Other elements are removed to save space -->
```

You need to add your custom text to the `Resources.xml` file where the other resources for the `CommentForm.ascx` control are stored (see the following code):

```
<?xml version="1.0" encoding="UTF-8" ?>
<root>
  <!-- Other elements are removed to save space-->

  <!-- Weblog Comment Form -->
  <resource name="Weblog_CommentForm_WhatDoYouThink">Leave a Comment</resource>
  <resource name="Weblog_CommentForm_CommentDisabled">New Comments to this post are
disabled</resource>
  <resource name="Weblog_CommentForm_AnonCommentsDisabled">Anonymous comments are
disabled</resource>
  <resource name="Weblog_CommentForm_Required">(required)</resource>
  <resource name="Weblog_CommentForm_Optional">(optional)</resource>
  <resource name="Weblog_CommentForm_Name">Name</resource>
  <resource name="Weblog_CommentForm_YourUrl">Your URL</resource>
  <resource name="Weblog_CommentForm_Comments">Comments</resource>
  <resource name="Weblog_CommentForm_RememberMe">Remember Me?</resource>
  <resource name="Weblog_CommentForm_NoComments">No Comments</resource>
  <resource name="Weblog_CommentForm_Said">said:</resource>

  <resource name="Weblog_CommentForm_Policy">Comments will be moderated</resource>


  <!-- Other elements are removed to save space-->
</root>
```

The result is shown in Figure 15-2.

Figure 15-2: Comment Form

Messages

Messages are another type of text value in Community Server. You are often confronted with messages when an error occurs in your application (for instance, when a post can't be found). Messages are stored in the `Messages.xml` file. Each message consists of an identifier, a title, and a body, which are stored in an XML structure similar to this:

```
<?xml version="1.0" encoding="UTF-8" ?>
<root>
  <message id="MessageID">
    <title>Message Title</title>
    <body>Message Body</body>
  </message>
</root>
```

Templates

Whenever a forum administrator tries to delete a post, he or she is redirected to a page to choose a reason for removing that post. The administrator may enter a message stating why a post was deleted or may choose from a list of common reasons. These reasons are called *reason templates*. Once a template is chosen or a reason is entered, the post's author will receive an email with the reason the administrator entered that lets the author know why the post was deleted.

There are some default templates for removing a post, but you can change them or add to them. These templates are stored in the `Templates.xml` file and have a simple structure, as shown in the following:

```xml
<?xml version="1.0" encoding="UTF-8" ?>
<root>
  <template id="TemplateID" type="TemplateType" sortOrder="TemplateSortOrder">
    <title>Template Title</title>
    <body>
    Template Body
    </body>
  </template>
</root>
```

Each template element has three attributes and two child elements; you see their description here:

❏ id — An identifier for template to be referred to later.

❏ type — The type of template. It's like a category for templates.

❏ sortOrder — An integer that helps to sort templates when they're being displayed to end users.

❏ title — The title of the template.

❏ body — The body of the template.

Emails

System emails may also be localized using files that are stored in the `Languages` folder. Emails are frequently used in Community Server for a variety of purposes. For example, when a user registers for a new account or sends an invitation to his or her friend, an email is used.

Emails are stored in the `emails.xml` file (in the emails folder) and use the structure shown here:

```xml
<?xml version="1.0" encoding="UTF-8" ?>
<emails>
  <email emailType="EmailType" priority="Priority">
    <subject>[Subject]</subject>
    <from>[FromAddress]</from>
    <body>
      Email body
    </body>
  </email>
</emails>
```

Email templates are straightforward, but you should note that all email elements have an `emailType` attribute that corresponds with an enumerator value in the Community Server APIs. In the preceding example, the `subject`, `from`, and `body` fields have variables shown in square brackets. There are a number of variables that can be used in the email templates. Many of the more popular variables include, but are not limited to [Subject], [SiteName], [Username], [TimeSent], and [adminemail].

Resource APIs

All of the things we've discussed so far are nothing without programmatic access to them. When you want to develop your own code and extend Community Server, you probably need to have access to the resource files via code. Community Server has opened all the doors for you. Some static methods in `CommunityServer.Components.ResourceManager` help you in this way.

`GetLanguageCharSets` is a function that returns a `NameValueCollection` of all supported `Charsets` in an application. The following code example specifies a `SupportsISO88591CharSet` method that checks if the `iso-8859-1 Charset` is supported in an application.

```
bool SupportsISO88591Charset()
{
    NameValueCollection charsets = ResourceManager.GetLanguageCharsets();

    for (int i = 0; i < charsets.Count; i++)
        if (charsets[i] == "iso-8859-1")
            return true;
    return false;
}
```

`GetSupportedLanguage` gets the name of a language and returns its key. `GetSupportedLanguages` returns a `NameValueCollection` of all supported languages in an application.

The `SupportsFarsi` method in the following code checks if Farsi is supported in an application:

```
bool SupportsFarsi()
{
    NameValueCollection Languages = ResourceManager.GetSupportedLanguages();

    for (int i = 0; i < Languages.Count; i++)
        if (Languages[i] == "Fa-IR")
            return true;
    return false;
}
```

You saw that it's possible to show string value of resources via Community Server controls in skins, but it's also possible to do this via code. The `GetString` method gets the name of a resource and returns its value. There are other overloads that let you pass the name of your own resource file to this method. The following code returns the string value for the home resource:

```
String GetHomeString()
{
    return ResourceManager.GetString("home");
}
```

Do you want to deal with a message in code? The `GetMessage` method helps you to pass a `CSException` enumerator and get its `Message` object. As an example, the `GetPostAccessDeniedTitle` function in the next code example returns the title of a message for `PostAccessDenied` exception:

```
String GetPostAccessDeniedTitle()
{
    Message message = ResourceManager.GetMessage(CSExceptionType.PostAccessDenied);

    return message.Title;
}
```

And the last static method in the `ResourceManager` class, `GetTemplate`, takes an integer value as the identifier for a message and returns a `Template` object. In the next example, the `GetIncomprehensiblePostBody` function returns the body of the Incomprehensible Post Reason Template:

```
String GetIncomprehensiblePostBody()
{
    Template template = ResourceManager.GetTemplate(3);

    return template.Body;
}
```

WYSIWYG Editor

The default WYSIWYG (what you see is what you get) editor for Community Server is TinyMCE, a simple but powerful editor. This editor has its own localization data, which are stored in JavaScript files in the `tiny_mce` folder off the root of your site. If you move your mouse over the editor buttons, you will see a Tooltip text that represents a description about that button. Localization data are stored for these Tooltips.

Community Server comes with default English localization files for this editor but you can download language packages from TinyMCE web site located at `http://tinymce.moxiecode.com/language.php)`. Thankfully, there are several language packs for many spoken languages on this site. If you can't find a pack for your language, don't give up. Read the online documentation at `http://tinymce.moxiecode.com/tinymce/docs/customization_language_packs.html`, and you can create your own language pack easily.

In order to localize the TinyMCE editor, you need to translate the files listed as follows. Note that you need to translate more files if any other plugin is installed on your editor.

```
/tiny_mce/jscripts/tiny_mce/langs/en.js
/tiny_mce/jscripts/tiny_mce/themes/CommunityServer/langs/en.js
/tiny_mce/jscripts/tiny_mce/plugins/contentselector/langs/en.js
/tiny_mce/jscripts/tiny_mce/plugins/iespell/langs/en.js
/tiny_mce/jscripts/tiny_mce/plugins/paste/langs/en.js
/tiny_mce/jscripts/tiny_mce/plugins/smilies/langs/en.js
```

All previous files have same structure that you see in the Editors Resource File Structure as follows:

```
tinyMCE.addToLang('',{
ResourceName1 : 'ResourceValue1',
ResourceName2 : 'ResourceValue2'
});
```

You just need to translate the string values that are embedded in single quotation marks (`ResourceValue1` or `ResourceValue2`).

For other editors installed on your application (such as `FreeTextBox`), refer to the editor documentation to learn about localization options.

Right-to-Left Languages

By default, Community Server is designed for left-to-right languages, but it's not a complicated task to make it ready for right-to-left languages. This task requires two major extra steps in localization:

❑   Enable right-to-left display — In this step, you change skin files and CSS codes to display the content in a right-to-left direction.

❑   Enable right-to-left typing — In this step, you add right-to-left typing functionality to the WYSIWYG editor to let your users type in their content from right to left.

This book provides a brief introduction of these two steps.

Right-to-Left Display

A new age came in web design with the advent of Cascading Style Sheets (CSS), which helps you design and modify an XHTML page easily. Community Server skins use CSS to lay out all controls and elements so that you have an easy way to manage the look of your site in a centralized location. You can change the text direction of all pages by changing the direction attribute of a CSS property quickly, but the result you get isn't attractive because there are some images and styles that have been applied to Community Server skins, and they should be aligned left. If you want to get a better result, you should try to change the text direction for subelements and any element that is necessary for this purpose.

The following code is a CSS modification of the `Common.css file`, which is located in `Themes/default/style`. This change enables a right-to-left display for sidebar content items. The result is shown in Figure 15-3. You can follow this example for other elements throughout your site.

```
/*
Generics
*/

body, html
{
   margin: 0px;
   padding: 0px;
   color: #000000;
   font-family: Tahoma, Arial, Helvetica;
   background-color: #606060;
}

/* Other properties are removed to save space */
.CommonSidebarArea
{
```

```
    width: 192px;
    margin: 22px 0px 0px 0px;
    overflow: hidden;
    direction: rtl;
}


/* Other properties are removed to save space */
```

Figure 15-3: Localized Sidebar

Right-to-Left Typing

Let's suppose that you've translated your application and changed its display directions. There is still another important step remaining: enabling right-to-left typing in the editor. TinyMCE is an editor that supports directions, but this option isn't available in the default Community Server editor. To enable this option, you need to add the directional plugin to your editor. If you download the public package for TinyMCE from their site, you will able to find all of the details to enable this plugin in Community Server by copying the content of the `plugins\directionality` subfolder to the corresponding folder in the Community Server `tiny_mce` folder. The last step that you will need to complete is to add this plugin to both the standard and enhanced editors for Community Server. To do this, you will need to modify the `Skin-Editor-Standard.ascx` and `Skin-Editor-Enhanced.ascx` files in the `Themes/default/Skins` folder to add the directional plugin. This example shows modified code for both controls:

```
<%@ Control Language="c#" %>
<%@ Register TagPrefix="CS" Namespace="CommunityServer.Controls"
Assembly="CommunityServer.Controls" %>
<%@ Register TagPrefix="TMCE" Namespace="Telligent.TinyMCEWrapper"
Assembly="Telligent.TinyMCEWrapper" %>

<TMCE:TinyMCE runat="server" id="Editor">
  <TMCE:TinyMCEOption runat="server" Name="fix_content_duplication" Value="false"
ID="Tinymceoption1"/>
  <TMCE:TinyMCEOption runat="server" Name="theme_advanced_resizing" Value="true" />
  <TMCE:TinyMCEOption runat="server" Name="remove_linebreaks" Value="false" />
```

```
    <TMCE:TinyMCEOption runat="server" Name="theme_advanced_statusbar_location"
Value="'bottom'" />
    <TMCE:TinyMCEOption runat="server" Name="theme_advanced_resize_horizontal"
Value="false" />
    <TMCE:TinyMCEOption runat="server" Name="plugins"
Value="'contentselector,paste,smilies,iespell,separator,directionality'" />
    <TMCE:TinyMCEOption runat="server" Name="theme_advanced_buttons1_add"
Value="'iespell,rtl,ltr'" />
    <TMCE:TinyMCEOption runat="server" Name="doctype" Value="'&lt;!DOCTYPE html
PUBLIC &quot;-//W3C//DTD XHTML 1.0 Transitional//EN&quot;
&quot;http://www.w3.org/TR/xhtml1/DTD/xhtml1-transitional.dtd&quot;&gt;'" />
</TMCE:TinyMCE>
```

```
<%@ Control Language="c#" %>
<%@ Register TagPrefix="CS" Namespace="CommunityServer.Controls"
Assembly="CommunityServer.Controls" %>
<%@ Register TagPrefix="TMCE" Namespace="Telligent.TinyMCEWrapper"
Assembly="Telligent.TinyMCEWrapper" %>

<TMCE:TinyMCE runat="server" id="Editor">
    <TMCE:TinyMCEOption runat="server" Name="fix_content_duplication" Value="false"
/>
    <TMCE:TinyMCEOption runat="server" Name="theme_advanced_resizing" Value="true" />
    <TMCE:TinyMCEOption runat="server" Name="theme_advanced_statusbar_location"
Value="'bottom'" />
    <TMCE:TinyMCEOption runat="server" Name="theme_advanced_resize_horizontal"
Value="false" />
    <TMCE:TinyMCEOption runat="server" Name="remove_linebreaks" Value="false" />
    <TMCE:TinyMCEOption runat="server" Name="plugins"
Value="'contentselector,paste,smilies,iespell,directionality'" />
    <TMCE:TinyMCEOption runat="server" Name="theme_advanced_buttons1"
Value="'fontselect,separator,fontsizeselect,separator,forecolor,backcolor,separator
,cut,copy,paste,pasteword,separator,code,iespell,ltr,rtl'" />
    <TMCE:TinyMCEOption runat="server" Name="theme_advanced_buttons2"
Value="'bold,italic,underline,strikethrough,separator,indent,outdent,separator,bull
ist,numlist,separator,link,unlink,image,contentselector,smiley'" />
    <TMCE:TinyMCEOption runat="server" Name="doctype" Value="'&lt;!DOCTYPE html
PUBLIC &quot;-//W3C//DTD XHTML 1.0 Transitional//EN&quot;
&quot;http://www.w3.org/TR/xhtml1/DTD/xhtml1-transitional.dtd&quot;&gt;'" />
</TMCE:TinyMCE>
```

Packaging for Distribution

Once you have localized Community Server in your local language, you may want to package your translation in order to share it with others. If you're going to release a language pack for a left-to-right language and haven't done anything more than translating localization files, your language pack shouldn't be more than a ZIP file of your language folder. In addition to this folder, you may translate WYSIWYG editor files. If you're localizing for a culture that needs extra steps to change themes and skins, you need to package your Themes folder and release it in addition to other files. You can accomplish this simply by zipping your Themes folder.

Sharing Your Localization Files

Community members welcome anyone who is willing to add to Community Server. If there isn't an international forum for your language, ask for it; otherwise, send your thoughts, questions, or suggestions that forum. Through the forums, the Community Server team will gather your language pack files and get them into the Community Server file galleries to spread your great work.

You can also share your language packs on your local Community Server site (if it exists) or write about it in your blog.

Summary

This chapter discussed the steps you need to localize Community Server for your local culture. It covered all the files that play a role in translation such as resources, messages, templates, and emails. This chapter also included discussions about resource APIs so that you could access resources programmatically. The translation of the WYSIWYG editor was also covered, and a general discussion was included about the steps you should follow to localize your application for a right-to-left language. Finally, it showed you how to package your results and share them with the community.

Commercial Add-ons

The various commercial add-ons can all be purchased online at the Telligent store. The store is located at http://store.telligent.com. This is also where you can purchase Community Server itself. In addition, there are support forums located at http://communityserver.org/forums specifically for each of the add-ons. The add-ons can also be downloaded at the Community Server web site, but they only function when the appropriate license file is installed.

Installing Commercial Add-ons

The various commercial add-ons are mostly packaged as Community Server modules. Therefore, you can generally follow the same basic steps that you would if you were installing any module (these steps can be found in Chapter 11. The largest difference between commercial add-ons and community-developed modules is the usage of the license file. Once you have purchased a license, you will receive a license file that you can then install using the Manage License page in the Control Panel System Tools section. In addition, there are configuration options specific to each add-on that you should also be aware of. There is documentation available for installing and configuring each of the add-ons located at http://docs.communityserver.org.

Single Sign-on Authentication

The different Single Sign-on Authentication Modules allow you to easily integrate Community Server with other systems that also require user authentication. This is helpful because it allows users of an existing system to only have to be authenticated in one system. The type of Single Sign-on Module that you should choose will depend on the type of system that is already in place and the type of authentication you plan on using in the future.

Microsoft Windows Authentication

The Windows Authentication Module allows users of Community Server to be authenticated using their Windows account. This is especially useful when Community Server is running on an intranet or extranet.

ASP.NET Forms Authentication

The ASP.NET Forms Authentication Module allows Community Server to be integrated into an existing application where user authentication already takes place. This can be especially helpful when you already have or would like to create an application that uses some, if not all, of the Community Server features. The ASP.NET Forms Authentication Module works by trusting the user ticket created by another application instead of requiring Community Server to create its own user ticket. Essentially, whenever users are authenticated in a different application, they can be issued a ticket that they then carry with them whenever they enter the Community Server system. The result of this is that a user is only required to log in to one system and yet is able to use many.

Passport Authentication

The Passport Authentication Module allows Community Server users to be authenticated using their Passport account. Passport is a system developed by Microsoft that maintains an easy-to-use user store that is available for applications to use. If you have a system that is currently using or plans to use Passport, then you can integrate that system into Community Server by using the Passport Authentication Module.

Cookie Authentication

This is an extremely useful module to have if you plan to integrate Community Server with a system that is not running on Windows or is not written in .NET. The Cookie Authentication Module allows Community Server to trust a user ticket that is stored in a common cookie. In this way, Community Server is able to integrate with a system that is developed on a different platform and can produce a cookie and user ticket. This provides a wide range of possibilities for allowing users to only be required to log in once.

Enterprise Search

The Enterprise Search add-on replaces the standard searching features of Community Server. If your community has more than 200,000 entries or more than 1 million impressions per day, you need to install Enterprise Search or your site's performance may be greatly degraded. The Enterprise Search add-on also allows for a new query syntax that can improve the user experience related to searching. Furthermore, with Enterprise Search installed, the files that are attached to posts and used throughout the file and photo galleries can be indexed and searched. This provides greater possibilities for users to find the content that they are searching for, even if that content is stored in a file in your gallery. For further information on installing and using Enterprise Search, consult the documentation at `http://docs.communityserver.org`.

News Gateway (NNTP)

The News Gateway is an essential add-on if you are using the Community Server forums functionality. It allows users of your site to post and read through the different forums by using a news reader such as Outlook Express. In this way, users can subscribe to different forum topics and stay up to date on those topics as they are discussed in the forums. Additionally, the News Gateway allows for users to receive content that can be read offline. If you would like to see this add-on in action you can use Outlook Express to connect to the News Gateway on `http://communityserver.org`.

FTP Server

The FTP Server add-on allows for the files in the file or photo galleries to be managed by using a variety of tools including the Internet Explorer FTP interface. Users in your community may be given access to the FTP folders using their community account name and password. Through the FTP Server add-on, users are able to easily manage their galleries by using a simple drag-and-drop interface.

Mail Gateway (SMTP)

The Mail Gateway add-on includes many useful features that allow authors and community members to update the community through email. An author can send an email to a specific address, and Community Server will use the email to create a post on either a forum or blog. It also allows a community to contact its members easily by providing for the creation of mailing lists. In addition, it allows for members to easily subscribe to posts and topics so that they are informed by email if the content on the site changes.

Resources

Support

Community Server Forums — http://communityserver.org/forums
Support forums for Community Server. If you ever have a question or would like to discuss any-thing related to Community Server, then visit these forums.

Community Server Documentation — http://docs.communityserver.org
Provides additional documentation on Community Server.

Community Server Blogs

Rob Howard — http://weblogs.asp.net/rhoward/

Scott Watermasysk — http://scottwater.com

José Lema — www.tankete.com

James Shaw — www.coveryourasp.net

Ken Robertson — www.qgyen.net

Wyatt Preul — www.wyattpreul.com

Dan Bartels — http://blog.danbartels.com

Kevin Harder — http://kevinharder.com

Scott Dockendorf—http://weblogs.asp.net/scottdockendorf

Jason Alexander—http://jasona.net

Ben Tiedt—http://getben.com

Dave Burke—http://dbvt.com

Keyvan Nayyeri—http://nayyeri.net

Jim Martin—http://jamesdmartin.com

Adonis Bitar—http://ooto.info

Other Resources

Community Server SDK Installation Guide—www.davestokes.net by Dave Stokes

Community Server Downloads—http://communityserver.org/files/

Community Server Site List—www.cs-listings.com

Telligent—http://telligent.com

For more work samples, please visit www.communityserver.org.

Index

SYMBOLS

A

B

Languages.xml code sample

R

S

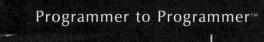